ORAL HISTORY, COMMUNITY, AND WORK
IN THE AMERICAN WEST

Oral History, Community, and Work in the American West

EDITED BY JESSIE L. EMBRY

THE UNIVERSITY OF
ARIZONA PRESS

TUCSON

The University of Arizona Press
© 2013 The Arizona Board of Regents
All rights reserved

www.uapress.arizona.edu

Library of Congress Cataloging-in-Publication Data
  Oral history, community, and work in the American West / Jessie L. Embry,
editor.
      pages cm.
  Includes bibliographical references and index.
  ISBN 978-0-8165-3017-5 (pbk. : alk. paper)   1. West (U.S.)—Social life
and customs—20th century.   2. West (U.S.)—Social conditions—20th
century.   3. Interviews—West (U.S.)   4. Oral history—West (U.S.)
I. Embry, Jessie L.
  F595.O73 2013
  978'.034—dc23

                                                                    2013009661

Publication of the book is made possible in part by a subvention from the Charles
Redd Center for Western Studies at Brigham Young University.

18   17   16   15   14   13   6   5   4   3   2   1

Contents

Preface

In 1973, I was finishing a whirlwind bachelor's degree at Brigham Young University and deciding what I wanted to do with the rest of my life. To delay that decision, I planned to start a master's degree program. Thomas G. Alexander suggested that I take an oral history class that the Charles Redd Center for Western Studies was sponsoring summer term. Gary L. Shumway, a professor at California State University, Fullerton, was the guest professor. I signed up with no idea what oral history was (I truly thought it had something to do with dental history). That class affected my career. I returned to the Redd Center in 1979 when I was hired as the oral history program director. Besides directing many oral history projects, my writing has been based on oral history.

I attended my first Oral History Association (OHA) meeting in October 1973. The organization was new enough that the founders were still in charge. After I came to work at the Redd Center, I continued to attend the OHA meetings and served as the editor of a pamphlet series for three years. The organization always interested me because it includes a mixture of historians, folklorists, journalists, family historians, storytellers, and social scientists. We all say we are doing oral history, but there are major differences in the motives, the interviewing techniques, and the end products. The essays contained in this volume show some of those differences. All of the interviews have been recorded and then excerpts have been transcribed so that the authors can include quotes in their articles. However, they do not agree on how much the verbatim transcripts should be edited. For example, I remove false starts and correct the grammar and complete the sentences. For me, that creates a more readable document. Others feel that I lose the verbal flavor of the interviews and the narrators' personalities by making those changes. Because there are advantages to both arguments, the authors have edited the excerpts from their interviews in many ways, and there has not been an attempt to standardize them.

In 2008, Redd Center Director Brian Q. Cannon asked me to put together a seminar on oral history and the American West. Following a pattern that had resulted in a book of essays *Utah in the 20th Century* (Utah State University Press, 2009), I asked participants to write papers and come together to share their work. I then edited the papers into a book. I put out a call for papers and received responses from historians and folklorists. I asked the seminar participants to step back from their oral history work and ask how their experiences in oral history increased their understanding of the American West. The impromptu discussion that followed that question helped all of us understand the focus for the rest of the day and for this volume. I knew the seminar was not about how to do oral history, but which of the two topics (oral history and the West) was more important? For me the question was easy: the American West had top billing since the Redd Center's mission is to promote the study of the West.

Editing the book posed a new set of challenges. To create a more balanced representation, additional essays were solicited. The authors represent a wide variety of oral historians. Some, like me, have been involved for years and have conducted hundreds of interviews on many topics. Others have had limited exposure to oral history. They have all seen the value and drawbacks of using oral history as a research source. Some conducted the interviews themselves so they wore two hats: creators and researchers. Some were only creators, and this was the first time they had used interviews to write a paper. Some were only researchers and used others' interviews. All of the essays provide valuable reflections on the role of oral history in researching the West and understanding community and work.

ORAL HISTORY, COMMUNITY, AND WORK
IN THE AMERICAN WEST

Introduction

THE ESSAYS IN this volume show ways that oral history helps increase the understanding of community and work in the American West in the twentieth century. This introduction sets the stage for the chapters by providing a backdrop of western history and oral history along with expanded definitions of community and work as they are used in this study. Finally, it outlines the book's contents.

Western American History

For years, western American historians wrote almost exclusively about white Anglo-Saxon Protestant men in the nineteenth century. Much of the genre's orientation reflected Frederick Jackson Turner's 1893 lecture "The Significance of the Frontier in American History."[1] Historian Patricia Limerick writes, "Turner was, to put it mildly, ethnocentric and nationalist; English-speaking white men were the stars of his story."[2] Turner's ideas were superseded by a focus on race, gender, and class in the 1980s in what is often referred to as the new western history.

Turner would not have been surprised that the frontier thesis did not endure. He observed, "Each age writes the history of the past anew with reference to the conditions uppermost in its own time. . . . The historian strives to show the present to itself by revealing its origin from the past."[3] The new western historians found new meanings as they examined groups left out of or underrepresented in the traditional western history. However, these new historians also focused their attention on the nineteenth century. Limerick, for example, occasionally steps into the twentieth century in her groundbreaking *Legacy of Conquest*, but her focus is telling the story of the people and lands Turner left out of his nineteenth-century analysis. Richard White includes more of the twentieth century in his study *"It's Your Misfortune and None of My Own,"* but again, only about a third of the book ventures past the nineteenth century.[4]

1

By 2004, historian David M. Wrobel declared that new western history was no longer useful. He acknowledged the life the new western historians had breathed into a dying field, but found they, too, had oversimplified a complex story.[5] The essays that followed Wrobel's comments in the September 2004 issue of *The Historian*, written by many of the new western historians, acknowledge that the field had moved beyond the "showdown at the political OK corral."[6] Historian Richard W. Etulain summarizes what many of the other bibliographical essays suggest: "These more complicated paradigms . . . should help us to avoid the too-positive triumphal approach of many early-twentieth century historians, and, conversely, move beyond several late-twentieth century scholars placing too much emphasis on negative conflicts in the West. This larger view sees the American West as an arena in which different cultures met, sometimes conflicted, but also compromised and intermingled."[7]

For some historians, expanding western history also meant looking into the twentieth century. In *The Oxford History of the American West*, historian Carol A. O'Connor declares, "Once a backwater of the nation, the West had grown in wealth and population and become an economic and political powerhouse. . . . The West's history in the twentieth century, no less than the nineteenth, combines elements sordid and sublime, tragic and triumphant. . . . The fullest understanding of the American West requires historical appreciation of this watershed era."[8] Peter Iverson agrees, "We need to present American Indian history as a continuing story. All too many historians have remained hesitant about entering the rather murky waters of the recent past."[9]

Oral History

Oral history is one way to expand the view of the American West because it can give a voice to people who rarely leave a written record. Oral history gives a voice to people of color, people from many economic classes, and people with different religious views. Iverson's claim that with "interviews . . . historians can write a richer history of American Indians" is true of other ethnic groups.[10]

Historian John Mack Faragher points out that ethnic studies are "notable for [their] use of oral history."[11] These interviews allow a more personal and less ideological view than can be drawn from written documents alone.

Interviewing is not a new technique in historical research, but, like history itself, its uses have evolved over the years. As it is practiced today, oral history began as an elitist movement at Columbia University in the 1940s. Historian Allen Nevins used oral histories to supplement the written documents available on leading US politicians. However, the technique quickly became a way to record the experiences of everyday Americans who left little or no record of their experiences. Oral history preserves stories for families, historians, folklorists, anthropologists, social scientists, scientists, business leaders, activists, journalists, educators, and museum professionals, to name just a few of its many consumers. Interviews enrich history by giving what radio broadcaster Paul Harvey famously called "the rest of the story."

Oral history connects the past, the present, and future. It matches what novelist George Orwell meant when explained the slogan of the Party in 1984: "[H]e who controls the past controls the future; who controls the present controls the past."[12] Historians Paula Hamilton and Linda Shopes claim, "Oral history . . . is at heart a deeply social practice connecting past and present, and at times, connecting narrative to action. [It] . . . span[s] the borders of established academic disciplines, contemporary professional practices, and community activism."[13] Or as Michael Frisch puts it, oral history is "a powerful tool for discovering, exploring, and evaluating the nature of the process of historical memory—how people make sense of their past, how they connect individual experience and its social context and how the past becomes part of the present, and how people use it to interpret their lives and the world around them."[14]

Community and Work

The common themes in this volume are how oral history helped the authors better understand the role of community and the role of work. These sound simple, but like the evolution of western history, they are just the beginning of complex interrelationships. A 1975 Webster's dictionary and a 2010 web version define *community* as "a unified body of individuals as a: state. commonwealth. b: the people with common interests living in a particular area; . . . d. a group of people with a common characteristic or interest living together in larger society."[15]

Although most of the authors in this book talk about communities that share the same geographic area, the common interests vary with each essay. For some it is a similar ethnic group. Others share an occupation. Still others find their community in religion. Sometimes the community is an unlikely combination, such as the rancher and federal inspector in Leisl Carr Childers's study of rural Nevada. Many scholars have struggled to explain community and how it has changed over time. Robert N. Bellah worried about people forming "lifetime enclaves" and no longer having interaction. Robert Wright wrote about "The Evolution of Despair" that this lack of community caused in 1996. Hillary Rodham Clinton quoted an African saying that "it takes a village (or a community) to raise a child."[16] These oral history interviews add to that dialogue.

Work is equally hard to define. While I am inclined to think of work as what I do for a living, the 1975 Webster's dictionary definition reminds me of the many other ways I use the word *work*. In fact, the first definition listed is "to bring to pass," and the second is "to fashion or create by expanding labor or exertion upon." The definition in a 2010 dictionary matches my usual view. *Work* is an "activity in which one exerts strength or faculties to do or perform something: a: sustained physical or mental effort to overcome obstacles and achieve an objective or result b: the labor, task, or duty that is one's accustomed means of livelihood c: a specific task, duty, function, or assignment often being a part or phase of some larger activity."[17]

Work also has a variety of meanings in the essays contained herein. In many cases, people's occupations bring them together as a community. But work can also be volunteer labor. For example, the Mormons in Fort Collins, Colorado, worked together to build a church building and a church community. In a similar fashion, women in Utah worked on promoting conservative ideals through the Eagle Forum. Sometimes the work that brings people together is often not referred to as work at all. Jose Alamillo expected that the Latinos created a community by working in the lemon groves of California. But when he asked about work, it was baseball and the Cinco de Mayo queen contests that his interviewees felt were more memorable and uniting. Working with lemons is what they did for a living, but it was not what defined them as people.

Of course, this is true of work and community throughout the world. In fact, in many ways the world became very much the same during the second half of the twentieth century. But there were unique elements that played out differently in the West. The articles that follow show what oral history can add to understanding some elements of community and work in the American West. They do not try to cover all aspects that connect the West, oral history, community, and work. They do, however, suggest some valuable interconnections. To help make those connections, the essays are divided into three categories.

The first part contains reflections on the uses of oral history. As the "oldest" practitioner in the group, I explain what I have learned about oral history and the West over the years. Then Barbara Allen Bogart, a folklorist who conducted her first interviews in 1978 as part of her dissertation research, talks about her experiences in western communities. Laurie Mercier first conducted interviews in Montana in the early 1980s and has since used oral history in her research on western mining and women's history.

The second part looks at how oral history gives voice to groups that were neglected in the old western history and continue to be underrepresented in the new western history, often because of limited sources. But the articles include more than just untold stories. They allow members of groups to speak for themselves. The authors "introduce voices that counter [conventional views of the past]; they can complicate our understanding of what happened and what it means."[18] For example, many western historians have documented Native Americans' work in California from the employers' point of view. William Bauer allows the Indians to talk about how they felt about the work. Similarly, Jose Alamillo describes the work and play of Mexican immigrants in the lemon groves of southern California.

Few historians combine ethnic groups, but Skott Vigil uses his Hispanic and Native American family to talk about migrant workers in Colorado. Georgia Wier allows Japanese Americans in Colorado to explain their unique experiences. These immigrants came to Weld County before World War II and felt accepted. Claytee White provides a unique perceptive of blacks in Las Vegas; though their numbers were small, these African Americans were involved in many businesses and activities.

Women's work has also been misunderstood. Their experiences were completely left out of the old western history or they were seen as reluctant followers of men. Later, while their work experiences were often limited by social norms, their life stories show their abilities to expand those limitations. Joanne Goodwin explains that Las Vegas women are more than showgirls and prostitutes. Even if they held these jobs, they explain their experiences differently than the standard stereotypes. Sandra Mathews uses her aunt's experiences in Alaska to show how women moved into the West for adventure even if they worked in traditional jobs, such as teaching. John Sillito, Sarah Langsdon, and Marci Farr look at another stereotypical women's job—in this case, nursing—but go beyond the stereotype to show how the women felt about their training. Melanie Newport looks at the Eagle Forum in Utah. This group of conservative women is often belittled, so her interviews allowed these women a forum to voice their political views and activities. All the articles show strong, independent women who make a place for themselves in the urban and rural West.

In nearly all cases, oral history provides material not available in traditional sources. The final articles in part 3 show how oral history is often the only source of information. The essays in this part show some unique ways that oral history changes how scholars and participants recall the past. Linda Myer studies the Mormon community in Fort Collins, Colorado. Usually there are many sources about the LDS Church in an area, including congregational histories, membership lists, newspaper articles, and journals. For Fort Collins, these records do not exist or are very sketchy. The only way Myers could learn about the local LDS Church was to talk to people. The stories from the interviews explain how the Mormons worked and grew together as a community. Leisl Carr Childers shows how nuclear testing in Nevada was more than just a footnote in the cold war. The testing affected people (where the official government position was that there were no people) and led to an unlikely friendship between a rancher and a federal tester. Kristi Young looks at family connections and stories that are not always historically accurate and reflect more on the narrator's views than they do on past events. Folklorist William A. "Bert" Wilson taught me that people believe what they think happened is more important than what actually did happen in the past.

Notes

1. Frederick Jackson Turner, "The Significance of the Frontier in American History," in *The Frontier in American History* (New York: Holt, 1920), 2. Historian Ray Allen Billington expanded on the idea in *Westward Expansion, a History of the American Frontier*. He writes in the preface to his first edition, "This book attempts to follow the pattern that Frederick Jackson Turner might have used had he ever compressed his voluminous researches on the American frontier within one volume." Ray Allen Billington, *Wesward Expansion, A History of the American Frontier* (New York: Macmillan, 1949), xi.

2. Patricia Nelson Limerick, *The Legacy of Conquest: The Unbroken Past of the American West* (New York: Norton, 1987), 20–21.

3. Ibid., 17.

4. Ibid.; Richard White, *"It's Your Misfortune and None of My Own": A History of the American West* (Norman: University of Oklahoma Press, 1991).

5. David M. Wrobel, "Introduction: What on Earth Has Happened to the New Western History," *Historian* 66 (September 2004): 440.

6. Ibid., 438–39.

7. Richard W. Etulain, "Meeting Places, Intersections, Crossroads, and Borders: Toward a Complex Western Cultural History," *Historian* 66 (September 2004): 509.

8. Carol A. O'Connor, "Introduction and Chronology," in *The Oxford History of the American West*, ed. Clyde A. Milner II, Carol A. O'Connor, and Martha A. Sandweiss (New York: Oxford University Press, 1994), 428.

9. Peter Iverson, "American Indian History as a Continuing Story," *Historian* 66 (September 2004): 529.

10. Ibid.

11. John Mack Faragher, "The Social Fabric of the American West," *Historian* 66 (September 2004): 444.

12. George Orwell 1984: and Related Readings (Evanston, IL: McDougal Littell, 1998), 39.

13. Paula Hamilton and Linda Shopes, "Introduction: Building Partnerships between Oral History and Memory Studies," in *Oral History and Public Memories,* ed. Paula Hamilton and Linda Shopes (Philadelphia: Temple University Press, 2008), viii.

14. Ibid., ix.

15. See http://www.merriam-webster.com/dictionary/community (accessed April 5, 2011).

16. Robert N. Bellah, *Habits of the Heart: Individualism and Commitment in American Life* (Berkeley: University of California Press, 1985), 72; Robert Wright, "The Evolution of Despire," *Time Magazine*, August 28, 1995, 50–57; Hillary Rodham Clinton, *It Takes a Village and Other Lessons Children Teach Us* (New York: Simon and Schuster, 1996).

17. See http://www.merriam-webster.com/dictionary/work (accessed April 5, 2011).

18. Hamilton and Shopes, introduction to part 1, *Oral History and Public Memories,* 3.

Part I

Reflections

1

Stories of Community and Work in the Redd Center Oral History Program

JESSIE L. EMBRY

Historian Jessie L. Embry discusses how community and work are two themes of the oral history projects she has conducted at the Charles Redd Center for Western Studies. A very personal reason for doing some of the interviews was that she wanted to preserve family history and understand how her family reflected larger regional and national experiences. The interviews were more than personal documents. Embry used them in books and articles to explain a larger historical setting. Other scholars have also found them useful for their research. As with all sources, these scholars' themes and their conclusions have sometimes been very different than Embry's. The research would have not been possible or as rich without the opportunity to talk directly with the interviewees.

LOOKING BACK ON my forty-plus years doing oral history, I believe interviews have been a valuable enterprise for my family, for my own research, and for other scholars. Because I work for a western studies center, my focus has always been on the American West. Oral history has been invaluable in documenting the towns and cities in the West and the larger communities of occupations, religion, sports, and ethnic groups. Although there are many themes in the oral history projects I have conducted and directed, two of the most valuable are community and work, and they fit the common threads found in this volume. These authors and I explain how people whose voices might have been completely lost are remembered as their stories are recorded. These individual stories complicate and add more layers to the simple stereotypes of life in the American West.

In my experience, oral history often starts at a basic level—the desire to know more about oneself. I grew up in North Logan, Cache Valley, Utah, and I have lived much of my life in Provo, Utah. I am a product of the western myths of open spaces and the individualistic "can-do-it" attitude. I am also a product of the Mormon community support system. I show the dilemma many westerners face.

Beyond that individual focus, I do oral history to flesh out my family history and understand my roots. My favorite interview is still the one I did with my father, Bertis L. Embry. He had always wanted to write his history, but he never put it together. When I sat down to interview him, I asked the first question, and he talked for three hours. I went back several more times and collected a total of eight hours of tape. At the time it seemed like a lot, and yet I sometimes wish I had asked him about other areas of his life. I am always glad I got some of his stories before dementia took over his mind.

My father was a product of the western American dream. His story fits Frederick Jackson Turner's frontier model. He came to Utah from Tennessee because his parents were seeking a community of Mormons and better work opportunities for themselves and their children. The West provided the open space and land for the Embrys that Turner suggested led to American democracy. My father's story adds some interesting twentieth-century twists to the narrative. My grandfather did not homestead on free land. Instead, he developed a business trucking fruit and cattle. He and my grandmother wanted more for his children and, like Turner, believed that the new frontier was education.[1] My grandparents relocated to Logan, Utah, so their children could attend Utah State University and live at home. It was a belief that continued for at least another generation. In our home, we understood that education was the ticket to a better life.

My grandparents bought a home in a Logan neighborhood known locally as "Little Berlin" because many of the residents were immigrants and spoke German. Most of them were from Switzerland and not Germany, but the Logan residents did not recognize the difference. My grandparents felt very much a part of the community and were accepted by the Swiss Mormons not only because they shared the same faith but also because they came from a similar lower-middle-class background. The connection to the community was strengthened because my father had served a mission in Germany. He met some of the Logan Swiss immigrants' children while he was on his mission, so he had another connection when the family moved to Cache Valley. My parents met on a blind date arranged by one of the Swiss women.

I interviewed my mother, but she was the hardest interview I ever attempted. She qualified as an interviewee for one of the Redd Center oral history projects, so I talked to her about her family life. I tried to talk to her about the rest of her life, too, but I only got an hour of tape. Now as I listen to the tape, I am surprised by how scared she sounds. She really did not want to be interviewed and agreed to do so only because she loves me. I enjoy listening to her voice, but I wish I had been able to allay her fears.

As limited as it was, her interview also taught me much about the freedom of the West. My mother grew up very poor in Nephi, Utah. Her parents had limited education, which constrained their lifestyle, although they made the best of what they had. My grandmother made beautiful quilts with scraps of fabric. She did not allow herself to use new material until my mother was employed and provided new fabric to make a quilt that my grandmother had only dreamed of making.

Like my father and Turner, my mother saw education as her frontier to success, so she attended the nurses' training program at Holy Cross Hospital in Salt Lake City. On the day she was to leave, her father said that if she left, she would not return to Nephi. He was right. Her training at Holy Cross opened up a whole new world for her.

These interviews with my parents help me understand my own life. I understood why my parents stressed education so much. I learned why I love the open spaces in the West. My conversation with my parents also helped my nieces and nephews. Among my favorite memories are listening to my brother read stories of my father's early life to his eight-year-old daughter on the day of my father's funeral and, five years later, hearing my nephew give a brief talk, based on her interview, at my mother's funeral.

I have been fortunate to be able to expand my family history and use these interviews in my research at the Redd Center. Oral history interviews with nonrelatives have further enriched my understanding of my family history, enabling me to see my parents' experiences in a larger western American context. For example, I learned more about my grandparents' experiences in Little Berlin when I conducted interviews with the Swiss immigrants and their Utah-born children who formed a community in northern Utah.[2] Their sense of community was strong because the missionaries who converted them were from Logan and encouraged them to settle there. The missionaries and their families befriended the newcomers. Others came to Logan, because they knew there were other Swiss, many from the same area of Bern. The families became even closer as they intermarried.

The Mormon neighborhood ward system created a strong sense of community for the Swiss and their neighbors. The bishops were Swiss. Meetings and socials reflected the European influence. The Mormon church leaders encouraged "all Saints of foreign birth who come here . . . [to] learn to speak English as soon as possible [and] adopt the manners and customs of the American people."[3] The oral histories show how the official and unofficial church policies helped the Swiss overcome the language differences and create a sense of belonging. Bertis L. Embry recalled, "Because they were much more at home in their language, . . . I can remember we would have almost as many testimonies borne in German as we did in English."[4] Rather than excluding those who did not speak German or Swiss, Anglo Opel Forsberg said she worked to become a part of the community. She learned to recognize the difference between the Swiss and high German dialects and understand a few words.[5] Anglo Elsie Embry Bastian especially enjoyed the dances "because they always did polkas, and it was so much fun. They had their own little music. They had their accordions. . . . They could really stir up the old rec hall." The daughter of Swiss immigrants,

Leah Holmstead remembered the Swiss people wearing native costumes, giving yodeling programs, and serving excellent food.[6] Oral history was the best way to document that sense of community; the local ward minutes did not include these details.

Many of the young men from the Logan Tenth Ward, like my father, were missionaries in German-speaking countries in the 1930s just as Adolf Hitler took control. My father's missionary journal and letters home document his skepticism about what Hitler was doing for Germany. He repeated that view in his oral history interview. As I expected, my father felt Hitler was an evil dictator, just as I have been taught in school and church. But I was surprised when other former missionaries spoke kindly of Hitler even years later. I think one explanation is that the missionaries wanted to feel a sense of community with the Germans and Hitler during their missions, and they remembered those feelings even years later.[7] Swiss American Elmer Stettler recalled, "We liked Hitler." He continued, "We would just eat up articles where some of his people were showing how the [Mormon] pioneers were organized into groups. We used it for material to disseminate the gospel." Swiss American Walter Jaggi, who had been my father's missionary companion for a while, claimed to have heard Hitler say, "If we want to become a great and mighty people, we have to endure like the Mormon pioneers," and that the two most perfect organizations in the world were the Germany army and the Mormon church.[8] These interviews reminded me that not all oral histories are controlled by current events. People can accurately remember their past feelings, even if those views become unpopular.

In my additional research I learned that my parents were very typical of many of the greatest generation that survived the Great Depression and World War II and that twentieth-century westerners were not very different from other Americans. That similarity is important for understanding the West. As the transportation and technology made it easier to communicate, the regions became more similar and less unique. For the fiftieth anniversary of World War II, I planned an oral history project on the impact of the war on the home front in Utah. I reasoned that many people had already interviewed the military personnel, but the war was an all-out effort at home as well as on the battlefield.

All the Redd Center interviewees saw life-changing events with the beginning of World War II. For example, at the beginning of the war, my father worked for the New Deal Rural Electrification Administration, teaching farmers in the rural South how to use electricity. My mother assisted the home economists. After the bombing of Pearl Harbor, my father worked as an engineer at Lawrence Livermore National Laboratory on what became the Manhattan Project. He might have been able to stay at that job, but when his draft notice arrived, he decided to enlist in the navy, where he could be an officer. He and my mother spent winters in Boston and summers in Florida during his training. The war ended before my father was sent overseas, but right after that he went to Europe as a translator, debriefing German naval officers. My mother worked as a nurse in some of the places my father was stationed. My parents and grandparents grew victory gardens, supported rationing, and worked in war industries at home. I was surprised that my Grandma Embry, who typed with two fingers, got a secretarial job.

The Redd Center oral histories helped expand my family's World War II home front stories. I learned from the interviews that Utahns were willing to make sacrifices for the war and respond to rationing. It was a sacrifice for the war effort, and the interviewees discussed other factors that influenced their reactions to shortages. For example, the first commodity rationed was gasoline. George Rowland Blake, a dairy farmer in Provo in the 1940s, recalled, "Because we had a tractor, we were allowed about as much gasoline as we needed. We had our own dispenser, a fifty-gallon drum that we pumped it out of." The family car, however, was limited. "We could have pumped gas out of that tank and put it in the car," he acknowledged. "There was nobody to supervise that and we were given about as much as we asked for. . . . But we felt it a matter of honor not to use tractor gas in our cars. Even though we had the gasoline, we didn't travel." Reinforcing his sense of honor were other characteristics: "sensitivity to national defense needs" and "we didn't have tires or time."[9]

Some interviewees did not realize that they were describing a black market when they discussed how they shared their rations. Farrin Mangelson's family did not use sugar in tea or coffee, so he felt they may have had some to spare. Even then, he recalled, they were "conservative on . . . desserts." As a result, the family had extra sugar stamps, which they would trade with others for shoe stamps "because the kids would wear through shoes." Zelda Packer recalled, "Some of the women here in the community would get together and compare the amount of sugar we had on hand. If one had more than the other one had, she would share. That was a great asset to the sisters in our community."[10] According to rationing regulations, trading or even sharing coupons was just as illegal as purchasing goods on the black market. Each family was to use its own allotment. Fifty years later, Mangelson and Packer did not recognize that their actions were prohibited. They told their stories as manifestations of patriotic compliance and neighborly goodwill that worked to everyone's advantage. These home front experiences are not unique to the West, but they are an important part of Utah and western history.

In the cold war that followed World War II, the United States and the Soviet Union struggled for influence throughout the world. In addition to military control, the two countries wanted to show that their system of government was superior, and both widened their focus to third-world countries. The fourth point in Harry S Truman's inaugural address was "a bold new program for making the benefits of our scientific advances and industrial programs available for the improvement and growth of underdeveloped nations."[11] My family and others from Utah were part of the Point Four Program/US Agency for International Development (USAID) experience in Iran, and that was the impetus for an oral history project about that experience.

When I was in the third and fourth grades in the early 1960s, my father worked as a Utah State University (USU)contract technician in Iran. He enjoyed his work with the Iranian farmers; he struggled with Iranian engineering students because he felt they were not very studious. While my father tried to share his technical skills with the Iranian people, he doubted that his two-year experience there would make any difference in a country with a thousand years of traditions. When I read the reports and interviewed other technicians who worked in Iran from 1951 to 1964, many of them seemed more hopeful about the impact they had on the country.[12]

My Iran contract interviews provided important information about community and work that were not available in other sources. Technicians from USU and Brigham Young University (BYU) created a small Mormon community. Mormons are often drawn to each other, even more so in Iran because these Americans were in a very different country. Richard Griffin, a USU technician who worked in Iran from 1955 to 1957 told me, "The Church was a big factor in our lives. . . . It meant a lot to us." Bertis L. Embry called the group a "pretty close-knit group" away from home. The USU and BYU group would have agreed with Leah Bryson Hart, whose husband worked for the State Department, "The Church was the best part of being [in Iran]."[13]

The technicians also summarized their success. Looking back after the 1979 revolution in Iran, the interviewees had some perspective on their work. I asked Louise and Deon Hubbard, who went to Iran in 1954, about their experience. Deon explained, "As I look back on Iran today, I say, 'What did we accomplish?' Had the shah's government continued in stability, I think we would have seen progress. I'm sure we laid a base there that was worthwhile. Many ideas and projects have not been completely uprooted. I'm sure that most foreign technicians who went there gained a technical experience in their fields that was worthwhile when they returned home. Our experience was great. Our experience was very worthwhile."[14]

My father however had less optimism. He recalled, "I tried to get them to adopt better irrigation methods and better use of farm machinery. In some respects, it was a lost cause. There was an awfully lot of money spent, and some good done but not nearly as much as they could have obtained from it." He remembered, for example, that "the power plant at the college was quite a problem. They insisted that the engines had to sleep." He complained that the professor in charge of farm machinery "didn't want to know anything about [improvements]. All he wanted was for the United States to build him a nice, big new building." But Embry felt that the government should not build anything unless there was a need.[15] My father would have made some of these comments at the time. Some he was able to make later because in retrospect he could see that if the program had improved irrigation methods and improved the lives of ordinary Iranians, they might have seen Americans in a more positive light.

The interviews expanded beyond my purpose in documenting the experiences of Utahans in Iran. Andrew D. Magnusson, a PhD candidate in Middle East history at the University of California, Santa Barbara, used my interviews to put the experience of the Utah Mormon technicians in the larger picture of twentieth-century Iranian history. For example, one of the BYU technicians, Max Berryessa, helped Iranian Prime Minister Mohammed Mosaddegh escape the US-led attempt to overthrow him. Even Kermit Roosevelt, the American mastermind of the attempt, was not sure how Mosaddegh escaped. Berryessa explains how it happened clearly in his interview. As Magnusson looks more closely at the interviews, I am sure he will find other stories that are only Mormon-related to me but are important for understanding the experience of a minority religion in a Muslim country. Although my focus was Utah and the American West, the interviews have a greater use.

Most of the Redd Center oral history projects have no connection to my family. The topics were selected with advice from the center's board and others and have usually been chosen because there is a lack of historical records on the topics. The dearth of information was the major reason for conducting the interviews. I went into the projects with no agenda about what I might find. I have used many of the projects when writing books and articles. Faculty and students from BYU and other institutions have also used them. The conclusions we reach are often very different, but I am convinced that none of them would be possible without the oral history interviews. They explain important parts of western American history.

The first large oral history project I was involved in was the Latter-day Saints (LDS) Polygamy Oral History Project. I was the first interviewer in 1976; the project was still active when I was hired at the Oral History Program Director in 1979. When I started, I was a little surprised at how many people refused to be interviewed. After all, I was a returned missionary coming from BYU. I felt that my motive to document Mormon history—quite apart from current polygamy—was clear. On further reflection, I realize I should have been surprised at how many people agreed to be interviewed because church leaders rarely discuss the topic to avoid providing information that could be used by the current polygamists.

There were other concerns. Many of the people who agreed to be interviewed came from the Mormon colonies in Mexico, where polygamy was openly practiced longer than it was in the western United States. This happened because some Mormon polygamists moved to Mexico after Congress enforced laws against the practice in the US territories. In 1890, Church President Wilford Woodruff wrote a manifesto, which said that the LDS Church would not perform marriages "contrary to the laws of the land." Although polygamy was technically against the law in Mexico, it was not enforced, so some new marriages were performed there and some Mormons arrived to have marriages performed. That ended when a new church president, Joseph F. Smith, issued a second manifesto that completely eliminated Mormon polygamy. When the Latter-day Saints abandoned the colonies during the Mexican revolution in 1912, they returned to the United States, where polygamy had not been practiced for years. The Payne and Farr families, who settled in Provo, and the Eyring family in Arizona worried about what might be said about their practice of polygamy. The children were told not to discuss polygamy at that time, and some were unsure if they should in the 1970s.

Despite these setbacks, the Redd Center interviewers were able to find people to interview using a snowball method. I had never taken a sociology class and was not constrained by the limitations of a representative sample. I still thought I needed a wide variety of people and thought it would not be a good idea to interview many children from the same family. I have since concluded that oral history is not about random samples. It is about as many stories as possible. I also discovered that I should interview as many people in a family as possible. Children's perceptions were often very different. For example, William Hendricks Roskelley married sisters, Margaret Ann and Agnes Wildman. The children of the first wife remembered that their mother got more time and resources because she had more children. A daughter of the second wife said that her father favored the first wife, and the wives did not get along.

As I processed the interviews, I began to wonder how different the LDS plural families were from the LDS monogamous families.

Polygamy was practiced for such a relatively short time in the LDS Church, so how did they decide how to organize their families? There were no instructions over the pulpit or polygamy handbooks. Many interviewees described family life in such a way that they did not seem all that different from monogamous families. Children were closer to their mothers than fathers, but that often happened in Victorian families during the nineteenth century. Mormon husbands, both plural and monogamous, were sometimes called on missions, leaving wives and children behind.

I decided that the best way to see if polygamous families were different than monogamous ones was to talk to children of monogamous families whose parents married about the same time as the polygamous families did. I used the cutoff date for marriages before 1904, the date of the second manifesto. I wrote a press release and submitted it to BYU Public Communications. This was my first lesson in how many people read newspapers. The Redd Center's telephone rang for weeks with people volunteering to be interviewed. They called from throughout Utah and as far away as Arizona. Some children from polygamous families also responded.

After looking at more than 200 interviews with children of polygamous families and nearly 150 interviews with children of monogamous families, I concluded that there was very little difference in the ways the children were raised. I used that conclusion as my thesis in writing *Mormon Polygamous Families: Life in the Principle*.[16] I had hoped I was writing the final word on Mormon polygamy, and I was surprised when a book called *Mormon Polygamy: A History* was published just before mine.[17] I now realize that there will never be a final word, but the oral histories provided essential details that were missing from other sources or harder to figure out. For example, the fathers' schedules were easier to discern because the children could say that the father came once a week or every third day. That information might be found in a journal, but it would require keeping track of each change in the households, and many journal keepers do not always record everyday details.

In many ways my book is a reaction to Kimball Young's *Isn't One Wife Enough?*[18] I had access to written notes by Young, a sociologist, and his graduate students. As I read the notes and the book, it seemed to me that Young found it difficult to leave out any good story; as a result, he often suggested that very unusual stories were the norm rather than the exception. So I used percentages to see what the norms were for my sample. I knew that I did not have a representative sample, but I wanted to make sure that if I said something was typical, then it was at least typical of the people that the Redd Center had interviewed and the other sources had consulted, including Young's. With the interviews from the polygamous and monogamous families, I felt comfortable concluding that there were few differences between the two, likely because the polygamists adapted their monogamous traditions. For example, most fathers were relatively disconnected from their children, and children were closer to their mothers.

The polygamy and monogamy interviews showed me that the interviewees often remembered general trends like kneeling at the table every day for prayer more than the specific prayers. Scholars have discovered the same things with other oral history interviews. They have found that most people summarize similar stories rather than tell a lot of specific incidents. My father talked in general about his problems with local Nazi leaders on his mission. In his journal, he described each incident in detail. Oral historian Alice Hoffman found that her husband combined many stories when he talked of his experiences as a private during World War II.[19] Although these summaries might appear to be problematic because they oversimplify what happens, they were advantageous in trying to piece together a family lifestyle in plural marriage. The children remembered what chores their mother shared with their father's other wives, and they discussed their relationships with all members of the family. I asked questions about discipline and family prayer to get a sense of who was in charge of each home. Having the opportunity to talk to my sources was also important because I could ask for clarification and more details.

Although I used the LDS Polygamy and LDS Family Life Oral History Projects to write my book, I am glad I haven't been the only one to use them. The interviews housed in the BYU L. Tom Perry Special Collections have been used extensively. As with my personal experience, family members of the interviewees continue to contact the Redd Center and Special Collections, delighted to find out that there was a tape and transcript from a beloved family member who has passed on. Students working on history papers at BYU and other universities have found readymade primary sources on a topic that interested them. Faculty members interested in polygamy have found the interviews valuable. For example, B. Carmon Hardy, a professor at California State University, Fullerton, has written extensively about the Mormon colonies in Mexico and Mormon polygamy. He used these interviews in his research. Several times, students in my history capstone class at BYU have found it interesting to research one family and compare their experiences with my conclusions.

The interviews tell much more about early Utah/Mormon life than just marriage patterns. I used the interviews to research the life cycles of Utah's women. Based on my reading of interviews with daughters, I concluded that up until World War II, girls learned what was expected of them as women from their mothers. Most expected to be wives and mothers, and they saw very few other options.[20] Charles S. Peterson, a professor at Utah State University, read the interviews for his research on Utah agricultural history. Recently, I asked Peterson how he had used the interviews. He explained that he did not consider them essential for his research but added that they provided excellent supportive stories.

I have had similar experiences with other oral history projects. I started the LDS African American Oral History Project when Alan Cherry suggested that there was little information about African Americans who had joined the LDS Church when blacks were banned from the priesthood. There was also almost no information about those who joined after 1978, when the priesthood was extended to all worthy males. I hired Cherry to conduct the interviews because I believe that it is better for insiders to do interviews because they understand the culture and share common experiences. Although the 225 interviews that Cherry conducted extended beyond the American West, they tell a great deal about the Church of Jesus Christ of Latter-day Saints, which has its headquarters in the West. The church has influenced western studies, especially Intermountain West history, and has been influenced by being in the West.

My book *Black Saints in a White Church* used Cherry's view that black Mormons experienced unusual integration because they wor-

shiped with white Latter-day Saints.[21] Martin Luther King Jr. once
called the eleven o'clock hour on Sunday the most segregated hour
in the United States. They may have been in the same Mormon
wards but black Mormons, especially in Utah where there were very
few blacks, sometimes experienced cultural misunderstandings. The
interviews and a survey supported that conclusion. Sociologist
Cardell Jacobson helped me analyze the interviews, and we found
that the LDS African Americans interviewed and surveyed were
middle class and believed in traditional Protestant values, the same
reasons other Americans give for joining the LDS Church.

Students and scholars have found the LDS African American
Oral History Project helpful in understanding the experiences of
black Latter-day Saints and have often come to very different conclusions based on their reading of the interviews. In 2010, Brigida
Delon, a BYU student in my history class, used the interviews
from Oakland, California, to look at the sense of community that
the black Latter-day Saints felt in the church. Delon grew up in
New York City. She had definite ideas that minority members, including African Americans, were discriminated against in the LDS
Church. She found that the African Americans' views of the church
in Oakland were very mixed. Eva Joseph and Vivian Troutman felt
discriminated against because of race and economics. Both came
from West Oakland, a poorer section of town, and they felt that
the women from the elite community of Piedmont were not very
accepting. Whereas my book had focused on a larger picture of
community, Delon looked at one specific area and found a lack of
community.

Sociologists have also used the interviews and come to different
views based on their discipline. In 1995, O. Kendall and Daryl
White published an article in the *Review of Religious Research*. The
Whites claim that Cherry "was unable to find a random sample,"
although that was never the goal in the project. They agreed that
"like typical oral histories, interviews were minimally structured."
They were surprised that "unlike some oral history projects, participants were identified by name, transcripts of interviews returned
to them for comments, and the final manuscripts copyrighted."
These are typical ways that historians do interviews, and it differs
from interview methodoligies in other disciplines. Still, the Whites

found that the interviews provided helpful information to determine how LDS African Americans explained priesthood restriction. Although the Church has never had a clear reason, the interviewees cited conditions in the United States at the time the church was organized, a curse dating back to Cain, and ignorance on the part of Mormons.[22]

Mormon sociologist Armand L. Mauss was also concerned about the snowballing method of obtaining LDS African American interviews because those no longer attending the Mormon church were underrepresented. But he still felt that "all of these interviews are, however, very valuable for illustrating recurrent experiences, ideas, and feelings of various individuals and certain types of interviewees." The interviews were "numerous enough to reveal a great range of social characteristics and life circumstances."[23]

African American historian Stephen Finley's reading of the transcripts identified some cultural characteristics very different than mine. While I sensed that the black Mormons were for the most part accepted within the LDS religious community and adapted to a new culture, after reading the interviews Finley felt that "culturally, African American Latter-day Saints stay connected to black churches and supplement their attendance in LDS services with black Protestant Christian services. They describe this continued connection in religious, not simply social and cultural terms." He also noted that "theologically, black Latter-day Saints describe an expanded ecclesiology. While many note the historic claims of the LDS Church to be the restored Christian Church in exclusive terms, many African American Latter-day Saints implicitly and explicitly understand neither God nor religious authority to be the province solely of the LDS Church." I was most surprised when he concluded, "African American Latter-day Saints make great efforts to construct meaningful racial identities, in the sense that it is important for them to be seen as black, but that African American communities at-large and the LDS Church are both fronts on which they view their struggles for acceptance and inclusion."[24] These examples show me that I bring my own biases when I read interviews. Although I wrote about acceptance and a sense of community, others with a different worldview perceived the stories very differently.

My career as a Mormon and western American historian has centered around the use of oral history. I recognize that there are problems with using interviews. Memories are often faulty; people's views might change over time. But I contend that any source has problems, so it is best to look for as many accounts as possible, and oral history can play an important role in understanding the community and employment of westerners, especially in the twentieth century. Interviews are often the only sources available. When there are other sources, interviews can provide more direct information; as Charles Peterson said of the polygamy collection, they provide excellent supportive stories. Interviewees are very passionate, and their excitement comes through the printed and recorded records. In addition, an oral history interview allows me the opportunity to question and gather more and sometimes deeper information. I know that my interviews have enhanced my research, and they will continue to be of value as primary sources to other scholars researching community and work in the American West.

Notes

1. Frederick Jackson Turner, "Pioneer Ideals and the State University," in *The Frontier in American History* (New York: Holt, 1920), 284, 287. Turner wrote, "In the transnational condition of American democracy which I have tried to indicate, the mission of the university is most important" and "The university has a duty in adjusting pioneer ideals to the new requirements of American democracy."

2. For more information, see Jessie L. Embry, "Little Berlin: Swiss Saints of the Logan Tenth Ward," *Utah Historical Quarterly* 56 (Summer 1988): 222–35.

3. Stephen Cameron McCracken, "German-Speaking Immigrants Living in Cache Valley: An Oral History," master's thesis, Utah State University, 1986, 107.

4. Bertis L. Embry, conversation, January 20, 1987.

5. Opel Forsberg, interview by author, 1987, 9, LDS German-speaking Immigrants Oral History Project, Charles Redd Center for Western Studies, L. Tom Perry Special Collection, Harold B. Lee Library, Brigham Young University, Provo, Utah. (Unless otherwise noted, all interviews are part of the Redd Center Oral History Program and the notes only list the project. The rest of the citation is the same.)

6. Elsie Embry, interview by author, 1987, 3; Leah Holmstead Oral History, interviewed by Jessie Embry, 1987, 4, 6–7, LDS German-speaking Immigrant Oral History Project.

7. For more information, see "Deliverer or Oppressor: American Mormon Missionaries' Views of Adolph Hitler in the 1930s," in *Regional Studies in LDS Church History: Europe*, vol. 4 (Provo, UT: Department of Church History and Doctrine, 2003), 47–63, and Embry, "Little Berlin."

8. Embry, "Little Berlin," 232–33.

9. George Rowland Blake, interview by Michael Van Wagenen, 1991, Utah World War II Home Front Oral History Project, 8–9.

10. Farrin Leon Mangelson, interview by Michael Van Wagenen, October 9, 1991, Home Front, 11; Zelda Bartlett Packer, interview by Michael Van Wagenen, October 19, 1991, Home Front, 2, 6.

11. *Technical Aid—An Investment in People: The Point Four Program in Iran* (Provo, UT: Brigham Young University Press, 1960), 3.

12. For more information on this subject, see Jessie L. Embry, *Mormon Wards as Community* (Binghamton, NY: Global Publications, 2001), 83–104; Jessie L. Embry, "Point Four, Utah State University Technicians, and Rural Development in Iran, 1950–64," *Rural History* 14 (April 2003): 100–113.

13. Embry, *Mormon Ward*, 88–89, 102.

14. Deon and Louise Hubbard, interview by author, 1999, 16, Utah Universities in Iran Oral History Project.

15. Bertis L. Embry, interview by author, 1984, 18, 84, 86. Copies in author's possession and at the Utah State University Special Collections.

16. Jessie L. Embry, *Mormon Polygamous Families: Life in the Principle* (Salt Lake City: University of Utah Press, 1987). The book has been republished by Greg Kofford Books (2009).

17. Richard S. Van Wagoner, *Mormon Polygamy: A History* (Salt Lake City: Signature Books, 1982).

18. Kimball Young, *Isn't One Wife Enough?* (New York: Holt, 1954).

19. Alice M. and Howard S. Hoffman, *Archives of Memory: A Soldier Recalls World War II* (Lexington: University Press of Kentucky, 1990).

20. Jessie L. Embry, "Women's Life Cycles, 1850–1940," in *Women in Utah History: Paradigm or Paradox?*, ed. Patricia Lyn Scott and Linda Thatcher (Logan: Utah State University Press, 2005), 394–415.

21. Jessie L. Embry, *Black Saints in a White Church: Contemporary African American Mormons* (Salt Lake City, UT: Signature Books, 1995).

22. O. Kendall White and Daryl White, "Integrating Religious and Racial Identities: An Analysis of LDS African American Explanation of Priesthood Restriction," *Review of Religious Research* 36, no. 3 (March 1995): 298–300. The five areas that the Whites identified were that LDS African Americans accepted the traditional views that blacks could be members without priesthood, a belief that blacks were denied the priesthood because of revelation but no

explanation of the reason, a focus on the present and not concentrating on the past, use of historical and sociological reasons for the ban, and a belief that whites had to become more accepting of blacks.

23. Armand L. Mauss, *All Abraham's Children: Changing Mormon Conceptions of Race and Lineage* (Urbana: University of Illinois Press, 2003), 282, 243–44.

24. Stephen C. Finley, Charles Redd Fellowship in Western American Studies Report, Charles Redd Center files.

2

A Two-Way Street

Explaining and Creating Community through Oral History

BARBARA ALLEN BOGART

*Folklorist Barbara Allen Bogart's essay on homesteading in Oregon
and mining in Wyoming raises an interesting question: Did oral history explain the community, or did the oral histories help create the
community? This question is especially important when oral historians study rural communities, where researchers can impact how residents view themselves. Bogart concludes that oral history does preserve
the history of communities, and it also allows communities to share
what the residents feel is important. In addition, the stories help create a sense of community with past and present residents because they
see more value in their own experiences. As Bogart writes, "The oral
history project and the exhibit ... legitimiz[ed] the boom ... as a
significant element of their past. It was no longer just something they
had lived through."*

THE WESTERN LANDSCAPE has an endless appeal to me—not just the
sweeping vistas of mountains and plains but the small communities
that lie between them. If we seem closer to nature in the West, I
believe we are also closer to history here. The most direct route to
the past, I also believe, is through the memories of those who inhabit this extraordinary region. As an oral historian, I have been

guided by the principle that oral history reveals the shape and meaning of the past from the narrator's point of view. By extension, when
oral history is collected and used in a community setting, it can reveal the dimensions of members' collective view of the local past.
This orientation was forged in my first major fieldwork project, in a
tiny settlement in south central Oregon, and it shaped the final project of my professional life, in a town of about 12,000 in southwestern Wyoming. Both communities were established during key historical periods in the Intermountain West: early twentieth-century
homesteading and ranching in Oregon, the transcontinental railroad, and mineral extraction in Wyoming in the 1970s.

The projects I undertook in both these communities created no
ripples in the academic world, but I believe they had an impact on
the communities themselves, especially by influencing how residents
of the communities saw and interpreted their own history as a result
of the oral history that I collected in each place. Let me explain.

Story Hunting in the Oregon Desert

A freshly minted doctoral candidate in folklore studies from UCLA,
I arrived in the dusty high desert of the Fort Rock Valley in south
central Oregon on a hot summer day in June 1978. I pulled into
my sister's long lane in my small car, which was stuffed with clothes,
books, and a box of blank cassette tapes, notepads, empty file fold-
ers, and a handheld tape recorder.

I moved into a twelve-foot travel trailer parked in my sister's
front yard—my home for summer. From the windows of the trailer,
I could see for miles in three directions. In those vistas, fewer than
half a dozen houses were visible. Beyond a low range of hills to the
west was the hamlet of Silver Lake, dating from the 1870s, consist-
ing of a post office, a store, a school, two or three businesses, and
perhaps two dozen homes. To the northeast was the even smaller
crossroads community of Fort Rock, established in the 1910s.[1] In
1978, there were roughly 300 residents of the Silver Lake–Fort
Rock area.

I was there to conduct fieldwork for my dissertation. My thesis
was that when asked to talk about local history, people would re-

spond with stories. I knew virtually nothing about the area before I arrived. I had chosen it for my fieldwork only because my sister and her husband lived there and could provide an entree into the community.

Before arriving in the Fort Rock Valley, I spent several days at the state and university libraries in Salem and Eugene, reading the few historical accounts of eastern Oregon and Lake County, trying to get a handle on the area's past but discovering little of interest or usefulness. "Nothing ever happened here," I wailed to myself. "This will be the shortest field project on record." Of course, I was wrong. There is nowhere on the planet where "nothing ever happened." By the end of the summer, I had discovered that plenty had happened in this postage stamp of a place, and I had recorded only a minute fraction of its human history. So I plunged into the fieldwork in a mood that combined fevered excitement and cold feet.

I decided to conduct open-ended interviews without a questionnaire—partly to encourage people to tell stories about the local past and partly because I still knew so little about the area that I had no specific topics to ask about. In the interviews, people gave me information about area history, but it wasn't in story form. Within two weeks and after just half a dozen interviews, my thesis was in shambles.

My first response was panic. I had moved out of my apartment in Los Angeles, put all my belongings in storage, and banked on this project to provide material for my dissertation. The idea of returning home and starting all over on a new project made me break out in a cold sweat. So I took a second look at the material I had gathered. Even if it wasn't in the form of the stories that I had expected, it must be *something*. The best thing to do, I decided, was to continue as I had begun—that is, keep using the same format for the interviews. That way, at the end of the summer I might not have anything of substance, but at least it would have the virtue of consistency. I soldiered on.

During my stay in the Fort Rock Valley, I interviewed about three dozen people, out of the hundred or so who lived there. Most of them were second- or third-generation residents of the area, like the two women in their eighties, whose French-born father, a professional chef with no farming experience, had brought his wife and five young daughters to the valley in 1909 (see figure 2.1). The sisters still lived in the homestead cabin their father had built, and they still ranched. I had several interviews with a man whose Finnish immigrant parents had also arrived in 1909. His home combined the original homestead cabin with an old schoolhouse, where he lovingly produced mimeographed articles on various topics of local history, based on information he had gathered over the years from area residents. The local rancher who was my sister's landlord regaled me with stories of his parents' experiences in the valley, along with the exploits of local characters.

Gradually over the summer, the story of the community emerged—in spite of my clumsy technique—and I began to see the material I was gathering for what it *was,* rather than what I thought it would be. Once I focused on what people were telling me, instead of how they were saying it, I began to hear repeated references to homesteading and stories filled with images of that era. What was especially striking to me about this emphasis on homesteading was that this topic was virtually absent from the published materials I had read before arriving in the valley. By the end of the summer it was abundantly clear to me that, as far as area residents were concerned, homesteading was the pivot around which all local history revolved. Every one of the three dozen people I inter-

Figure 2.1 The tiny hamlet of Fort Rock as it appeared in 1912. The rock formation that gave the community its name is visible on the right. Credit: Fort Rock Valley Historical Society.

viewed—old-timers and newcomers alike—had something to say about it. When I counted the times various subjects were mentioned, homesteading topped the list. When I plotted those subjects on a timeline, the homesteading period and the years surrounding it dominated the chart. Clearly I had tapped into a collective understanding of local history that had been shaped over the years by the ongoing conversations that residents shared among themselves about where they lived.

As I tuned into what people were talking about, I began to think of the topics in the interviews as a kind of seismograph. A new thesis began to emerge: when asked to talk about local history, narrators will focus most intently on what they consider to be its most important aspects. In the Fort Rock Valley, people talked most often and at greatest length about the dryland homesteading that brought nearly 1,200 people into the valley in the 1910s and the drought that drove almost all of them out again by the early 1920s.

Over and over, people told me of families arriving with little more than a few sticks of furniture and no farming experience to take up 320 acres of land under the Enlarged Homestead Act of 1909. They described the 10′ by 14′ or 12′ by 16′ cabins of milled lumber and tar paper in which the families lived. They explained how drought, jackrabbits, and killing frosts in the summers eventually drove the homesteaders out. Sometimes I heard the same story from two or three people—of houses abandoned with coffee cups still left on the tables, school buildings hauled off their foundations to become additions to existing ranch houses, whole families piling their few belongings into wagons and leaving the valley after years of hard, fruitless work. These were clearly the touchstones, images that symbolized the homestead era for residents of the area. They were also hard evidence for me that residents had formed a communal understanding of the homesteading era as the focal point of the local past—and local identity.

When I finally drove out of the valley at the end of August, the landscape was full of ghosts for me, dotted with the small homestead shacks, schools, and stores that had filled it in the 1910s. The richness of the area's human history had been laid out for me in the words and stories of the people who lived there. It was no longer an empty place where nothing had ever happened.

I wrote my dissertation based on the interviews I had conducted over that summer, arguing that the shape of the local past from the insiders' perspective was clearly revealed in the topics they chose to emphasize in the interviews.[2] In 1985, I returned to the valley to do more research in primary sources and to talk with a few more people. Eventually, I wrung a book about the homesteading era from all my research, including the interviews.

The book was published in spring 1987.[3] That fall, I returned to Fort Rock to attend the annual Homesteaders' Reunion. I brought copies of the book with me to give to some of the narrators who still lived in the area. One woman in her eighties, who had been born in the valley and lived there most of her adult life, beamed at me when I handed her the book. On the dust jacket was a photograph of a group of women, along with a young girl, in front of a homestead cabin. She was the twelve-year-old girl in the picture. "Who would ever have thought I would be on the cover of a book?" she said wonderingly. Her remark gave me a thrill of pride for what I had apparently done for her. During the reunion, as copies of the book circulated among the attendees, I watched and listened as people flipped to the index looking for familiar names, recognized and re-peated stories in the text, wondered why certain families were not mentioned. I was gratified at the apparently positive response, but I also became aware that the material in the book was on the brink of entering the slipstream of community historical tradition, that it would become fodder for future conversations about the local past, including discussions of what I had gotten wrong and what had been left out.

In the early 1990s, the Fort Rock Historical Society put together a small museum, where my book was sold. In 2007, the book was reprinted by a regional publisher, so it continues to have a life in the area.[4] As I think about that, I realize that the story it tells, as-sembled from the memories I gathered from a more or less random group of people in the area in 1978, may have had the effect of consolidating the local view of history—preserving it in amber, as it were. My argument that homesteading was the keystone of local history may have become a self-fulfilling prophecy.

Drilling for Meaning in Wyoming

Oddly enough, the book on Fort Rock led me by a long and winding road to Evanston, Wyoming, the setting for the other bookend of my oral history career. In 1989, I participated in a conference in Billings, Montana, celebrating the statehood centennial of the northern Rocky Mountain and Plains states. Standing in the book exhibit room at the conference, I overheard a woman asking about my Fort Rock book at the sales table. Thrilled by the attention, I introduced myself to her. She was from Rock Springs, Wyoming; after our conversation, she invited me to participate in a program at Western Wyoming Community College the following summer. I fell in love with Wyoming during my visit, and I moved there permanently by summer 1991. Three years later, I was settled in Evanston in the southwestern corner of the state.[5]

Historically, Evanston was a railroad town, founded when the tracks of the Union Pacific Railroad reached the Bear River Valley in southwestern Wyoming in late fall 1868. From the moment I arrived there, I heard references to "the boom," a period from the mid-1970s through the mid-1980s when Evanston and the surrounding area had been in the throes of oil and gas exploration and production. By the mid-1990s, the boom had been over for ten years, but it had clearly left its mark on the local psyche. Conversations were peppered with the phrases "before the boom," "during the boom," and "since the boom." Applying the principle I had developed in Oregon—that people will talk most about what looms largest in their historical consciousness—I realized that the boom and the subsequent bust constituted a watershed event in local history. The longer I lived in Evanston, the more this impression was confirmed.

I gradually became part of the community, working as a historical consultant, operating my own bookstore, serving on various historic and civic boards, and eventually becoming director of the county history museum. Through those years, I maintained my original curiosity about the boom, believing that it offered a ripe opportunity for oral history and a deeper understanding of the community from the inside. After all, for all I knew, the town might as well have been built the day before I moved there. My

chance to pursue the boom as a research topic finally came in
2005, when, as museum director, I launched an oral history project with the goal of mounting an exhibit based on the material
gathered. The museum secured funding from the Wyoming Humanities Council, corporate sources, and the Charles Redd Center for Western Studies at BYU to conduct and transcribe the interviews and produce the exhibit.[6]

There was no question that the periods of boom and bust were
significant in the community's history, and I wanted to discover its
dimensions from those who had lived through it. In selecting narrators for the project, I sought people with direct experience of the
boom from as many sectors of the community as possible. They
eventually included both lifelong community residents and people
who came during the boom and stayed. Among them were elected
city and county officials, police officers, teachers and school administrators, attorneys and judges, nurses, city workers, real estate
agents, bankers, pastors, oilfield workers, oil company employees,
and retail business owners. My goal was to construct a seismograph that revealed the contours of the boom from the insiders'
perspective.

Having learned from my initial disastrous experience in Oregon
that completely open-ended interviews were not very effective, I
used a questionnaire as a framework for the interviews, asking people about their involvement in the boom and about its effects—
both good and bad—on the community. It was relatively easy for
me to do because at this point I had lived in Evanston for ten years
and understood something of its history—an advantage I did not
enjoy in Fort Rock.

Over a six-month period, I interviewed forty-four people.[7] All of
them spoke about their experiences and perceptions of the boom.
People talked about the early signs of change coming as oil companies began buying up oil leases, surveying, and drilling explor-
atory wells. They spoke at length about the social chaos created
when the community was flooded with thousands of mostly young
single men looking for work in the oilfield and on construction
sites. They explained the more permanent and visible changes in
the community as roads, schools, a hospital, and other public buildings were constructed, and new housing developments exploded

the community beyond its original boundaries and tripled its geographic size.

Just as many of the narrators in Fort Rock had focused on a few vivid images of the homesteading period, so those narrators in Evanston often mentioned specific elements from the boom period that encapsulated its impact on residents—a railroad underpass bottleneck that regularly caused miles-long traffic jams, oilfield workers flinging $100 bills around town, a notorious row of bars on a downtown street, people living in tents along the highways leading to the oilfields, and the shoddy construction of hastily constructed boomera houses. Nearly everyone spoke about these topics, which symbolized the physical and social chaos of the period.

For everyone I interviewed, the hallmark of the boom was change—the changes it wrought in the community, both physically in the built environment and socially in the influx of outsiders who came during that period. The population of Evanston ballooned from 4,000 in 1970 to an estimated peak of 18,000 in the early 1980s. Even after the boom ended, the population did not return to its preboom levels. (Even by 2000, the population was still 11,000.) The economic structure of the community, historically dominated by the railroad and ranching, now included oil and gas extraction. The social and religious structure of the community expanded dramatically from its predominantly working-class, Mormon base to include engineers, attorneys, physicians, and other professionals drawn to the community during the boom. Many of these new residents became involved in creating arts and philanthropic organizations, establishing new congregations for a wide range of religious denominations, and provided the impetus for a strong historic preservation movement in the community. In speaking of these changes, many of the old-timers mourned the loss of their small, tight-knit, homogeneous hometown, whereas newcomers, who were the agents of change, viewed the changes more positively.

The exhibit created from the interviews, *Boom and Bust in the Overthrust*, opened for a nine-month run at the Uinta County Museum in September 2006. The four dominant themes in the interviews—early signs of the changes coming, the social chaos of the period, the physical and social transformation of the community as a result of the boom, and reflections after the fact on the boom's significance—became the exhibit's infrastructure, and the narrative line was carried in excerpts from the interviews. Distilling the boom experience into discrete themes had the effect of shaping people's perceptions of the period and of their own experiences. At the same time, the themes were deeply familiar to the exhibit visitors. Lurking on the periphery of the exhibit area, as I frequently did, I heard visitors tell their own stories in response to the images they were seeing.

The exhibit attracted many new visitors into the museum—presumably drawn by the prospect of seeing their own lives and experiences reflected there and giving them the opportunity to tell their own stories as well. It also brought a wealth of artifacts into the museum on loan, including a collection of hundreds of boom-related stickers and patches, three large trash bags of oilfield-era ball caps resurrected from a garage, and a working scale model of a drilling rig, which has since become part of the museum's permanent collection. Once people saw the exhibit—especially those who had worked in the oilfield during the boom—they were eager to contribute the material evidence of their experiences. So the exhibit was almost continuously expanded during its run.

Just as the oral history interviews called on narrators to reflect on their experiences, the exhibit prompted visitors to see those experiences, along with their own, in a larger context. For me, an outsider to the community who had not lived through the boom, the project created an awareness of how utterly the boom transformed the community. The town I walked into was not the same place that residents had known before the boom.

A few people were initially puzzled by both the oral history project and the resulting exhibit. The subject did not seem historical to them. In fact, one man whom I interviewed told me bluntly, "When you first called and told me what you were doing, I didn't get it. This wasn't history. This was just something we lived through." But after my interview with him, he said, "Now I *do* get it. This is part of our history, too." In the long run, the oral history project and the exhibit had the effect of legitimizing the boom in the community's consciousness as a significant element of their past. It was no longer something they had just lived through. It gave them a way to think about the boom beyond their own experiences, to recognize the subtle as well as the obvious effects of the period.

In an incident reminiscent of the woman from Fort Rock who was delighted to find herself on a book cover, a former oilfield worker discovered himself in the exhibit quite by accident. In the late 1970s, he had taken a year off from college in Massachusetts and had come to Wyoming to work as a roustabout in the oil fields. He eventually returned to school, earned his doctorate in chemistry, and became a very successful chemist. In 2007, while attending a professional conference in Salt Lake City, he rented a car and drove up to Evanston "for old time's sake" as he later explained. Driving around town, he spotted the exhibit sign outside the museum and decided to come in. There he saw himself in a photograph of several oilfield workers in 1979. He was shocked and delighted at the same time. The picture not only brought back memories but made him realize that he, too, had had a hand in the changes the boom had brought to the community.

What It All Means

Oral historians understand that oral history is a process that creates a historical record. They also understand that the very act of asking people about their experiences can give these narrators a new awareness of the significance of those experiences. Both of these aspects of oral history were part of my work in Fort Rock and Evanston. Those projects also suggest that oral history projects in a community context have another dimension as the work of the oral historian becomes interwoven with the existing historical traditions among community residents. Here oral history has the power not only to inform but also to transform people's ideas about their history.

In the Fort Rock project, my published study of homesteading put the local understanding of what had happened there into a broader regional context. In Evanston, the interviews and the museum exhibit offered residents an opportunity to see what had happened to the community in larger strokes and allowed them to measure their own understanding of the boom against the narrative I constructed from the stories I had gathered in the interviews.

In both communities, residents' memories were filtered through my perspective as an outsider, then re-presented to them. I believe the work I did made a contribution to a community's understanding of its history. I am also keenly aware that the version of history I created through oral history has probably become part of a feedback loop into the community's view of its own past.

If oral history in a community setting has the potential to affect and shape community's view of its own history, to become woven permanently into local historical consciousness, then oral historians must recognize that we are not just documenting history; we are part of the process of shaping people's understanding of it.

Sailing between Scylla and Charybdis

Oral historians working with communities to document their history straddle two worlds. One is the community in which the oral history is recorded; the other is the academic community to which we all belong to some degree or another. I came to an awareness of this duality only after my fieldwork in Oregon was completed. I approached that project from an academic point of view: I was there to record information that would be useful in completing my doctoral program. I had no idea then that the material I gathered and the wisdom I gained would broaden my perspective to include the possibility that the community's own view of its past had a validity equal to that of the outside academic historian. In my book on Fort Rock, I was careful to present the local past in light of the larger historical context of early twentieth-century homesteading while retaining the community's interpretation of it. In Evanston, I undertook the oral history project as both an academic enterprise—to document people's memories of the boom and bust period as part of the museum's archival records—and as a project derived from and constructed for the community.

To which world do we swear our first allegiance, and where does our primary responsibility lie? How do we reconcile the community's perspective on its past with that of the larger world of historical research? How do we tell the community's story to the broader historical community? How do we negotiate the channel between the whirlpool of Charybdis, which can suck us into the community's view of its past with no reference to the outside, and the monster of Scylla, who feeds on our work with no reference to the community's perspective on it? That metaphor is a little exaggerated, but the divide between the two is quite real, as all oral historians working in public history settings understand. The trick is to recognize the challenges and demands of both worlds and find the balance that will create a fully dimensional view of the past from both the inside and the outside.

Notes

1. The community was named for a nearby rock formation—a tuff ring more than 4,000 feet in diameter and standing about 200 feet above the surrounding plan. Its tall, straight sides resemble a fort, thus giving the formation its name.

2. Barbara Allen, "Talking about the Past: A Folkloristic Analysis of Orally Communicated History," PhD diss., University of California, Los Angeles, 1980.

3. Barbara Allen Bogart, *Homesteading the High Desert* (Salt Lake City: University of Utah Press, 1987). Eventually, all the interview tapes and other materials I gathered in researching the area were donated to the Special Collections of the University of Oregon Library.

4. Barbara Allen Bogart, *Homesteading the Oregon Desert* (Wallowa, OR: Bear Creek Press, 2007).

5. Evanston was established in December 1868 as an end-of-the-tracks town on the Union Pacific Railroad. It was platted a year later. Until the early 1970s, the railroad was the dominant economic force in the community. Other economic activities that shaped the community's identity were coal mining and ranching.

6. The interviews were conducted between November 2005 and June 2006. The exhibit, *Boom and Bust in the Overthrust, 1975–1985,* was on display in the Uinta County, Wyoming, Museum from September 2006 through June 2007.

7. The tapes and fully transcribed interviews are part of the collection of the Uinta County Museum in Evanston. Copies of the transcripts are also on file at the Uinta County Library.

3

Probing Memory and Experience

The Untapped Potential of Oral History (Re)Collections

LAURIE MERCIER

Historian Laurie Mercier's long work in oral history in the West pro-
vides a setting for her to reflect on interviewing and then using the
interviews in historical research. In this essay, she laments that many
early oral histories are only gathering dust on archive shelves even
though they have much to tell about memory and historical events. As
she reexamined interviews she did years ago, she found new values for
oral history. First, she found that memory can be both collective and
individual—and those memories change over time. Unlike other
sources, it is possible to ask an interviewee how he or she felt at the
time, exposing the different ways that people evaluate the past. As
Mercier finds with a collection of interviews with Montana women,
sometimes what interviewees do not say—the silences—are as impor-
tant as the stories.

OVER THE YEARS, state historical societies, museums, and universities in the American West have created impressive and rich oral
history archives. These represent a tribute to the many dedicated
oral historians who have persisted in collecting and preserving so
many interviews despite financial obstacles and lack of institutional
support. These archival projects have been designed with future

historians in mind: they have anticipated the loss of memories about specific events and lifeways and endeavored to record and preserve them. The collections reflect the diversity of people and life in the West, whether documenting reindeer herding in the Northern Slope or the impact of flooding from a dam break in southeastern Idaho.[1]

Sadly, these collections have been underutilized by scholars. Researchers typically dip into individual interviews that offer specific information, or they conduct their own interviews for particular projects and donate them to an archive. Scholars, producers, and curators may use archived interviews for their publications, exhibitions, radio, and other media productions. Rarely do they turn to collections as a whole for understanding the region and particular eras and events. As archivists and scholars, many of us have straddled the often different worlds of creating and interpreting oral history interviews. It is only recently, with two book projects, that I have begun to look more broadly at some oral history collections.[2] Through this process, it has become clear that these collections often speak as a group, revealing insights that individual interviews cannot. They present new possibilities for studying people, communities, and regions, and reveal the role of memory and storytelling in accounts of the past. Moreover, oral history collections can help us understand the West in new ways. This essay suggests that we might take measure of four decades of collecting oral history in the West to see how it affects our understanding of the region's past.[3]

Oral history collections have not merely recorded and preserved people's reminiscences about forgotten events and experiences; they can provide a glimpse of memory at specific points in time. They represent snapshots of how people reconstructed the past and the way they chose to translate their experience in light of all kinds of influences, including community pressures, changing political and social values, and the presence of a particular interviewer and his or her questions. This chapter focuses on two different kinds of memory: the collective or social, and the individual. Both point to the ways that archival collections can help us more clearly understand the complexity of people's lives, based on my fieldwork in Montana in the 1980s and my more recent analysis of some of those same interviews three decades later.[4]

A review of any oral interview collection reminds us that memory is socially produced. People construct narratives out of their own cultural expectations and influences and, in turn, relate accounts that have meaning to others sharing that milieu. Anthropologist Elizabeth Tonkin argues that oral narratives are constructed and reinforced by daily discourses that stabilize existing social relationships and are "less individual than is commonly supposed."[5] The broader social and cultural context, communities, the nation, and ideologies shape memories or the recounting of stories about the past.

Two examples from Idaho and Montana illustrate how a changing political culture can change the construction of memories and how interviewers can help narrators override those pressures to conform. Folklorist Sam Schrager wrote about his fieldwork in northern Idaho recording the role of the Industrial Workers of the World (IWW, or "Wobblies") in the 1917 timber workers strike. Schrager heard repeated stories about how terrible logging camp conditions prompted the strike, and narrators consistently credited the IWW, not the companies, for bringing about necessary changes in the camps. Schrager noted that this kind of collective oral story contrasted to written accounts of the Wobblies, in which they were portrayed as tramps and troublemakers. What strikes me in rereading Schrager's essay is that his narrators are appreciative observers of, not participants in, the IWW, even though we know that almost 90 percent of Northwest woods workers in 1917 joined the IWW in going out on strike. For example, Dick Benge said that he did not go out on strike because he had to support his parents, but he was pleased with the results: "'They put in steel bunks for us. They furnished us our bedding, blankets, pillow, sheets, everything! Of course I didn't *help* 'em any with it, but . . . I enjoyed what they done.'"[6] I suggest that perhaps narrators distanced themselves from anything that might be viewed as controversial according to contemporary sensibilities.

But narrators can construct variations in their telling, and interviewers can play a critical role in helping the narrator push against social codes and better articulate meaning. By the questions interviewers ask, narrators are motivated to transform their personal anecdotes into a more self-reflective form that, as Alessandro Portelli has noted, includes the larger historical and social significance of what has happened to them. Interviewers and narrators are engaged in "dialogic discourse," constantly negotiating the story that is told.[7]

In interviewing woods workers in western Montana in the early 1980s, I found this same appreciation for but distancing from the IWW. For example, former logger Bert Wilke felt a need to rationalize his participation in the union—it was clear that the intervening years dominated by the cold war and the negative portrayals of the IWW made him hesitate to admit his sympathies. As interviewer, I made it clear that I was interested in hearing more about the IWW and historicized his involvement by returning to the question, "But what did you think at the time?" By acknowledging that he was the product of and involved in a particular time that spawned the IWW, he was able to recall and talk freely about his earlier, more enthusiastic identification as a Wobbly without fear of current judgments.

As interviewers creating and researchers using oral history collections, we must attend to these social influences on the construction of the past, including how one's community helps shape those narratives. Interviews are often intended to embody a community perspective, focusing on the dreams, opinions, and fates of others in the community as much as about individual experience.

The fluidity of collective memory is apparent in two sets of interviews I conducted in the blue-collar, company-dominated but very union town of Anaconda, Montana. The interviews reveal that within the span of the decade following the closure of the town's major industry, people began to recast their memories of the role of the Anaconda Copper Mining Company in the community. Shortly after the smelter shut down in 1980, workers and residents were quite critical of the company and faulted poor management for the plant closures. But years later, in a deindustrialized and desperate economy with high unemployment, with few Anaconda workers now belonging to a union, many shifted their blame for the closure from the company to environmental and labor demands.[8]

An alert interviewer familiar with past interviews can question why stories have changed. As I heard these revised interpretations, I was in the position to question people about why this collective story about the company had changed so dramatically. Union activist Howard Rosenleaf noted the contradictions evident in the community stories circulating: "Of course the company told 'em, 'Hey, it's your fault.' And they believed that . . . the unions went too far, asked for too much. I negotiated probably seven or eight times with the Anaconda Company, never once in all the years that I negotiated did anyone ever tell me, 'You got too much.'" Instead, Rosenleaf remembered, rank-and-file members complained, "'You sold us down the river, you son-of-a-bitch. Is that all the better you can do? [But] that plant wasn't down fifteen minutes and somebody said to me, 'Well you finally did it, you pushed 'em too far.'" Rosenleaf's account and his frustration with changing perspectives recognize that community memory had been sabotaged in some way by intervening events. Other narrators admitted that they were no longer company critics because of their changed circumstances. Former employees, such as Jerry Hansen, noted, "We all hated the work, but now we wish we were back."

Other longtime unionists noted the dramatic changes in community life and the contradictions embedded in postshutdown conversations. "Now they complain, they say it's all the union's fault [for closing the smelter], I hear that a lot," Erma Bennett commented. "People that wouldn't have anything if it hadn't been for unions. . . . Would have worked their whole lives and died in the poor house, got nothing" had it not been for unions. Katie Dewing noted the change in her restaurant workers union: "We have a union but nobody pays any attention to it. If the waitresses were to go out on strike tomorrow wouldn't make a bit of difference. People would still go in the Park Café and eat. But in the old days they wouldn't have."

Attentive interviewers can help narrators reflect more deeply about changing memories by asking them to contrast then and now, and thus acknowledge that one's assessment of the past is shaped by the present. The Anaconda narrators were able to assess quite clearly how the revised community narrative reflected the changing political climate of the 1980s, the loss of alternative perspectives as formerly expressed by organized labor and a more diverse media, and a public willingness to target unions and environmentalists rather than more complex structural economic factors.

Not many oral historians have the opportunity to return to their narrators years later and interrogate the contradictions embedded in their changing stories, so these examples underscore how collective stories can change and how oral history collections can illuminate those historical processes. We have generally moved away from what Luisa Passerini calls the "facile democratization" of oral history that relied on letting people "speak for themselves," but at the same time, oral histories need to be considered on their own terms and not merely plugged into the standard historiography as "fragments through which the past . . . may be reconstructed."[9] In the past twenty years, oral historians have come to recognize what Alessandro Portelli has called the "distortions" of memory as a value rather than weakness, as narrators seek to "make sense of the past and to give a form to their lives."[10]

Let us turn to the second form of memory that we most expect from oral history: individual memory. Oral history, after all, provides the personal insights about past events that illuminate our understanding of a larger history. For the past decade I have been struggling to write a book that will profile selected oral history interviews with Montana women, part of a project completed in the 1980s. In returning to this collection, I am struck by persistent themes that had not occurred to me as I completed the interviews. I think of these as individual stories, because I do not believe that the women had practiced telling these tales with other listeners, as we find in the collective stories already mentioned. Although the women came from different communities and backgrounds, and their stories lack the uniformity that we find in many community oral histories, they share much generationally and economically. They all came of age in the 1920s–40s, and all struggled to support themselves and their families.

In many ways these end up as collective stories based on gender—based on the narrators' expectations that they, their partners, and society had about their roles as women. Indeed, one might ask if there is anything but a collective narrative. The interview transcripts reveal that the women also place their narratives in the context of the time of the interview and respond to the social location of the interviewer. They framed their accounts to contrast what they perceived to be different choices for women a half century before the gains of the feminist movement in the 1970s. For example, they often emphasized moments of triumph despite great

social odds. They also responded to me in certain ways because of
my age and gender.

There are two dominant, striking themes emphasized by all of
these female narrators. The first is material survival—about how
much the women endured hardships, had to make do, sacrificed,
and sometimes triumphed. This is a familiar theme in other oral
histories with western women and also in popular film and the writings of professional historians about women in the West. The other
dominant theme concerns intimate relationships. These stories
challenge persistent myths about families and gender ideals; they
also reveal attitudes and silences that tell us much about women's
lives. How do women describe their relationships? They often claim
their independence owing to absent or ineffective husbands or as-
sert expectations for egalitarian relationships. At best, their stories
reveal some ambivalence toward husbands, which contradicts many
western stories of women as partners. In women's history research,
we ask questions about private and public spheres, but these narrators did not distinguish between the two. Clearly these interviews
tell us much more than the details of life in a particular place.

Women often chose to highlight how they asserted their independence despite the odds. Their insistence at maintaining egalitarian marriages illustrated this, as Helen Raymond explains: "I didn't
think about it much then, it was just up to me to go to work. And
I was never discriminated against much and the men I married were
people I got along with pretty good. And I didn't feel like I was
taking second place. I remember when I was married to my first
husband, we went hunting or anything and I was always in the
gang with him and I was part of everything." This assertiveness is
echoed by Lula Martinez, who referenced her attitudes "then"
compared to the recent feminist movement:

> I've always been [for women's rights] but I didn't even know
> it, and I think you will find the majority of women are but
> they don't know because they've never really knew what [fem-
> inism] was. . . . I had a good understanding with my first hus-
> band. And my second time, when I got married, I just laid it
> on the line the same way, you know, and we got along fine,
> really good. . . . I think as far as marriage is concerned, I think
> it's great but I think that a complete understanding before-

hand is due because I'm this way and I'm not going to change for nobody because I'm me.

In their narratives, Raymond and Martinez downplayed the role of their husbands in their lives even as they insisted on their roles as equal partners. They hinted that they could survive on their own without husbands, even if they enjoyed male companionship, as witnessed by their choices to marry again. Most other women featured in this collection had little to say about husbands, which may have had much to do with their desires to re-create their lives and for once put themselves at the center of their histories. Their silences about intimate relationships may also reveal ambivalences or pain. These individual oral histories, then, not only reflect that men and women often led separate, gendered lives but that they also become part of collective stories from women that indicate their modes of resistance in the face of limited power and economic opportunities. In the process of telling their stories, they seemed empowered or emboldened.

The fact that a significant number of the Montana women interviewed were on their own (from desertion or what was legally called "malicious abandonment," or separation) but never formally divorced also explains silence, resentment, or ambivalence toward relationships. The oral history collection leads us to this realization; one cannot often find evidence of desertion or separation in census statistics or court records. Others had married several times, and some casually mentioned an early marriage, a "kid" marriage, glossing over it as if it didn't count, but needing to mention it to explain the presence of children or the chronology of their lives.

That skipping over or avoidance of stories interests me now. How would these women tell stories about their lives that had remained hidden from or forgotten by their families and communities? As we have seen in looking at social/collective oral history, ordinarily people recount their lives in rehearsed "conversational narratives," frequently judged by family, friends, and community. But in the individual oral history account, until the interview, these women have not told their stories or even avoided them, or they tell them in new ways prompted by an interviewer's questions.

As a narrative bumps up against a social convention, narrators struggle with how to explain their lives within a perceived framework of acceptability. For example, Ida Duntly, who met and married a railroader in Minot, North Dakota, moved west to the Fort Benton area, where his family lived and they could take up a homestead. Later, with two young children and pregnant with a third, Duntly's husband deserted her. This is how she described the incident after I asked about her first year on the homestead that she acquired: "Well, I don't know what to say, I hate to tell you this . . . and I don't want to be recorded [she later consented], but my husband left, pulled out, and he never went out there so the little kids and I went out there by ourselves and that was tough going, all those years I was out there." Somewhat embarrassed, and still saddened by the painful episode so many years later, Duntly hesitated to explain the event but knew it was essential for understanding her choices and hard life that followed as a single parent. I then asked why she decided to remain on the homestead.

> Well, you have it and I didn't want to give it up, I had nothing you know, once you have it you might as well and I stayed, stayed out there. And then when I got it proved up, I had to borrow, borrow, borrow all the time and by that time, then I borrowed money on the homestead to pay off all my debts and I'm off the homestead . . . that's how I lost it. . . . Wasn't that beautiful? . . . And alone and everything and going through this other deal and everything.

Duntly spoke of the pain and shock of her predicament as a deserted young mother and expressed reluctance to record the story—the rest of her narrative emphasized her life of hard work and struggle to raise children and grandchildren, enduring one hardship after another, and through determination working to ensure that they received education and vocational training. In reexamining her story and others, it began to make sense why so many women emphasized their children's or grandchildren's lives in their oral narratives—their own lives had been so full of hurt and struggle in the first half of the twentieth century, and achievement was often expressed through the offspring's successes. Gender determined their job choices and opportunities and family circumstances, whether in marriage, divorce, or desertion.

Deserted by her first husband, Peggy Cyzeski found work in Malta at a hospital treating quarry workers with dust pneumonia to support herself and her two children. Then another tragic chapter in her story unfolded:

> I worked there till I met Mr. Roe and I married a Mr. Roe. And I supported him for ten years. He would not work, he would not hold a job, he would not work. He was a very good-looking man, he had personality plus and I had been a widow for eight years with my children and I married this Mr Roe. . . . I seen him very few times but I was lonely and alone and so I married him. And we lived together ten years and I supported him ten years.

The language that Cyzeski used to describe herself as a "widow" (instead of deserted) and references to her loneliness as an explanation for marriage again reveal the limited options for women and the social pressures to marry. But Roe did not follow social expectations to be a responsible provider and mate.

> [We leased a Missouri River ranch], bought an old truck, a team, a few chickens and a hog from my hospital money. . . . And there I was alone again. . . . He wasn't with me, he was supposed to go out and work on construction and make money and send to us, but he would come home every fall about huntin' time without a dime. . . . My neighbor loaned me a mowin' machine, there was a big crop of sweet clover had come up on the river bar, and the kids and I mowed it, raked it up with pitchforks, thrashed it out and sacked it and took it to town and we had enough money out of that clover to get them in school and pay the rent on the ranch for the next spring. I would take my kids to school in Malta and work in the wintertime. I worked as a nurse for a long time and then I worked in a cleaning shop as a alteration lady and I mended clothes.

Cyzeski frames her struggles to survive in contrast to Roe's irresponsibility. In her narrative about life and work in rural northeastern Montana and her many disappointments, she explains how she learned not to depend on men and describes how she raised children and grandchildren from her own hard work.

More than anything, women emphasized that responsibility for children (and sometimes grandchildren) shaped their choices in life. Ida Duntly, who described a long list of restaurant jobs she held after her homestead experiment, explained why she relocated from Great Falls to the small community of Geraldine, which had fewer economic opportunities:

> I found it too hard for me to try to raise those girls in Great Falls, I couldn't, and you can take care of them better in a small town. I couldn't have watched those kids and worked out in the city. And I had to do it, I had the girls and I had to take care of them. And I thought a small town would be better to do it in. That's why I started to work in Geraldine 'cause then I put the kids to school in Geraldine and stayed right there.

Sometimes women expressed ambivalence toward those children and hinted at lives they might have had were they unencumbered by family responsibilities. As a young woman, Bernice Kingsbury played the violin in a dance band in western Montana and recalled how her musical aspirations were cut short by a premature marriage and pregnancy:

> And so I married somebody else and had a child by him, but we never estab[lished] . . . just a kid marriage, you know. And so I went back to [Tacoma] with my folks and went to beauty school. My eldest sister took care of my little boy for me, but I'd spend every weekend with her in order to be with my son. . . .
>
> I was all set to . . . I found somebody that would finance me on the Dollar Steamship line and I was going to the Orient and have a beauty shop on the ship. It sounded like a great idea and I went to visit my son. . . . I thought nope, if I'm gonna have my baby, I'd better get to where I can have him every day.

With a loan from her mother and brother, Kingsbury opened a beauty shop in Valier. Her narrative suggests opportunities but emphasizes her obligations to raise her child that sent her in another direction, limiting her choices to life in a small Montana town.

Rose Larson of Roundup spoke about her own early failed marriage (another kid marriage) and the economic circumstances that constrained young couples and burdened them with family oversight. She describes how she asserted her independence while collaborating with her ex-husband to raise her children:

> My dad worked in the mines and each kid tried to get a little job of his own to see if he can make ends meet. . . . Then when I was sixteen I got married, then we lived in Klein for a while then the Klein mines shut down . . . because my husband was a younger man in the mine he was out of a job so we moved out in the ranch . . . with his uncle. That's where we opened a coal mine and we worked there until we couldn't do no more, you couldn't sell the coal, you couldn't give it away, and years were getting dry so we moved to town. I had two children, two girls, had to move to town account of school and I got a job and he got a job and that's how we made our living.
>
> Then we finally broke up . . . and of course I was just a young punk, I didn't know too much in them days either and he would sort of listen to all the old folks what they were saying so we broke up. But we raised the kids together and they went to high school and one was a hair dresser. . . . And I worked at one place to the next and I wind up at the Vienna Café, I worked there eight or ten years.

Helen Raymond also spoke of cordial relations with her ex-husband. Although they did not share children, they amicably divided property. In the 1930s and '40s they ran a hot springs and café in Silver Star and then a tavern in Virginia City.

> That was the time my husband, he was going to open up this tavern. He was the one that built it. It was an old building and

he refurbished it. And we decided to separate and I took Virginia City and he kept the [hot springs] lease in Silver Star. . . .

Yes, that was our settlement, as we would put it. But we
stayed friends, he was up to see me quite often, and it took
quite a while before it all worked out. But he had a sad thing
happen to him, he was killed by a train run over him in White
Hawk. He was riding with an old man and they were going to
go fishing, and I think the old man's eyesight was poor. . . .
Killed my ex-husband . . . he was only forty-two when he was
killed.

After describing her work running a bar and restaurant and supporting some mining ventures in Virginia City, Raymond mentioned another marriage but was vague about its details: "I married
Dick [Raymond] in '42. . . . And then we were divorced, about
nine years later. I always worked when I was here." Without paus-
ing to elaborate on this second marriage, she immediately resumed
talking about her work life.

Not surprisingly, there were lots of silences in these narratives, either from pain or embarrassment—women avoided discussion of
what they feared would generate societal disapproval and making
public what they had held secret and perhaps not clearly sorted out in
their own minds. But the women narrators recognized the importance for telling these stories so that their lives would add up—not in
terms of providing accurate chronologies for the sake of history but to
explain the decisions and choices made, always with the implication
that history might have turned out differently. This becomes evident
when reexamining a body of interviews, rather than depending on a
single oral history to illuminate a period, event, or woman's life.

Urvashi Butalia, in her profound book about the 1947 partition
of India, *The Other Side of Silence*, claims that "the way people
choose to remember an event . . . is at least as important as what
one might call the 'facts' of that history"; people's reluctance to
recall particular memories sometimes pointed to their own complicity in this history as well as their pain. She asks "how do we
reach beyond the stories into the silences they hide?"[11] It is difficult
to know about or interpret silences. It is equally difficult to determine meaning from the common patterns in particular stories. True

to narrative conventions, most of the women I interviewed turned tragedy into triumph. Emphasizing their endurance, the women narrators employed a narrative strategy that expressed a resistance in their narratives that may have reflected part of their experiences but not in total.

When an oral history collection is examined, it can lead us to new insights about individual resilience as well as avoidance about the painful past. In *Life and Death in the Delta*, which describes a collaborative oral history project about the Mississippi civil rights movement, Kim Lacy Rogers found that narrators had a variety of strategies, often reflecting their own class and activist positions, to describe the painful past. Some seemed reluctant to remember the worst abuses and created optimistic narratives about achievements gained through struggle; others emphasized the continuation of poverty and oppression despite gains. The common thread in these narratives, she finds, is the "residue of collective trauma." Rogers concludes that however politically transformed these African American communities became, they could not "fully escape the damage inflicted by the past."[12] The pain of the past, or the silences or words that disguise that pain, is evident in the narratives by Montana women, even if it was not clear to me thirty years ago as I heard them.

The prominent themes of survival, loneliness, and hardships in these narratives speak to the particular times in the American West—the first half of the twentieth century—and to experiences based on class and gender. Oral history reveals information about lives not available in other sources. But as Sherna Gluck has observed, a problem in women's oral history is that we speak to the survivors—the women who found coping strategies that worked and agreed to be interviewed. Those battered, silenced, or insane are not around to tell us their stories. We work with the stories that we collect. Oral history projects provide a window to the shifting collective view of the past, imbued with the values, politics, and ideas of the time. We can also find meaning in what is not explicitly stated but is in the telling or the "traces" left behind. These oral history interviews supply surprising insights if we attend to the gaps, the hesitancies, and the hints that provide a fuller accounting of the stories of subordination as well as resistance.

Notes

1. The great variety of collections is illustrated by simply searching on the keywords "oral history" in the Northwest Digital Archives, which returns several hundred examples. More and more of these collections are digitized, and this changes the way we record, preserve, catalog, and access oral history, and it enables more unexpected interpretations and imaginative presentations. Projects like Densho, the Japanese American Legacy Project (http://www. densho.org/), and Project Jukebox of the University of Alaska Fairbanks (http://jukebox.uaf.edu/site/) demonstrate how digital collections can be shared widely while still protecting the privacy and concerns of narrators.

2. The first project, *Speaking History: Oral Histories of the American Past, 1865–present* (New York: Palgrave Macmillan, 2009), coedited with Sue Armitage, features selections from oral history collections around the country. I am also returning to interviews I conducted twenty-five years ago for another book project I describe later.

3. This essay is a revised version of a paper presented at the April 2008 Pacific Northwest History Conference, held at Oregon State University in Corvallis. I extend special thanks to colleague Luz Mara Gordillo and the participants in the June 2008 oral history seminar held at the Charles Redd Center for Western Studies, especially Jessie Embry, Sandra Matthews, Joanne Goodwin, and Kathryn MacKay, for their helpful comments.

4. From 1981 to 1983, under the auspices of the Montana Historical Society, I conducted about 150 interviews with Montana men and women about their work in the first half of the twentieth century. The Montanans at Work project sought to include a representative sampling of the state's diverse peoples and places, focusing on the leading industries of the era—mining, logging, and agriculture. The interview questions focused primarily on work in all its variety, from homesteading to caretaking to the general piecing together of different seasonal occupations to survive in an economically challenging region. My recent analysis concerns a subcollection of women's interviews (about seventy-five of them), to be featured in a book tentatively titled *Surviving Montana: Women's Oral Narratives and the American West*. All of the Montana interviews mentioned in this essay are deposited with the Montana Historical Society.

5. Elizabeth Tonkin, *Narrating Our Pasts: The Social Construction of Oral History* (New York: Cambridge University Press, 1992), 12.

6. Sam Schrager, "The Stories that Communities Tell," *Oregon Historical Quarterly* 97, no. 2 (1996): 221.

7. Alessandro Portelli, *The Battle of Valle Giulia: Oral History and the Art of Dialogue* (Madison: University of Wisconsin Press, 1997), 3–23.

8. This is a phenomenon documented in other deindustrialized communities across the United States. See, for example, Barry Bluestone and Bennett Harrison, *The Deindustrialization of America* (New York: Basic Books, 1982);

and Sherry Lee Linkon and John Russo, *Steeltown U.S.A.: Work and Memory in Youngstown* (Lawrence: University Press of Kansas, 2003). On Anaconda, see Laurie Mercier, *Anaconda: Labor, Community and Culture in Montana's Smelter City* (Urbana: University of Illinois Press, 2001), and Laurie Mercier, "In Search of Working Class Voices: Montana's Oral Literature," in *Writing Montana: Literature under the Big Sky*, ed. Rick Newby and Suzanne Hunger (Helena: Montana Center for the Book, 1996), 282–99.

9. Luisa Passerini, "Work Ideology and Consensus under Italian Fascism," in *The Oral History Reader*, ed. Robert Perks and Alistair Thomson (London: Routledge, 1998), 53–54.

10. Alessandro Portelli, "What Makes Oral History Different," in *The Oral History Reader*, ed. Robert Perks and Alistair Thomson (London: Routledge, 1998), 69.

11. Urvashi Butalia, *The Other Side of Silence: Voices from the Partition of India* (Durham, NC: Duke University Press, 2000), 8, 10.

12. Kim Lacy Rogers, *Life and Death in the Delta: African American Narratives of Violence, Resilience, and Social Change* (New York: Palgrave Macmillan, 2006), 13, 18.

Part II

Examples of Neglected Groups

4

"Everybody Worked Back Then"

Oral History, Memory, and Indian Economies in Northern California

WILLIAM BAUER

Historian William Bauer shows the diversity of western labor history when he discusses Native American work in California. His essay shows three values of oral history in better understanding the West. First, few western histories have documented Native American views. Second, until recently most researchers have looked at the experiences of Native Americans only through European American sources. Bauer's interviews with the Native Americans break down the stereotype of lazy Indians and shows how they were very involved in agriculture. Finally he uses oral history to negotiate a middle ground that addresses indigenous scholars' criticism of the new Indian history.

FOR MORE THAN sixty years, a contentious issue in American Indian history and studies has involved the use of sources. The discipline of history requires scholars to spend countless hours in archives, where we sift through box after box of documents produced usually by non-Indian people. This method has created several problems for understanding American Indian history. American Indian studies scholar Jack Forbes once noted that the reliance on non-

Indian sources created "single-sided approach[es]" to Western Indian history, "In their writings the Indian may be raised to the level
of a human being—and some of them may even express sympathy
for the 'poor Indian'—but he is still somehow non-American. The
very term 'American' is used in United States history as to exclude
the Indian, and historians may be said to have approached Western
history with little objectivity in this regard."[1] Such criticisms led to
the development of ethnohistory—fusing historical and anthropo-
logical approaches to understand both sides of cultural contacts—
and the "new Indian history," now several years old, which placed
American Indians at the center of the narrative and emphasized
American Indian political history and ethnic survival.[2] The study
of American Indian history now appears to be at a crossroads. Critics of ethnohistory and the new Indian history argue that American
Indians remain marginal to American history.[3] Meanwhile, Indigenous scholars point out that written records are biased and incomplete when it concerns American Indian history. Rather than producing "rounder" histories, ethnohistory and the new Indian
history have created "non-Indian perceptions of American Indian
history."[4]

This essay uses oral histories from northern California's Round
Valley Reservation to examine California labor history and strike a
middle ground between these two criticisms. This work is built on
oral interviews I conducted with reservation residents in 2003.
Rather than merely mentioning Indian work, oral histories function as both *descriptive* and *interpretive* historical sources. Oral histories described past working experiences and the conditions under
which Round Valley Indians worked. Considering that there is a
prevailing belief that American Indian people are either perpetually
unemployed or "lazy," this contribution alone is certainly important and noteworthy.[5] Additionally, oral narratives emphasized that
migrant labor was a social experience, connecting California Indian families and communities. These interpretations clashed with
some interpretations of migrant labor in the American West, which
depict the migrant western workforce as male and atomized. Finally, oral histories provide opportunities for California Indians to
interpret and define economic and historical change. They, not
non-Indian anthropologists or government officials, define pov-

erty, inequitable working conditions, and the everyday importance of labor.[6]

Oral histories can help to answer many of the criticisms of the new Indian history and ethnohistory. Oral histories help produce "Indian perceptions of American Indian history." This essay pays attention to the ways Round Valley Indians described and interpreted their experiences at migrant workers in California. Additionally, this essay compares Round Valley Indian work and labor to other working people's experiences in the American West. This chapter brings Native perceptions into conversation with other labor histories in the American West and asks scholars to take seriously the role that employment, not unemployment, has played in American Indian history.

Since first contact, European and American observers have remarked on the apparent lack of work in American Indian communities. At the founding of the Jamestown colony, English colonists commented on the inability of Powhatan men to work. In 1621, John Smith noted, "The men bestowe their times in fishing, hunting, wars, and such man-like exercises, scorning to be seen in any woman like exercise, which is the cause that the women be verie painfull and the men often idle."[7] Remarks such as Smith's created a stereotype that American Indian men were lazy because they shunned agricultural work and American Indian women were oppressed and overworked drudges because they tended fields. These labels helped Europeans justify the appropriation of American Indian land, for they argued that American Indians failed to properly work or use it.[8]

The critical remarks about American Indian work, or lack thereof, existed in the historical records pertaining to the Round Valley Reservation. In 1917, Round Valley Reservation school superintendent Walter McConihe commented, "[The Indians] are out working picking hops and beans and working in the beet fields."[9] On one hand, this is a helpful statement: it indicated that Round Valley Indians actually worked. However, this source was too pithy to provide any detail. Who was working? Why? Indeed, there were numerous archival documents that said much the same thing and in many cases left me saying, "Well, I know that. I want more information!" Obviously, talking to myself in the archive nonplussed the people sitting next to me, but the point remains: archival documents provided few details about Round Valley Indian work and labor aside from the fact that they worked.

In addition to failing to describe Indians' working conditions, archival sources frequently criticized Round Valley Indian workers. McConihe wrote in 1923, "The reservation is full of possibilities for the Indian who will take hold and work but as I have, in my annual reports each year, shown how few of them will grasp these opportunities."[10] Immediately, this should strike us as a contradictory statement: McConihe claimed that there were few Indians willing to work, but we already know from his own typewriter that Indians picked hops, beans, and beets. In this instance, Indians were not "working" in the way McConihe wanted, thus producing critical assessments of Indian labor. Viewing Round Valley Indian labor through the perspective of a federal Indian policy that idealized yeoman farmers, McConihe wanted the Indians to stay in one place and work on their farms, not move about in search of wages.

The idea that American Indians lacked work and labor persists in contemporary descriptions of Indian country. When non-Indian observers discuss present-day American Indian issues, they frequently cite the galling unemployment rates that persist on reservations. In 1997, *Washington Post* writer Peter Carlson visited South Dakota's Pine Ridge Reservation, home to part of the Lakota Nation, and reported, "It goes on all day, day after day, a steady flow of supplicants coming into the tribal offices at Pine Ridge, which is in Shannon County, S.D., the poorest county in the America, a place where unemployment hovers around 80 percent." Carlson continued, "The country's 2.1 million Indians, about 400,000 of whom live on reservations, have the highest rates of poverty, unemployment and disease of any ethnic group in America."[11] In a sense, little changed between the seventeenth century and the late twentieth: non-Indian observers know American Indian communities for the absence of work and labor. This resulted from the fact that many archival sources about American Indian work and labor reflected the needs and desires of non-Indian people, rather than the thoughts and beliefs of actual working Indian people. From the Virginia Colony to the Round Valley Reservation to the Pine Ridge Reservation, non-Indians have described and interpreted Indian work and labor to generate support for colonial agendas, promote certain federal Indian policies, or generate sympathy for Native peoples.[12] If we only relied on archival documents or the remarks of non-Indian journalists to write and understand American Indian labor history, we would have an incomplete, if not prejudiced, narrative.

After interviewing a few people from Round Valley, it quickly became apparent that they worked in different occupations in the early twentieth century. The most common job was migrant agricultural work in Mendocino County. Kathleen Cook remembered, "Everybody here used to go to Ukiah. They start after they got the hops done [in Round Valley] and go to Ukiah and pick hops, and pears, and grapes, they were the last."[13] Claude Hoaglen also recalled picking hops in northern California:

> I picked hops for Grant and Walter Winters. I was fourteen or fifteen when I started. It was hot but a lot of fun. We would eat watermelon for lunch. A big truck would come and pick us up every morning. We would start work at about 8 a.m. [My brother] Acie drove a hop wagon. We wasn't paid too much. We would pick the hops, weigh them, and then they would give us a tag with the weight on it. Every evening, the ice cream wagon came by. Rollie Hurt's wife owned that. I stayed with my grandmother, Annie Feliz. Sally and John Piner, my aunt and uncle, lived near the Hop Ranch. I picked hops with a bunch of old guys. Floyd Wright was so slow that some of the girls would have to come back and help him. There were a lot of women, some with kids. There were some good-looking chicks. Those were good ol' days.[14]

In a very helpful way, Cook and Hoaglen provided more detail than I found in McConihe's letters and government reports. Rather than merely observing that Round Valley Indians left the reservation to work, Cook and Hoaglen recalled the type of work they performed, their work schedules, and the social and kinship relations that Round Valley Indians created in the fields of northern California.

Cook's and Hoaglen's memories of migrant agricultural work were embedded in the history of the growth and development of

Mendocino County's agricultural economy. In the late nineteenth and early twentieth centuries, Mendocino County farmers began to put more land in monoculture. Wine grapes have been a staple of California agriculture since the eighteenth century, with grape production in Mendocino County dating back to the 1860s. By the 1910s, Mendocino County produced large crops of grapes and today remains an important center of viticulture in northern California.[15] Meanwhile, hop production began as early as the 1870s and weathered several late nineteenth- and early twentieth-century busts. By World War I, Mendocino County was a center of the hop industry in California and remained so until the Great Depression.[16] Finally, in the 1920s and 1930s, pear production boomed in Mendocino and Lake Counties, aided by the construction of Highway 20, which linked these remote counties with more populous areas in central California.[17] As monoculture grew in Mendocino County, farmers increasingly turned to northern California Indians to fill their labor demands. Round Valley Indians, for instance, did not stick around growing areas once the picking season ended. Instead, they returned to the reservation. Furthermore, anti-Chinese hysteria in the nineteenth century made Mendocino County hostile toward Chinese immigrants, forcing growers to look for a workforce that would work for low wages. They settled on California Indians living on the Round Valley Reservation as well in the rancherias of Mendocino and Lake Counties.[18]

Round Valley Indians also harvested hay for ranchers. "I had to help during the World War II," June Britton remembered. "Us girls had to work because [my brother] was gone and [my other brother] was too little, and we had to do the hay. Them days, we didn't have all this equipment. We shocked the hay, and then hauled it and put it in the barn."[19] Francis Crabtree, who worked in the hay in Round Valley and Alturas (about 300 miles northeast of the reservation), remembered,

> they just stacked it up there in the field, just certain places. . . .
> They already had it bailed when we, we didn't do nothing to
> that. Down here, they put it all in a barn and stuff. Then they
> made big haystacks too, loose hay, big rounds, I don't know,
> like a big pole with a pulley on it and they'd stick a big fork in

it, and lift it up and drop it on top, and a couple of guys up there putting it out. . . . Spreading it out, they'd do it all out in a field. Like the bailed hay, they take, after they got all the stacks they wanted they took a lot of loose hay and put it on top, keeps the water from ruining it.[20]

Cutting, shocking (putting the hay in bundles to aid in the curing process), hauling, and stacking hay was an essential aspect of the pastoral economy in Round Valley. Native and non-Native ranchers stored hay to feed their livestock during the winter months, when animals had grazed over pasture. Round Valley Indians also exchanged work in the hay fields for assistance in other agricultural ventures. Because many Round Valley Indians did not own farm machinery, they worked in the hay fields for those who did. In return, Native and non-Native machinery owners plowed Native fields.[21]

Round Valley Indians also frequently mentioned shearing sheep. Aloya Frazier remembered, "[My dad] was a sheep shearer, but he never did herd sheep. I guess you could call him a professional, because, I don't know why, I always thought about that too when I was a kid, all these young guys, all these old guys, everybody around here sheared sheep, that is what they did in the spring, you know. They sheared sheep by hand, you know. And then when they went to a machine, and they all quit." Frazier continued, "[My dad] went clear into Montana shearing sheep. . . . They'd go to Sacramento, Sacramento Valley, and they'd shear over there. Well, they'd shear all summer. They'd start about [March] and they ended about September in Humboldt County. They'd shear in Sonoma County [too]."[22] By the time Frazier's father traversed the American West clipping wool, Round Valley Indians had been shearing sheep for decades. Non-Indian ranchers introduced sheep to the area in the 1870s when a high tariff increased the price of US wool. In the spring, Round Valley Indians left the reservation for nearby ranches and spent a couple of weeks shearing sheep with hand-held clippers.[23]

Sheep raising created other jobs for Round Valley Indians. Although Aloya's father did not herd sheep, many people in Round Valley certainly did. Claude Hoaglen recalled, "My father drove

sheep for [non-Indian rancher] John Rohrbaugh, up on government land near Deer Creek. He herded cattle for Rohrbaugh when
he was younger, and when he got older he drove the sheep. We
used dogs to move the sheep. We did that north of the Ranger Station, up near Leech Lake. We had to pack our food and move to
the mountains. There weren't too many roads up there in those
days. Rohrbaugh had sheep and cattle."[24] Francis Crabtree's family
also worked for Rohrbaugh. He remembered herding sheep: "Well,
[it was] a lazy man's job, a lot of fun. Start them up in the morning
and go up ahead and go to sleep. On the ridges, keeping them
from going further. The dogs did all the work when you herd
sheep. About three months, from June, first part of June to September 15th, we had to be out of there, before that. It was on the
Forestry and that was the way they had it." Crabtree continued,
"Oh, I didn't care too much about it when we just, our dad was
doing it so we were just with him. We missed a lot of fun, going to
anyplace; you had to stay out there when everything was going on.
Sit up on a hill and look back toward Covelo and think about the
rodeo going on."[25]

Round Valley Indians worked in industrial jobs as well. During
the late nineteenth and early twentieth centuries, the timber industry of Humboldt County expanded to meet the demands of urban
development, energy consumption, and construction.[26] Francis
Crabtree's father worked in Humboldt County's woods in the
1910s. "He packed wood for the donkeys [small steam engines
used to pull logs up hills] on his mules," Crabtree explained. "He
had four foot wood, that he'd carry to the donkeys, they had it already cut and in piles, and he'd carry it to the donkeys and that is
what they fired their donkeys with." Crabtree himself worked on
the Northwestern Pacific railroad as a teenager, "I was seventeen,
almost eighteen, I guess. I worked on [the railroad] I don't know
different times, I don't know how many times. Quit and then we
work and then go back for the winter. . . . Then in the spring we'd
quit, come down, and go back in the fall again."[27] In the early
twentieth century, the Northwestern Pacific Railroad connected
the San Francisco Bay Area with timber-rich Humboldt County.
The railroad constructed a 140-mile line from Willits to Scotia (a
mill town). Not only did Round Valley Indians work on the con-

struction of the railroad that winds its way through the Eel River canyons, they also maintained the track lines once the railroad was completed.

Oral histories clearly reveal that Round Valley Indians participated in a dynamic labor system, which included agricultural, pastoral, and industrial jobs. Rather than remembering a history of unemployment or laziness, Round Valley Indians described a past full of seasonal employment opportunities and hard work. But too often California Indians are ignored as members of the state's agricultural and industrial workforce. The processes of mechanization, Native population decline, and racism marginalized Native peoples in some areas of agricultural labor.[28] Oral histories, however, effectively restore Round Valley Native peoples to California's labor force.

The types of jobs that Round Valley Indians performed are easily found in the archives, as well as the reasons employers hired them. What we lack are the meanings and interpretations Native peoples invested in the labor experience. Historians of migrant labor in the American West argue that young men dominated the occupation. Furthermore, most of these young men were alone and on the move, leaving behind families in eastern cities or Europe. Historian Carlos Schwantes described the workforce of the American West thusly: "It was foremost a predominately male community of manual labor dependent upon others for wages in the extractive industries of the sparsely settled Rocky Mountain and Pacific Regions of the United States and Canada."[29] The all-male character of the migrant agricultural workforce also prevailed in New Mexico, where Hispanic women stayed in villages while men traveled to work in the beet fields of Colorado.[30]

California historians have noted that migrant work was problematic for Native families and communities. In Los Angeles, historian George Harwood Phillips found that integration into southern California's agricultural workforce produced cultural disintegration. The changing economic and labor conditions in Los Angeles caused high rates of California Indian unemployment and antisocial behavior.[31] In California's central valley and mining areas, meanwhile, historian Albert Hurtado discovered that wage labor undermined California Indian communities and family security. During the 1850s and 1860s, wage labor drew California Indian men from their communities, thus leaving their wives and children vulnerable to attack by Americans and Mexicans. Native women, meanwhile, worked as domestic servants in non-Indian communities and found themselves "vulnerable to physical and sexual exploitation."[32]

The work experiences in northern California, as told and interpreted in Round Valley Indian oral histories, differed significantly from those in other parts of California and the American West. Significantly, Round Valley Indians remembered migrant labor as a family, not a male, endeavor. Robert Anderson recalled,

> A lot of the families, I can remember yet, we'd be picking hops down there at the old Johnny Johnson ranch, and a lot of the Indian people would be camped down by the river and they would stay there all summer. And they had not only, not only did they have hops, but they had prunes as well. A lot of the local people, the other ranchers around there, would, when they weren't working for Johnny Johnson, they would go across the field and work for old McGarvey and some of them other old ranchers along the river down there, that had, you know, fruit to pick and hops to pick. And the Indians, I can remember them, a lot of the families from here, just like a little community down along the river, everybody camped out, you know. And they stayed down there until all the fruit was done, and then they came home.[33]

If anything, migrant labor strengthened the Native family in Mendocino County. Round Valley Indians used kinship ties to find work. Bobbi Anderson recalled, "After the hops were done, we moved on to Ukiah [where my uncle] was a foreman there. And he'd come and pack us all in a big truck, we'd all go there, and he'd have a house for us to stay in. We stayed down there and my dad was kind of like a foreman, until the prune crop was done and then we come home."[34] Other families relied on wage work to buttress a viable household economy, which included raising livestock and tending gardens. Barbara Pina's family did not camp at the Hop Ranch when they picked hops, "we had to commute. We had the farm to take care of. That was a morning, noon, and night project." Often, work on the family farm had to be completed before hop picking began. "We were milking ten to twelve cows at that time. Mom and Dad and [my brother] were over in the Sacramento Valley . . . working in the rice. Then we went and picked hops for our [school] clothes. It only lasted about two weeks but we still had those cows to milk."[35] Indian families astutely divided family labor to enable these economies to function. June Britton explained that her family relied on everyone to contribute to the family's wherewithal (see figure 4.1). "I went [to pick hops with my mother]. We went as a family. . . . We didn't pick hops until we got older. She didn't go until we got older and then we would all go and pick."[36]

Round Valley Indians recalled that in addition to strengthening the Native family, migrant labor supported a sense of community, rather than atomizing Indian workers. "I enjoyed the company of being out amongst people [picking hops] and I enjoyed the money," June Britton stated. "We didn't associate with many people, we were raised up on [the north] end of the valley. . . . [Our parents] never took us no place. We stayed home. If I could get out and pick hops I could see different people."[37] Jobs produced opportunities for social interaction outside of the workplace, too. Aloya Frazier remembered that he used his wages to participate in regionally important recreational events. "Well, the biggest ambition at that time was to work like hell and then go to Willits for the Fourth of July rodeo. We had to get to Willits for the rodeo and we had to work like a bastard."[38] Migrant wage labor helped create and maintain a sense of community in northern California. Round Valley Indians knew that they could interact with other Native people in the fields and in recreational and social spaces away from the job site.

Unlike in Los Angeles, where gambling demonstrated social decay, games of chance united Indian workers and became essential aspects of migrant labor in Round Valley and Mendocino County.[39] During hop picking season, one of the most popular events was "grass game," a gambling game that predated first contact. Arvella Freeman recalled how Native people played the game: "They'd give you twelve sticks and two pair of bones. I don't know what, I'll get my son to look for dead coyote, I think that is what they made them out of, grass game bones. I think it was a coyote bone, off the

Figure 4.1 Wailacki June Russ Britton hoeing her garden as part of a 4-H program administered by the Office of Indian Affairs. When interviewed in 2003, June remembered the necessity of family members cooperating to plant gardens and work in the hop fields. Photo courtesy of the National Archives and Records Administration, San Bruno, California.

leg. 'Course my dad made a pair and somebody stole it. But they'd be nice to have. I've never seen them nowhere. They would have four people on that side and four on this side. And whoever bet on which side, they got a big ol' dish towel and tie that money up in that and set it right in the middle where you were playing. I said they wouldn't dare do that now."[40]

Grass games were quite popular at agricultural worksites. Leland Fulwilder remembered, "the grass game players, everybody wanted them and then they would, like, hop season time come up in and bring a big old truck, hard wheel trucks. They would take them to Ukiah, Lake County and all around there, end up gambling, after they finish work, they'd play grass game."[41] Claude Hoaglen recalled, "Some of the people camped at the Hop Ranch. They built a roundhouse with a ditch around it. They danced and sang in there. They also played the grass game and sang. It was a good time. Sometimes, I watched the dances through the holes in the building. I didn't play the grass game then. I played when I was older and after I got to drinking wine."[42]

In addition to associating with other Native people, grass games featured opportunities for family interaction. Arvella Freeman tenderly remembered, "They'd have grass game over in the other field, and my dad would take me, and my dress was just dirty I guess, and he'd turn it around, turn it inside out. And there were some women there and they would say, 'oh, can I take this little girl home?' I guess because I was so dirty and everything. And he'd say, 'no, she stays with me.' He'd play grass game all night and I would lay on his back. I remember all of that. But I wouldn't leave him. I would lay on his back."[43] Rather than separating Round Valley Indians from one another, migrant labor opportunities united them and created strong social networks in the twentieth century.

Round Valley Indians ensured that wage labor and economic activities were deeply rooted in social and kinship relationships. Aloya Frazier recalled that when hunting, "Three or four of us would go out and the most [deer] we ever killed was two. [Then we would d]ivide it up."[44] Kathleen Cook remembered that sharing economic resources continued in the 1930s. "See, people used to come here and borrow lard and everything from mom. Flour and different things. But I guess people had a really hard time, but I can't remember that. We had our own gardens."[45] It is no wonder, then, that agents criticized Indian workers. Many rejected aspects of the capitalist ethos that emphasized the individual pursuit of wages and wealth. Instead, Round Valley Indians upheld tradi-

tional economic practices by redistributing and sharing their resources.

These comments illustrate that Round Valley Indians were not
the typical migrant worker in the American West. Most labor histories of the American West emphasize that migrant workers were
young, unattached, and itinerant men. Furthermore, for Native
peoples in California, wage labor sometimes led to antisocial behavior and undermined the strength of the Native family. Instead,
Round Valley Indians used wage labor to maintain community and
the Native family. They used migrant labor to interact with other
Native people in northern California in the workplace and the recreational activities in which they participated after the workday concluded. Additionally, Round Valley Indians traveled and worked as
families and divided their labor power to maximize its potential.
Indeed, they used migrant labor to create a sense of community
during an era when the federal government and other groups attempted to undermine Native identities and social cohesion.[46]

Round Valley Indian oral histories accomplished more than describing the migrant labor experience and investing their own
meanings in the process. The oral interviews also offered interpretations of important concepts in American Indian history. Round
Valley Indian memories of agricultural labor conflicted with other
observations of Indian economies in the twentieth century. For one
thing, Round Valley Indians and non-Indian observers created different meanings for Indian poverty. During the Great Depression,
Columbia University anthropology graduate student Amelia Susman reported, "Living conditions vary, but the survey found about
one third of the houses to be ramshackle shanties. About half have
inadequate clothing and bedding. . . . Most families have a sewing-
machine and big family portraits in heavy gilt frames, purchased after
the land sales."[47]

Susman's comments might lead one to assume that Round Valley Indians were desperately poor. However, they rejected this notion out of hand. One day, Anita Rome was reading a group of archival documents about her family in the 1930s. She remarked,
"Those documents say we were poor, but we did not think we were
poor. We had pigs and chickens."[48] Rome's comment suggests that
Round Valley Indians equated poverty with the lack of food, not

the absence of material goods or the quality of a house. Other statements confirm this notion. When asked about the Great Depression, Kathleen Cook remarked, "It seems like we had something; maybe we had hard time, but I don't remember. I know my mom had a milk cow and we had milk, 'cause I was the milker. We made our own butter, we had our own milk, we made our own cream, and she had her own chickens and so we had all the eggs we wanted. . . . I don't remember really having a hard time. It seems like to me that we always had something."[49] Rome and Cook simultaneously contradicted Susman and defined poverty from a Native perspective. Susman emphasized the acquisition of material goods as the index of poverty: Indians lived in "ramshackle shanties" with few, if any, objects in their homes. Oral histories, on the other hand, pointed to the ability to provide one's sustenance, to feed oneself, as the reason they were not poor.

All of this is not to say that Indians did not recognize the asymmetrical labor and economic relations in Mendocino County. Many Round Valley Indians lived in a situation resembling debt peonage. Barbara Pina stated, "Dad said that the people here on the reservation would go down and get the supplies, and then they would work off in the summer. . . . We would have a big old bill, and dad would go sheep shearing and pay it all off. It was about $1500." Aloya Frazier added, "You'd go down there once a year, every six months, pay it up and start it again."[50] Similar arrangements existed throughout Mendocino County, where Indians were perpetually indebted to ranch owners. Yet the oral histories attempted to restore some control over these relationships by embedding them in the social relations created by wage labor. Barbara Pina remarked, "they were good people." Aloya Frazier elaborated, "But you know, a lot of people don't know this either, that is why George Ells, [George] Bauers, and old Ed Gravier, a lot of these old Indians that was their bankers, they'd loan you fifteen cents. That is why these old Indians went to the old ranchers, they were their bankers. They'd handle their money and their business."[51] Even though Round Valley Indians were indebted to local ranchers and farmers, they remembered that the relationship was a social one, not necessarily economic. To be perceived as "good people," the "bankers" (ranchers and farmers) had to be generous and helpful to

Round Valley Indians. Otherwise, they might take their business and work elsewhere.

Round Valley Indians also critiqued the agricultural wage scale. Wages were small for Indian workers, frequently one penny per pound of hops picked. Those who remembered hop picking probably agreed with Norman Whipple's statement: "You know, it took a lot to make a pound."[52] Aloya Frazier said simply and insightfully, "Pick hops all day and go down and buy an ice cream, and that was our profit."[53] Francis Crabtree remarked, "Spent it every way and any way. There wasn't much anyway. Didn't have to worry about spending it."[54]

In addition to low wages, Native workers had to wait for their compensation. Aloya Frazier recalled, "The old mill they had down here, I don't know how many they had working, they go out and fall them with their old handsaws, and buck it, fall it, and then they'd drag it in the mill, and then they'd all work to cut it up, and then the bosses take it down and sell it and then they'd get paid."[55] By articulating a labor theory of value, rather than a monetary or market one, Frazier emphasized that Round Valley Indians provided the hard work that allowed non-Indian farmers to sell hops or timber on the open market.

In their totality, these oral histories revealed the generational nature of agricultural labor. Working in the hop fields was one of the common experiences that united Indians who lived in Round Valley between 1870 and 1940 (see figure 4.2).[56] Kathleen Cook remembered, "Everybody used to go down there and work. It give everybody a job. They were like migrant workers. Like they do now with Mexican people, that was how the Indians used to work. A few non-Indians worked in there that was poor and that wanted to work."[57] By incorporating Round Valley Indians into and making them viable contributors to California's agricultural working class, Cook revealed one of the ways these Natives survived the nineteenth and twentieth centuries.[58]

Far from being the "lazy Indian," Round Valley Indians were revealed by oral histories as having worked in a number of agricultural and industrial jobs in the early twentieth century. They picked crops and fruit, worked on railroads, and harvested hay. Indians moved from job to job throughout the year and cobbled together a

Figure 4.2 An elderly Pomo woman and a Pomo boy pick hops near Ukiah, California, in the 1940s. Northern California Indian families frequently migrated to and worked in the hop fields in family units, thus maximizing earnings. Photo courtesy of the Parsell Collection, Mendocino County Museum Archives, Willits, California.

workable household economy. In the process, they described the family economy that existed in northern California. They divided their labor by gender and age to combine as many resources as possible. Finally, Round Valley Indians offered a cutting and insightful analysis of economic change in California. By insisting that they were not poor and discussing the uneven economic relations of the past, these narrators' oral histories become a useful tool for reinterpreting and reanalyzing California Indians and the state's labor and economic history. If scholars want to truly write Indian-centered histories, we must be willing to use oral histories. Interviewing

American Indian workers helps us avoid the frustration stemming from the pithy and often biased documents historians find in archives. With assiduous use, oral histories help provide an Indian-centered history and reveal the manner in which Indigenous peoples of North America remember and interpret historical changes in their lives.

Notes

1. Jack D. Forbes, "The Indian in the West: A Challenge for Historians," *Arizona and the West* 1 (Autumn 1959): 209.

2. James Axtell, "Ethnohistory: An Historian's Viewpoint," *Ethnohistory* 26 (Winter 1979): 1–13; Robert F. Berkhofer Jr., "The Political Context of a New Indian History," *Pacific Historical Review* 40 (August 1971): 357–82.

3. Nicolas Rosenthal, "Beyond the New Indian History: Recent Trends in the Historiography on the Native Peoples of North America," *History Compass* 5 (July 2006): 962–74; Jeffrey Ostler, *Plains Sioux and U.S. Colonialism from Lewis and Clark to Wounded Knee* (New York: Cambridge University Press, 2003), 3–5.

4. I borrow the phrase "Indigenous scholar" from historian Susan Miller, who identifies Indigenous scholars as "A small cadre of American Indians in the discipline [who] have rejected the consensual narrative of American history and the Euroamerican paradigm that frame it to develop a separate and competing narrative." Susan Miller, "Native America Writes Back: The Origin of the Indigenous Paradigm in Historiography," *Wicazo Sa Review* 23 (Fall 2008): 9. See also the important remarks in Devon Mihesuah, "Introduction," 1–22, Angela Cavender Wilson, "American Indian History or Non-Indian Perceptions of American Indian History?," 23–26, Wilson, "Grandmother to Granddaughter: Generations of Oral History in a Dakota Family," 27–36, all in *Natives and Academics: Researching and Writing about American Indians*, ed. Devon Mihesuah (Lincoln: University of Nebraska Press, 1998). The idea of ethnohistory producing "rounder" historical narratives is taken from Wilcomb Washburn, "Ethnohistory: History 'in the Round,'" *Ethnohistory* 8 (Winter 1961): 31–48.

5. Historian George Harwood Phillips makes a valuable critique of California Indian labor in the eighteenth and nineteenth centuries. He argues that many scholars and contemporary observers identified California Indian work and labor but rarely described them. George Harwood Phillips, *Vineyards and Vaqueros: Indian Labor and the Economic Expansion of Southern California, 1771–1877* (Norman, OK: Arthur H. Clark, 2010), 17–18, 34. Unfortunately, Phillips does not use oral histories to add more descriptive and interpretive weight to his study of Indian workers in Los Angeles.

6. Other scholars have made efforts to include oral histories in their interpretations of American Indian work and labor history. See Brian Hosmer, "'Dollar a Day and Glad to Have It': Work Relief on the Wind River Indian Reservation as Memory," in *Native Pathways: American Indian Culture and Economic Development in the Twentieth Century,* ed. Brian Hosmer and Colleen O'Neill (Boulder: University Press of Colorado, 2004), 283–307; Colleen O'Neill, "The 'Making' of the Navajo Worker: Navajo Households, the Bureau of Indian Affairs, and Off-Reservation Wage Work, 1948–1960," *New Mexico Historical Review* 74 (October 1999): 375–405; Kurt Peters, "Continuing Identity: Laguna Pueblo Railroad Workers in Richmond, California," *American Indian Culture and Research Journal* 22:4 (1998): 187–98.

7. David D. Smits, "The 'Squaw Drudge': A Prime Index of Savagism," *Ethnohistory* 29 (Autumn 1982): 281.

8. Ibid., 281–306.

9. W. W. McConihe to E. B. Merritt, August 24, 1917, National Archives and Records Administration, Washington, DC, Record Group 75, Records of the Bureau of Indian Affairs, Central Classified Files, 1907–1939, Round Valley Agency (hereafter CCF), Box 1: 72106-1917.

10. W. W. McConihe to the Commissioner of Indian Affairs, November 14, 1923, CCF, Box 63: 52422-1923.

11. Peter Carlson, "The Unfashionable," The Washington Post Magazine, February 23, 1997, 8.

12. In a way, this resembles the experiences of jute workers in Bengal. See Dipesh Chakrabarty, *Rethinking Working-Class History: Bengal, 1890–1940* (Princeton: Princeton University Press, 1989).

13. Kathleen Cook, interview by author, January 9, 2002, Covelo, CA, tapes and manuscript in author's possession.

14. Claude Hoaglen, interview by author, June 18, 2002, Dos Rios, CA, tapes and manuscript in author's possession.

15. Orie Loucks, *Sustainability Perspectives for Resources and Business* (Boca Raton, FL: CRC Press, 1998), 250; David Bentsen, *Mendocino County Hop Production. Statistical Report of the California State Board of Agriculture for the Year 1920* (Sacramento: California State Printing Office, 1921), 279.

16. Bentsen, *Mendocino County Hop Production,* 279.

17. Elizabeth Mitcham and Rachel Elkins, eds., *Pear Production and Handling Manual,* University of California Agriculture and Natural Resources Publication No. 3483 (Berkeley: University of California Agriculture and Natural Resources, 2007), 7–8; Bentsen, *Mendocino County Hop Production,* 279.

18. William Bauer, *"We Were All Like Migrant Workers Here": Labor, Memory and Community on California's Round Valley Reservation, 1850–1941* (Chapel Hill: University of North Carolina Press, 2009), 82–85. For a discussion of anti-Chinese sentiments in Mendocino County in particular and race relations in the county in general, see Linda Pacini Pitelka, "Mendocino: Race Relations in a Northern California County, 1850–1949," PhD dissertation, University of Massachusetts, 1994, 180–200.

19. June Britton, interview by author, March 19, 2002, tapes and manuscript in author's possession.

20. Francis Crabtree, interview by author, March 22, 2002, Redwood Valley, CA, tapes and manuscript in author's possession.

21. Amelia Susman, *The Round Valley Indians of California: An Unpublished Chapter in the Acculturation of Seven [or Eight] American Indian Tribes*, Contributions to the University of California Archaeological Research Facility 31 (Berkeley: University of California Press, 1976), 52.

22. A. P. Frazier and Barbara Pina, interview by author, March 22, 2002.

23. Lynwood Carranco and Estle Beard, *Genocide and Vendetta: The Round Valley Wars of Northern California* (Norman: University of Oklahoma Press, 1981), 185, 196–97; Bauer, *"We Were All Like Migrant Workers Here,"* 66–68.

24. Hoaglen interview.

25. Crabtree interview.

26. Daniel Cornford, *Workers and Dissent in the Redwood Empire* (Philadelphia: Temple University Press, 1987), 14–20.

27. Crabtree interview.

28. Albert Hurtado, *Indian Survival on the California Frontier* (New Haven, CT: Yale University Press, 1988), 193–210; Richard Steven Street, *Beasts in the Field: A Narrative History of California Farmworkers, 1769–1913* (Palo Alto, CA: Stanford University Press, 2004), 135–57.

29. Carlos Schwantes, "The Concept of the Wageworkers' Frontier: A Framework for Future Research," *Western Historical Quarterly* 18 (January 1987): 41. See also Richard White, *"It's Your Misfortune and None of My Own": A New History of the American West* (Norman: University of Oklahoma Press, 1991), 270–97; Carlos A. Schwantes, "Wage Earners and Wealth Makers," in *The Oxford History of the American West*, ed. Clyde A. Milner II, Carol A. O'Connor, and Martha A. Sandweiss, (New York: Oxford University Press, 1994), 431–67; Michael P. Malone and Richard Etulain, *The American West: A Twentieth Century History* (Lincoln: University of Nebraska Press, 1989), 45–53; Gunther Peck, *Reinventing Free Labor: Padrones and Immigrant Workers in the North American West, 1880–1930* (New York: Cambridge University Press, 2000); Frank Tobias Higbie, *Indispensable Outcasts: Hobo Workers and Community in the American Midwest, 1880–1930* (Urbana: University of Illinois Press, 2003).

30. Sarah Deutsch, *No Separate Refuge: Culture, Class and Gender on an Anglo-Hispanic Frontier in the American Southwest, 1880–1940* (New York, 1989); Skott Vigil, "Los Vigils: Genealogy, History, Labor, and Identity of a Mixed-Blood Ute Family, 1807–1956," M.A. thesis, University of Wyoming, 2006.

31. George Harwood Phillips, "Indians in Los Angeles, 1781–1875: Economic Integration, Social Disintegration," *Pacific Historical Review* 49 (August 1980): 427–51.

32. Albert Hurtado, "California Indians and the Workaday West: Labor, Assimilation and Survival," *California History* 69 (Spring 1990): 2–11.

33. Robert and Barbara Anderson, interview by author, June 19, 2002, Covelo, CA, manuscript and tapes in author's possession.

34. Ibid.

35. Frazier and Pina interview.

36. Britton interview.

37. Ibid.

38. Frazier and Pina interview.

39. Phillips, "Indians in Los Angeles," 432.

40. Marian (Arvella) Freeman, interview by author, June 20, 2002, Covelo, CA, tape and manuscript in author's possession.

41. Leland Fulwilder, interview by Skip Willits, April 23, 1990, Covelo, CA, Round Valley Oral History Project, Round Valley Public Library, Covelo, CA.

42. Hoaglen interview.

43. Freeman interview.

44. Frazier and Pina interview.

45. Cook interview.

46. A similar process occurred on the Fort Hall Reservation and the ghost dances of the late nineteenth century. Shoshones and Bannocks used the ghost dances to articulate ethnic identities at the same time that non-Indians attempted to eradicate those same identity markers. Gregory Evans Smoak, *Ghost Dances and Identity: Prophetic Religion and American Indian Ethnogenesis in the Nineteenth Century* (Berkeley: University of California Press, 2006).

47. Susman, *Round Valley Indians*, 53.

48. Anita Rome, interview by author, June 22, 2002, Covelo, CA, manuscript in author's possession.

49. Cook interview.

50. Frazier and Pina interview.

51. Ibid.

52. Norman Whipple, interview by author, July 1, 2004, Covelo, CA.

53. Frazier and Pine interview.

54. Crabtree interview.

55. Frazier and Pina interview.

56. Thus, wage labor resembled attending an off-reservation boarding school as a generational experience in Indian communities and nations. Compare my insights on wage labor with Brenda Child's on boarding schools in Brenda Child, *Boarding School Seasons: American Indian Families, 1900–1940* (Lincoln: University of Nebraska Press, 2000).

57. Cook interview.

58. Labor is a significant but often ignored part of California Indian life. Readers of the work of Greg Sarris will note that the seminal events in Indian lives occur at worksites in northern California. See Greg Sarris, *Mabel McKay: Weaving a Dream* (Berkeley: University of California Press, 1994) and *Grand Avenue: A Novel of Stories* (New York: Penguin Books, 1994).

5

Bittersweet Memories

Oral History, Mexican Americans, and the Power of Place

JOSÉ M. ALAMILLO

Historian José Alamillo uses oral history to better understand the experiences of Mexican Americans in the lemon groves of southern California. Through interviews, he learned that in spite of the constraints of living and working in a single agricultural industry town, Mexican immigrant workers used leisure and cultural activities to build community solidarity and forge relations with employers, city officials, and Anglo residents to achieve greater political power. He also learned that leisure activities were highly gendered. Oral history allows these Mexican Americans to focus on what is most important in their lives rather than what the historian planned to research.

ON APRIL 20, 1998, I arrived at the home of Natividad "Tito" Cortez, prepared to interview him about his working experiences in Corona's citrus industry. Before we began, he wanted to show me his old scrapbook. His scrapbook included photographs and newspaper clippings of his baseball career. Cortez began pitching for a company baseball team, the Foothill Lemoneers, then for a city amateur team, Corona Athletics, and later for the Tucson Cowboys, a farm team of the Cleveland Indians. One sports news headline declared him "Tucson's No. 1 pitcher" because of his reliable curveball and effective relief pitching. His promising career was cut short, however, when he was accidently hit in the left eye with a ball. As he reflected on his short-lived professional baseball career, I noticed his trophies and framed pictures carefully placed around his living room. Despite the unfortunate incident, Cortez continued to talk about his athletic achievements and his love for baseball. Why was he more interested in discussing baseball rather than agricultural work? According to Cortez, "Baseball was the only recreation we had since there was no television. We worked hard every day of the week except Sunday when we could relax and play baseball."[1]

Baseball was a main form of recreation for Mexican American men in the citrus town of Corona. For Mexican American women who worked inside the citrus packing houses, their leisure experiences were more limited. They looked forward to church-related events and Cinco de Mayo celebrations. On May 5, they participated in the parade, staffed the food booths, and attended the street dances. If they sold enough tickets, they could earn the Cinco de Mayo Queen title. This was one of the few times that parents allowed young girls to attend a dance without a chaperone. Aurora Delgado, former queen candidate, admitted, "I could use [the queen contest] as an excuse to get out of the house. I'd rather sell tickets than do housework."[2] To win the title, each candidate had to sell five-cent raffle tickets at the street dance. When I visited the home of Gloria Granado, she was excited to show me her photographs of her coronation as the Cinco de Mayo Queen of 1945. She admitted that as young, shy girl, being a queen candidate forced her "come out of her shell" by meeting new people and gaining more confidence.[3] Like Cortez's pride in his athletic achievements, Granado's pride in her crown resonated years later.

Oral histories of Mexican Americans convinced me that I needed to expand my research beyond the workplace and explore different forms of leisure and cultural activities that gave their lives meaning. In this chapter I examine how oral history transformed my original focus on labor history toward greater emphasis on leisure and gender. Many of these memories were rooted in physical spaces and places in town where they created a sense of community. These spaces were not the same for men and women, however, but reproduced existing gender inequalities. Oral histories produced invaluable new information not found in company archives and newspapers about the Mexican American experience in this southern California town. Oral history interviews conducted in the city of Corona, California, between 1996 and 1999 forced me to reconsider the original focus of my dissertation and later incorporated these changes in my book, *Making Lemonade out of Lemons*.[4] Additionally, visiting the places of leisure (bakery, veteran legion hall, baseball diamond, park, and recreation center) was important for my informants' recollections. Their physical presence in these places triggered new memories and unexpected emotions that made me more reflective about contextualizing and interpreting oral history narratives.

The Circle City

When I first visited Corona in 1996, I got lost trying to find the main library in the center of town. After returning to where I began, I realized I was traveling on a circular street called Grand Boulevard. When the city was founded in 1896, it was laid out as a circular design three miles around. Two decades later, this street was transformed into a racetrack. Between 1913 and 1916 the city hosted the Corona Road Races to promote tourism and attract new businesses to the city.[5] The racing event ended tragically in 1916 when a driver crashed his car, killing three spectators and injuring five. It was not the circular boulevard or road races that made Corona famous, however, but its large acreage of lemon groves. There were also thirty packing houses and the nation's only lemon by-products plant that gave the city the popular nickname "The Lemon Capital of the World."

In 1989, the Corona Library's Heritage Room acquired records from a citrus company that included some information about its predominantly Mexican labor force.[6] According to librarian Gloria Scott Freel, the records of Verity & Sons were almost thrown away until she saved them by loading up her station wagon three times with over thirty-five linear feet of ledgers, correspondence, marketing, and financial records. Two months later the packing house burned down. The records remained in storage for seven years until the library received a grant from the California State Library to process the collection. Several years later, the Corona Library received an even larger donation (approximately 5,000 linear feet) from the Orange Heights Orange Association. This company archive included more than twenty-five citrus companies that ultimately merged into one association.[7] This archival collection documented the rise and fall of the citrus industry in Corona and southern California. As I reviewed the minutes, correspondence, annual reports, and employee records of both collections, I found very little information about its employees. Company archives provided limited information on their workers. As Chon Noriega observed, "The archive is a political institution that excludes much more than it includes. Without a presence in the archive, excluded groups are less able to tell their stories within the marketplace of ideas."[8] For this reason I turned to oral history to recover the workers' voices. Oral history has long been instrumental in the research and writing of Mexican American history in the United States.[9] With recent theoretical developments, scholars have turned to oral history to explore people's contested memories and attachment to place.[10]

Places of Leisure

One day before going to the library, I stopped for coffee and *pan dulce* (sweet bread) at a Mexican bakery located inside the Corona Ranch Market. While I was standing in line at Joe's Bakery, a group of elderly men seated at a corner table started singing, "Alla en el Rancho Grande" (Over at the Big Ranch), a traditional Mexican ballad made popular by the 1936 Mexican film by the same name. Everyone listened with a big smile and applauded when they finished. When the singing stopped, I thanked them for evoking fond memories of my small Mexican ranch. I introduced myself as a college student researching the history of Corona's Mexican American community. At first, the four men (Rudy Ramos, Reynaldo Aparicio, Onias "Ace" Acevedo, and Alfred "4F" Martinez) confused me for a newspaper reporter poking around for local news stories. Even though we had similar ethnic heritage, I was still marked as an "outsider," so I needed to come clean about my own positionality as a working-class, male, Mexican American student.[11] Once I shared more information about my family's immigrant and labor history in the Ventura County lemon industry, they began to trust me. Some of these men had dropped out of high school to work as citrus pickers during the 1930s, and some were military veterans of World War II who used their GI Bill to complete their education. Others were business owners who were involved in community and civic affairs. For the next couple of weeks, I returned to Joe's Bakery to listen to their ballads and the stories of their hometown. They complained about the suburban sprawl, declining citrus groves, and extreme hot weather conditions, and they decried the lost sense of community.[12] After repeated requests, each one agreed to do a personal interview with me in their home, away from the noisy bakery.

Their memories centered on social spaces and geographical places throughout the city and surrounding citrus ranches. The first of these was Sixth Street, a principal business thoroughfare that cuts through Main Street. The Mexican American veterans mockingly nicknamed Sixth Street the "38th Parallel" because it served as the racial divide between the Mexican communities in north side from the Anglo community on the south side. ("38th Parallel" also refers to a circle of latitude used as the boundary between North Korea and South Korea.) This spatial barrier reflected the system of de jure and de facto racial segregation that characterized many southwestern cities prior to World War II. Racialized spaces in Corona also included residential neighborhoods, stores, restaurants, schools, swimming pools, theaters, parks, and recreational facilities. These racialized spaces lead to unequal racial outcomes in American society or, as George Lipsitz succinctly puts it, "it takes places for racism to take place."[13] The history of residential segregation was still very alive in the memory of Onias "Ace" Acevedo, the city's first Mexican American councilman, who recalled how property deeds restricted where Mexican people could rent or purchase homes. "There were many times a listing would come in and they would have down at the bottom, 'Don't show to Mexicans.'"[14] He ignored these racially restricted covenants because he believed in doing business with everyone. However, when he showed available dwellings to nonwhite prospective homebuyers, Acevedo received angry phone calls from white homeowners.

One afternoon, longtime photographer Rudy Ramos offered to drive me around the Northside barrio to show me the remaining dwellings that survived the 91 Freeway construction and urban renewal projects.[15] As he drove into the Mexican neighborhood on the Northside barrio, he recalled the community struggle to pave the streets. He showed me a *Corona Independent* article that described his fight to pave the roads and install street lights in his neighborhood. Ramos attended a city council meeting along with members of Los Amigos (first Mexican American civil rights organization in Corona) and demanded immediate action. He explained that street dirt and dust "was a menace to the community and health." He insisted, "We have been waiting a year for answers and action. Can't we do something to settle it? We don't mind paying taxes, but we would like to see some of the money put into use in this area. Whenever we ask for improvements there are always too many problems."[16] After six months of inaction from the city, Ramos picked up his camera, took pictures of unpaved streets and dark alleys, and convinced the editor to print his photos on the front page of the *Corona Independent*. His photographs galvanized public support that ultimately forced the city to fund several infrastructure improvements. By the look in his face, I could tell he was proud that his photographs helped improve his community.[17]

I relied on my informants at Joe's Bakery to direct me to the important social spaces and physical places in the community. They suggested I attend the next citrus worker reunion at the Joe Dominguez American Legion Hall. The citrus worker reunions began in 1993 with the idea of recovering the history of Mexican Americans in the city and providing a space for friends and family to share old photographs and stories of working in the industry and living in the labor camps and barrio neighborhoods. The idea for a reunion began over coffee between Rey Aparicio, Onias Acevedo, and Rudy Ramos at Joe's Bakery. It began with someone complaining that the only time they saw their old friends was when they died or attended the same funeral. Since very few Mexican Americans graduated high school (because they worked in the citrus industry), they created their own version of a high school reunion. Although these reunions were called citrus worker reunions, it also included residents who did not work in the industry. Many of the attendees were connected through Washington Elementary School, a segregated school that only admitted mostly Mexican students and a few Italian and black students. "This is the only reunion we have," explained Alex Rivera, a former Washington student and truck driver. "We know each other because we grew up in the neighborhood. It was a rough time back then because there was little education and a lot of work."[18]

On September 1, 1996, I attended the third annual citrus worker reunion at the American Legion Post 742 Hall on Yorba Street. More than 200 were in attendance, some traveling from northern California and as far away as Arizona and Texas. Afraid that I might feel out of place, I asked Rudy Ramos if I could go with him so he could introduce me to his friends. I encountered many friendly people who were naturally curious about how I was connected to Corona. After I revealed that I was attending graduate school at University of California, Irvine, and researching the history of Corona's Mexican American community, some responded with limited information and others became excited that I wanted to learn their family's history. I gravitated to those enthusiastic to share their stories about family's history in Corona. I sat at a table decorated in lemon and orange colors; the delicious aroma of barbecued beef came from the kitchen. Dolores Salgado, one of the main organizers of the reunions, instructed me to get in line before the food ran out. According to Salgado, the Post's Ladies Auxiliary developed a good reputation for making delicious food using cherished family recipes.

Founded in 1948, the Ladies Auxiliary was composed of wives and daughters of veterans, who cooked the food, took over the job of raising funds for student scholarships, and supported local child welfare programs. American Legion Joe Dominguez Post 742 was founded two years before the Ladies Auxiliary by twenty-nine Mexican American veterans of World War II after being rejected from the all-white post named after Charles Jameson, a prominent citrus grower in southern California. These veterans turned bitter memories of segregation into an opportunity to build their own organization to cultivate community leaders. Many post members became active in civic affairs and electoral politics. According to the post's first commander, Rey Aparicio, "We wanted to improve our image, our community and maybe change a few things in Corona."[19] The American Legion Post 742 was named after Joe Dominguez, a Mexican American soldier from Corona killed in 1943 while serving in the US Army.[20] Onias Acevedo also played an important role in developing the post. He explained why they selected Joe Dominguez. "He wasn't the first Hispanic to be killed in World War II from Corona but he was their classmate from elementary school to high school and was very friendly and popular in the community."[21] After several decades of meeting in garages and raising funds, in 1982 post members designed and built a lodge with a large meeting room, kitchen, and cocktail lounge. After a long struggle to secure a space of their own, the American Legion Joe Dominguez Post Hall continues to host community events and family reunions.

After attending my first citrus worker reunion, I found it obvious that this event was a rich source of historical information. I felt that the local library should be part of capturing these memories and photos. Although library staff attended the first reunion, where they registered each attendee, they needed volunteers to help conduct oral histories. I offered to interview many of the reunion attendees and donate the recordings to the library. However, I needed to spend more time with local residents to gain their trust and visit the places where their memories resided. Although the Washington Elementary School, Teatro Chapultepec, and St. Edward Catholic Church—constructed with fieldstone from surrounding riverbeds—have all been torn down, many residents still remember these places where they built a shared memory. The power of place nurtured a shared sense of community. According to Dolores Hayden, "The power of ordinary urban landscapes to nurture citizen's public memory, to encompass shared time in the form of shared territory—remains untapped for most working people neighborhoods in most American cities, and for most ethnic history and most women's history."[22]

Even though the reunions brought together former pickers and packers from the citrus industry, their memories did not revolve around their work experiences. Many shared their recollections of the fun times they spent with family and friends. Despite the economic hardships that many immigrant and working-class families faced and the racial segregation that limited recreational opportunities, they found ways to have fun. One of the memorable leisure places was the sandlot that was the home of the Corona Athletics Baseball Club. When I interviewed Reynaldo Aparicio at his tax preparation business, he remembered fondly the baseball field. "They had a field up on the corner of Railroad and Sheridan. There's a little shopping center there now. It used to belong to the [Santa Fe] railroad company but railroad let them put up a backstop and they used to play baseball in that. When they hit a home run they would blow the car horn. There were some very good teams that came out of there."[23] One of these was the Corona Athletics. Considered one of the most successful independent semiprofessional teams in southern California, the Athletics won several regional championships and produced several Major League players.

For many young Mexican Americans, high school sports were not an option because they had to drop out of school and work to support their families. Instead, they played in independent baseball teams sponsored by local businesses, companies, and churches. Jess Uribe began playing at the age of sixteen and continued into his adult years. He recalled how they earned money to pay for equipment costs by passing around a donation basket and organizing dance fundraisers. Uribe used his organizational and leadership skills in his grocery store job. "I helped to organize the workers in the grocery store to vote in favor of the union. The union helped me and my family for many years."[24] Baseball allowed Ray Delgadillo to travel abroad, so when he received an invitation to play in the Mexican Baseball League, he signed a contract and played for one season. He had to return to the United States in 1943 because he was drafted by the US military.[25]

Former Corona Athletics player Jim "Chayo" Rodriguez was instrumental in redirecting my strict focus on labor issues to more of an emphasis on sports. Rodriguez's playing and coaching career in the Inland Empire has spanned a remarkable seven decades and was responsible for bringing fast-pitch softball to the city park.[26] When I met him at one of the reunions, he invited me to his home. He converted his garage into a baseball museum that included team photos, jerseys, hats, gloves, bats, and other memorabilia. I was so impressed that I encouraged him to display this variety of memorabilia at the Corona Public Library. Like many former players, Rodriguez maintained a close attachment to the sport through photographs, visiting former players, and watching games in the same playing fields where he had spent much of his leisure time.

Rodriguez accompanied me to the locations where he played baseball and softball. At every place, his spatial memory revealed new insights about sports history in Corona. For example, when we visited Corona City Park, he remembered his friend's experience in the minor leagues. "Bobby Perez pitched minor league ball in Reno for the Pittsburgh Pirates. Those minor league teams keep you out there if you are good, but they only want you to be the 'meat squad' for batting practice."[27] Unlike professional leagues, community-based baseball was a family affair in which different generations could participate as players or spectators. This memory brought on by the park visit reminded him why he dedicated so much to coaching and promoting baseball and softball in the city and region.

Rodriguez started playing at the age of thirteen in junior high school with mostly white kids. Because of his dark skin and Mexican heritage, he admitted, "They used to call me *la mosca en la leche* or fly in the milk."[28] He was often mistaken for an American Indian when his team played at the Indian reservations and Sherman Institute. This mistaken identity did not stop him from playing and coaching for over sixty years. Because of the few Mexican American coaches, he decided to coach and promote fast-pitch softball in Corona's city park. During the 1970s, Rodriguez formed The Chicanos softball club to steer troubled Chicano youth away from gangs and prisons. Inspired by the Chicano movement, he sought to instill cultural pride by selecting Pancho Villa, a Mexican revolutionary leader, as their mascot. He recounted his early struggles against the city officials to bring the Chicano Fast Pitch Softball Tournament to Corona City Park during Labor Day and Memorial Day weekends. For sixteen years, the tournament attracted more than sixty teams from Arizona, Texas, and Mexico. With Rodriguez's coaching and mentoring, the Chicanos lived up to their team mascot by winning several championship titles.

Gendered Leisure Places

Because Joe's Bakery, Joe Dominguez American Legion Post Hall, and the baseball stadiums were primarily male spaces, I needed to expand my network to find more women's voices. One day I visited the Corona Senior Center, where I encountered a sewing circle of elderly women. I was reluctant to meet them at first but was encouraged by the center director. Some of the women told me the well-known story of the legendary Mexican bandit Joaquin Murietta, who hid in Corona evading police authorities. Others recalled the famous Corona bootlegger Juan Salvador, the main character in Victor Villasenor's novel *Rain of Gold*.[29] When I asked about female bootleggers, there was an uncomfortable silence. There was neither confirmation nor denial of their existence. Visiting the Corona Senior Center was more difficult because it was a tight-knit sewing circle of women, some reluctant to be interviewed for personal reasons.

In gathering the memories and life stories of Mexican Americans, I found that their remembrances of leisure places differed according to their gender position. When I asked my female informants about their leisure experiences, some recalled how they were prohibited from certain public spaces by their parents, especially at night. As a young girl, Margaret Santos was frequently warned by her parents not to visit Main Street because of its negative reputation. "Corona from 5th Street all the way down to the boulevard was a happening town, with full of cantinas, pool halls, lots of music and dancing. But we girls could not walk down there by ourselves."[30] Even though they were prohibited from visiting this part of town, some women showed boldness. For Margaret Muñoz Rosales, it was one of few places where she could go dancing. "We were young and after work, we would take a quick shower and go to the dances. They use to have swing music and that was a lot of fun. That is where I met my future husband. I was dancing swing when I met him."[31]

The ladies at the Corona Senior Center suggested I meet Frances Martinez, whom they jokingly referred to as *sacafiestas* (party starter) because of her very active social life, even in her late eighties as a full-time babysitter for her great-grandchildren. When I visited

Frances at her red cinderblock home on Merrill Street, in Corona's South side, I also met her daughter and granddaughters, who wanted to meet me and understand my research. After I discussed my research project, they allowed me to interview Frances but warned me that she had a good memory and would talk for hours. They were correct; between 1996 and 1999 I conducted four oral interviews that lasted three to four hours each. These sessions with Martinez convinced me to rethink my focus on labor and explore the gendered dimensions of leisure spaces.

Martinez was born in Durango, Mexico, in 1912. After her mother died during childbirth, her aunt, Tiburcia Aguirre, brought her to live with family relatives in Corona. She was sent to a St. Mary's Parochial School in Los Angeles, where she learned to dance and play the violin and piano. Upon returning to Corona in 1928 to start high school, she began using her artistic talents in two main kinds of festivals: (1) religious fiestas that included seasonal and rites of passage celebrations, and (2) secular festivals that included folkloric dance and patriotic holidays.

Martinez played the piano for 11:30 a.m. mass and was also hired for funerals, weddings, and other special occasions. She recalls how she joined the choir when she was fifteen: "I can still remember what a bold front I put up when [Mrs. Mary Schrick] came to call on me. It seems there was no one to play the organ the church and she wanted to organize a choir. She had heard from our pastor that I could play and sing a little. Financially the going was terribly tough, but I was determined to finish high school."[32]

As a young girl living with a strict aunt, Martinez was not allowed to attend social events unless they were church-related and she was accompanied by a chaperone. She remembered, "When I came to Corona in 1928, there was nothing going on. They used to have these *jamaicas* at the old stone church. It is not like it used to be. My cousin and I used to go every Sunday afternoon. They had the girls selling food. Then they had a jail and if the guys did something bad the girls were allowed to take them to jail."[33] Jamaicas were festive church bazaars organized by parishioners of St. Edward Catholic Church to raise money for charity and provide free entertainment for families. For young men and women, these parish events offered opportunities to carry out their courtship.

"The young lovers were clever," admitted Martinez. "They met secretly at church events." It was during church services that Martinez could see her boyfriend. "George and I knew each other through St. Edward Church. I played the organ and sang in the choir. I sat up sort of high so I could look down at George. Eventually we ran off and got married."[34]

Martinez and I visited the former location of Teatro Chapultepec, a family-owned theater that screened silent films and Mexican films. There was no trace left after urban renewal and construction of the Corona Mall during the 1960s. She pointed to a narrow alley and off to the north where the quaint brick building once stood. She remembered the extra money she earned playing piano for silent films. It was not an easy job because she had to improvise and synchronize the music with each scene. "I made up the stuff and tired to match the noise with the action. . . . When there was a kissing scene, I had played treble trills. When they showed a motion picture about the girl tied up on the railroad tracks, I had to pound on the keys really hard and scream."[35] She felt nostalgic and wished there was some historic memorial to remember this important community space. She pointed to other locations that have been forgotten and made me promise to document them.

A major turning point for Martinez came when she visited her estranged father and other relatives in Mexico. During her visit, she "felt proud about Mexican heritage because they don't miss any opportunity over there to make a holiday." She added, "I came back determined that if there was anything I could do to lift the spirit of my people in this country I would try."[36] As a result, her aunt first nicknamed her Sacafiestas because "she was always asking me what party I had up my sleeve next time." Martinez added, "I knew how to get a party started."[37] As a result, she explained, "We put our own fiestas on . . . We had dances in the streets. We closed the east and west streets and we would have some pretty good bands in the 1930s."[38]

One of her articles in the local newspaper focused on the Feast of Our Lady of Guadalupe. She wrote, "If you wake up hearing strange sounds Friday morning, Dec. 12th, don't be alarmed, relax. It isn't spring yet. It is the Feast of Our Lady of Guadalupe, the Virgin of the Americas, which will be celebrated at St. Edward's Church."[39]

After describing historic significance of La Virgen to Mexican history and national identity, she commented, "After all, why can't the Americas have a patron of their own? Italy has St. Anthony; Ireland has St. Patrick, to name a few."[40] Frances's oral testimonies and writings on the Virgin of Guadalupe celebration and Mexican religious traditions gave legitimacy to the public expression of a unique Mexican American religiosity.[41]

Mexican American women's leisure activities extended beyond the Catholic Church but were still constrained by parental authority, gender, race, and economic factors. Two events that allowed women to exert themselves in the public domain were the annual Cinco de Mayo celebrations and afternoon dances near the river. Because of the hot weather during the summer months, residents would gravitate toward nearby rivers and creeks for swimming and dancing. The *tardeadas*, the afternoon dances held before sunset, attracted the most attention. "Tardeadas were like our holiday," explained Martinez. "Every Sunday people came from San Bernardino, Chino, and Pomona to River Road [and Temescal Wash]. There used to be cabins there and there was a dance floor. My aunt did not let me go to the afternoon dance but I found a way, either we found a chaperone or sneaked out." These dances were rather informal gatherings but attracted some of the more talented musicians in the area. In 1938 the Santa Ana River flooded, and it wiped out the dance floor. The residents found new places to dance.

Street dances during Cinco de Mayo festivities were one of the few occasions when Mexican Americans could claim public space in this agricultural town. On Saturday, May 2, 1998, I attended a Cinco de Mayo parade and fiesta to see why so many considered this event a Corona tradition. The parade started at 10 a.m. and had floats, marching bands, dance groups, and car club cars. It ended at the city park, where food and entertainment awaited the spectators. Corona's Cinco de Mayo celebration started as a small community event in 1923 and has continued to the present day. The celebration begins with a street parade on Main Street, music concert at the city park, the coronation of the queen and street dance party (see figure 5.1). Al Varela, professional photographer and member of the Corona Cinco de Mayo Committee, met with me during a Cinco de Mayo celebration to discuss how this holiday has changed

Figure 5.1 Cinco de Mayo procession on Main Street, circa 1930s. Used by permission of the Board of Trustees of the Corona Public Library.

over the years. "This event has become more than a Mexican holiday," he explained. "It has evolved into a civic event with funds from committee fundraisers, local businesses, nonprofit groups, and the city contributes between $3,000 and $4,000 to stage the event."[42] Even though the parade had grown bigger with more than 10,000 people in attendance it still had a personal touch with spectators lined up on Sixth Street talking with parade participants. The grand marshal is selected from a pool of "community heroes" because, according to Varela, there is "a long tradition of Mexican Americans being involved in local politics and community organizations. We don't need movie stars or Hollywood celebrities to give it legitimacy."[43] He proudly added Corona has one of the longest running Cinco de Mayo celebrations in southern California and "by having a fiesta here, we're digging our roots deeper into our culture here."[44]

Memory and place were interwoven into these Cinco de Mayo celebrations as a means of carrying out cultural practices and claiming political power in this agricultural town. These fiestas were not organized simply for the pleasure of the community but also to build political power and resolve community problems. When the police began harassing suspected zoot suiters and *pachuco* gangs, Frances Martinez and other Mexican American residents saw a need for a youth recreation center. When they approached the city, they received little support, so they began to redirect the proceeds from the Cinco de Mayo celebrations to finance La Casita building. They worked on raising money for the recreation center from 1947 to 1949 and the La Casita became a reality in 1950. Alice Rodriguez and Lupe Delgadillo, close friends of Frances Martinez who worked together in the citrus packinghouses, also raised funds for the building. To many of my interviewees, Recreation Center represented a community success story and the rise of a powerful Mexican American voting bloc.

Alice Rodriguez started working at the Foothill packing house when she was fifteen, following in the footsteps of her older sisters. She wanted to remember not the long hours of packing lemons but what she did for fun during weekends. She discussed her organizing efforts in making the Cinco de Mayo Queen contests a successful funding source for La Casita (see figure 5.2). "We were already fired up," remembered Lupe Delgadillo. "Since I was the only girl with a car I did most of the traveling back and forth to Los Angeles to buy materials for the fundraisers." When I visited

Figure 5.2 Cinco de Mayo Queen Eloisa Hernandez, 1948. Used by permission of the Board of Trustees of the Corona Public Library.

the La Casita Recreation Center with Rodriguez and Delgadillo, we found a dilapidated building with closed doors and windows. Their memories of struggles to raise enough money for its construction quickly turned to anger against the city for neglecting the center. They discussed how the city sold La Casita to a group of local Anglo businessmen without consulting them in the early 1960s so they could finance moving city hall to the high school building.

Conclusion

Oral history is not just a research method but a political project. The process of engaging people with memories of their lives requires patience, self-reflexivity, careful listening, and political risk. One example of memory becoming politicized was when I asked about the 1941 citrus strike. The strike created internal divisions within the community that reverberated decades later. Several union supporters who worked for the city's packing houses felt betrayed by workers from the labor camps, who refused to join the picket line and the union. It was very difficult for my informants to discuss this strike; it was much easier to talk about baseball, the pool halls, and Cinco de Mayo parades. Longtime Corona residents fiercely guarded their memories of the past by teaching me about how certain historical events should be publicly remembered. They taught me that their leisure pastimes were as important as their working experiences. Even though some attempted to compartmentalize work and politics from leisure, these were often blurred, especially when important union and civil rights organizing took place on the baseball field and during Cinco de Mayo fiestas. It was the female informants who taught me to think critically about these leisure spaces, because on the surface they appear entertaining and festive but underneath they reveal relations of gender and class power that constrain collective struggle for liberation.

Visiting the Mexican bakery, veteran legion hall, baseball fields, and recreation center was important in gaining new insights about their past, hopes, aspirations, and disappointments. Ultimately, my informants convinced me to reconsider how their cultural struggles in specific kinds of leisure places helped challenge the oppressive working and living conditions in an agricultural town. By telling me their stories of work and leisure, they were not only reconstructing their past but also envisioning a better political future for their grandchildren. Many expressed a deep concern about the lack of recreational opportunities for youth and the need for more parks and open green spaces. Small traces of Corona's "old small-town charm" and citrus legacy remain in the physical landscape, but newcomers from Orange County and Los Angeles County know very little about the town's labor and ethnic history. Some of my informants suggested the need for more memorials, monuments, street naming, and museums as important sites for remembering. When Jim Rodriguez was invited to donate his baseball memorabilia to the Corona Heritage Park and Museum, he did not trust that they would interpret his stories accurately and display his collection to a wider audience. It is important that less privileged groups become more adept at using memory as an instrument to redefine mainstream public history and challenge their own subordination. In summer 2012, I attended the reunion of former members of the Corona Athletics Baseball Club and the Corona Debs at the American Legion Joe Dominguez Post Hall. Organized by Richard Cortez, son of Natividad Cortez, this event brought multiple generations of baseball fans who shared their stories about how baseball helped build a sense of community and a shared history.

Notes

1. Natividad Cortez, interview by author, Corona, CA, April 4, 1998.

2. Aurora Delgado, interview by author, July 15, 1999.

3. Gloria Granada, interview by author, June 18, 1999.

4. José M. Alamillo, *Making Lemonade out of Lemons: Mexican American Labor and Leisure in a California Town, 1880–1960* (Urbana: University of Illinois Press, 2006).

5. Johanna Rachelle Tucker, "Corona's Grand Street Racing," June 1979, unpublished manuscript, Heritage Room, Corona Public Library, Corona, CA. In one of his *California Gold* episodes on public TV, Huell Howser attempted to re-create the road races with vintage race cars and help from a former attendee of the 1916 race.

6. Joe Gutierrez, "Documents Packed with Corona History," *Press-Enterprise*, March 16, 1996. The citrus packing house opened in 1908 and closed down in the 1980s.

7. Datwa Morales, "Citrus Records Tell Tale," *Press-Enterprise*, September 25, 1998.

8. Chon Noriega, "Preservation Matters: Research, Community and the Archive," in *A Companion to Latina/o Studies*, ed. Juan Flores and Renato Rosaldo (Malden, MA: Blackwell, 2007), 190–91.

9. Some of the early work on the use of oral history in writing Mexican American history include Oscar Martinez, "Chicano Oral History: Status and Prospects," *Aztlan: A Journal of Chicano Studies* 9 (1979): 119–31; Debra Weber, "Oral Sources and the History of Mexican Workers in the United States," *International Labor and Working Class History* 23 (Spring 1983): 47–50; Hubert Miller, "Oral History: A Tool for the Study of Mexican American History in the Lower Rio Grande Valley of Texas," *Oral History Review* 15 (Fall 1987): 80–95; Raquel Rubio-Goldsmith, "Oral History: Considerations and Problems for its Use in the History of Mexicanas in the United States," in *Between Borders: Essays on Mexicana/Chicana History,* ed. Adelaida del Castillo (Northridge, CA: Floricanto Press, 1989), 161–73.

10. Nancy Raquel Mirabal, "Geographies of Displacement: Latina/os, Oral History, and the Politics of Gentrification in San Francisco's Mission District," *Public Historian* 31, no. 2 (May 2009): 7–31; Mary Ann Villarreal, "Finding Our Place: Reconstructing Community through Oral History," *Oral History Review* 33:2 (2006): 45–64; Horacio N. Roque Ramirez, "Memory and Mourning: Living Oral History with Queer Latinos in San Francisco," in *Oral History and Public Memories,* ed. Paula Hamilton and Linda Shopes (Philadelphia: Temple University Press, 2008), 165–86.

11. On this point see Patricia Zavella, "Recording Chicana Life Histories: Refining the Insider's Perspective," in *Insider/Outsider Relationships with Informants,* Working Paper No. 13, ed. Elizabeth Jameson (Tucson: University of Arizona, Southwest Institute for Research on Women, 1982), 12–14.

12. Jenny Cardenas, "Living the Good Life in Corona: Old-timers Look Back with Humor," *Press-Enterprise*, April 12, 1992.

13. George Lipsitz, *How Racism Takes Place* (Philadelphia: Temple University Press, 2011), 5.

14. Onias "Ace" Acevedo, interview by author, October 15, 1998.

15. Ramos's love of photography began at Corona Junior High School, and with the help of a teacher and earnings from picking lemons, he bought his first camera. What was once a hobby turned into a lifelong ambition; in 1958, he opened a professional photography studio in the south side of town. Rudy Ramos, interview by author, October 10, 1998.

16. *Corona Independent*, May 4, 1949.

17. Inspired by Rudy Ramos's photograph collection, the Corona Library's Heritage Room held several "Shades of Corona Photo Days" during summer 2008, inviting city residents to bring their family albums and personal photograph collections "to help preserve the history of Corona's ethnic communities." "Shades of Corona" pamphlet, July 25, 1998, personal collection.

18. Jerry Solfer, "Memories of Hardships, Friendships," *Press-Enterprise*, September 4, 1994.

19. Sandra Tapia, "Legion Post 742 Turns 50," *Press-Enterprise*, September 6, 1996.

20. "Joe Dominguez's Death Brought War Home," *Corona Independent*, May 25, 1990.

21. Acevedo interview.

22. Dolores Hayden, *The Power of Place: Urban Landscapes as Public History* (Cambridge: MIT Press, 1995), 9.

23. Reynaldo Aparicio, interview by the author, January 17, 1998.

24. Jess Uribe, interview by the author, February 20, 1998.

25. Ray Delgadillo, interview by the author, June 24, 2001.

26. Jerry Soifer, "Chayo Is a Corona Landmark," *Press-Enterprise*, November 3, 1989.

27. Jim "Chayo" Rodriguez, interview by the author, March 16, 1998.

28. Ibid.

29. Victor Villasenor, *Rain of Gold* (New York: Delta Books, 1991).

30. Margaret Santos, interview by the author, March 16, 1998.

31. Margaret Muñoz Rosales, interview by the author, August 2, 2000.

32. Frances Martinez, interview by the author, July 14, 1999.

33. Frances Martinez, interview by the author, January 26, 1998.

34. Ibid.

35. Ibid.

36. Ibid.

37. Frances Martinez, interview by the author, January 22, 1998.

38. Joe Gutierrez, "Tranquil Times, Even While Dealing with Segregation," *Press-Enterprise*, Nov. 20, 1994.

39. Frances Martinez, "Guadalupe Feast Observances at St. Edwards Friday," *Corona Independent*, December 10, 1947.

40. Martinez interview, January 26, 1998.

41. For more information on the construction of a Mexican American ethno-Catholicism, see Roberto Treviño, *The Church in the Barrio: Mexican American Ethno-Catholicism in Houston* (Chapel Hill: University of North Carolina Press, 2006).

42. Al Varela, interview by the author, June 19, 2001.

43. Ibid.

44. Ibid.

6

"That's All We Knew"

An Oral History of Family Labor in the American Southwest

SKOTT BRANDON VIGIL

Historian Skott Brandon Vigil uses his family history to understand two groups neglected in western history: Mexicans and Utes. His oral histories illuminate the experiences of migrant families who created a place for themselves in the American West while providing an essential agricultural workforce in the region. Focusing on Mexican migrant workers, Vigil shows that the migration to the West came from the South as well as the East. His interviews deconstruct many stereotypes of Indians and Mexicans and provide a way for him to reexamine his role as a "second generation migrant wanting to remember where [he] came from."[1]

IN 1942, AUDENAGO Vigil and his two sons, Nick and Jose Bill, left their humble home in Pilar, New Mexico, for Denver, Colorado. The Great Depression had hit the family particularly hard. There was little work available in their rural home, just southwest of Taos, and the family survived on "sweet gravy" (a flour and sugar mix), rabbit meat, and poached livestock. Audenago heard about the prospects for good wages and abundant work in Colorado. The nation's agricultural production had begun to increase in response to the war raging in Europe, and Colorado farmers devoted more land to the cultivation of sugar beets. The Vigil men packed their meager belongings, bid their family farewell, and boarded a bus for central Colorado. On arriving in Denver, the trio found transportation to Berthoud, where, for the next fifteen years, the Vigil family (and eventually Audenago's wife, Erminia, and their nineteen children) worked as migrant farmworkers in northern Colorado. In the 1950s, when mechanization of the sugar beet harvest reduced the amount of work available near Berthoud, Audenago packed his family into a two-door Chevrolet and moved to Santa Maria, California. There, the family picked strawberries, carrots, and string beans in an effort to find a piece of the California dream. These migrations left an indelible imprint on the family's oral history. For the nineteen Vigil children, now fully grown, the decades removed from their migrations and agricultural work did not dull their memories and descriptions of work in the American West. Family oral histories are one of the few ways that readers can understand the work and labor of the region's agricultural workforce.

This essay uses oral histories from the surviving members of the Vigil family to uncover the experiences of a migrant worker family in the American West. The Vigils' stories provide an intimate look into the lives of migrant laborers and the challenges they faced in the twentieth-century American West. The Vigils vividly remembered the difficulties of picking sugar beets in Colorado and strawberries in California. Oral histories also revealed that they organized their labor within their household. All family members contributed labor power by picking crops, hauling wood, watching younger family members, pooling their wages, and enforcing work codes and discipline on each other. The family also remembered conflicts with their employers, not over labor conditions in the fields but when employers attempted to undermine kinship and family relations within the Vigil household. The Vigil family's story provides one example of how oral history can help us show the experiences of poor, working families and how they created a place in the post-Depression American West.

Oral history is essential to understanding this family history. Often even the best written sources lack the powerful and emotional accounts contained within oral testimonies. The oral histories of the Vigil family are important because, as scholar Ingrid Scobie observes, "Interviews serve to remind historians of the individual cases which comprise the generalized picture."[2] Oral accounts deepen and strengthen our knowledge of the past; without them our understanding of history is less textured.

During summer 2005, my family and I traveled throughout Colorado, New Mexico, California, Wyoming, and South Dakota in an effort to conduct interviews with fourteen of Audenago's children. These interviews provide the foundation for an examination of the lives of this multicultural working-class family. Without oral history, we would lose the opportunity to see their struggles and experiences. The Vigils were one of many families that saw in westward migration an opportunity to find a better quality of life and improve their social station. Their story and oral history speaks to the creation of the American West as one of the most diverse regions in the United States.[3]

Audenago Vigil, the family patriarch, was born in 1906 in Pilar, New Mexico. His birth created quite a scandal in the small hamlet. Pilar, Audenago's father, was a fairly prosperous man in the village. He was descended from a mixed Ute-Hispanic family formed during the trade of human captives in the early nineteenth-century Southwest. Audenago's ancestors did not live on the Ute reservation, but made a life for themselves in the Hispanic and Pueblo communities of northern New Mexico, such as Picuris and Pilar (the town).[4] In the late nineteenth century, Pilar married a woman named Libradita Cortez, and they had several children. In the early twentieth century, Pilar began an affair with a woman named Andrellita Sauzo, the daughter of Pedro Antonio Sauzo and Nazcita Garcia, widow of Jose Guadalupe Vigil, and mother of several children. Libradita was still alive during the affair, and it caused her severe anguish and may have contributed to her death. Pilar and Andrellita's children, too, were upset about the affair and opposed the couple's later decision to marry.[5]

Pilar and Andrellita's union produced two children, Audenago and Carolina Vigil, who were born into difficult circumstances. Andrellita's family treated her like an outcast because of her affair with Pilar, and the poor treatment extended to Carolina and Audenago. Audenago's aunts and uncles ridiculed him and called him a bastard. Worse than this, Pilar initially refused to recognize Audenago as his son. It was not until his teenage years that Andrellita even told Audenago his father's name. Audenago confronted Pilar, who admitted his paternity.[6]

To escape the abuse and mistreatment in his home, Audenago left the town of Pilar to look for work. His journey took him across the Mountain West and into what historian Sarah Deutsch has called the "regional community" of northern New Mexico. In the late nineteenth century, the arrival of Anglo Americans in northern New Mexico upset social and economic relations in the Hispanic communities. To compensate for shrinking communal grazing lands, the destruction of the pastoral economy, and the arrival of Anglo American "modernity," many Hispanic men left their home villages to work in the railroad industry, mines, and beet fields.[7] Audenago joined this army of male itinerant workers. He cut railroad ties in Chama, New Mexico; pushed coal carts in Ouray, Colorado; and herded sheep in Big Piney, Wyoming. Working in Wyoming was especially harrowing. One day, a bear entered the camp and attacked his sheep dogs. The bear attack so startled Audenago that he hid for two days before he felt safe to venture out again.[8] Jose Bill recalled how these early experiences affected his father's later life:

> I can just sense the agony of a man, of a young kid, you know, of the great fear. And I think that he became the man that he was because of the treatment and fear that he suffered under his uncles and under that environment that he had to be in when he was in Wyoming. He was a very angry person, [who lacked] self-esteem. . . . I can understand now why he may have been the way that he was.[9]

The anger to which Jose Bill alluded did not manifest early in Audenago's life. He was a carefree young man when not defending his camp from bear attacks. He saved enough money to buy a car, and, each year, when he returned to New Mexico, he and some friends cruised around, drank alcohol, and acted wild. In his fancy suit and car, Audenago became popular among the younger people in Pilar. During one of these visits, Audenago caught the eye of a young woman named Erminia Romero. Jose Bill recalled his parents' courtship. "As I understand it, my mom got pregnant before wedlock . . . but dad went and asked permission to marry her but it was sort of a shotgun wedding." In the early twentieth century, sexual liaisons like that between Audenago and Erminia were common in northern New Mexico. Seasonal and migrant workers often had relationships with the young women who stayed in villages and communities. Often, though, these men left their illegitimate children behind as they participated in a circuit of seasonal labor opportunities. Audenago was not one of those men; he married Erminia and continued to participate in migrant labor.[10]

Shortly after they married, Audenago returned to herding sheep in Wyoming. In the middle of the 1930s, he added winter work on ranches in Winnemucca and Elko, Nevada, to his seasonal migrations. In between the Wyoming and Nevada ranching seasons, Audenago returned to his wife and ended up getting her pregnant nearly every year. Their first son, Nick, was born in 1931, then Jose Bill in 1932, Jose Thomas in 1934, Audenago Jr. in 1935, Juan in 1937, Delores in 1939, Mary in 1940, and Esther in 1941.[11] Audenago and Erminia's living conditions were quite common in northern New Mexico. Despite the tendency of men to travel in search of work for a good portion of the year, Hispanic men and women created a life together and with their community after they married. Although the family's oral history is silent on Erminia's strategies, she probably integrated herself into a large community of women in Pilar. Hispanic women formed social and economic relationships with other women in the community through *comadre* and **madrina** relationships. Women also had their own religious events and roles in male-dominated religious services. Finally, women shared labor and the products of their work to make ends meet while their husbands were away working.[12]

The Great Depression created extremely difficult circumstances for the family. While Audenago was away, Erminia moved her growing family into a vacant adobe house next to Pilar, Audenago's father. She probably moved closer to Pilar to secure help raising an ever-growing family.[13] While living in the town of Pilar, the family had very little to eat, and Erminia did what she could to take care of and feed her family. Jose Bill remembered, "[We] had nothing but sugar and flour in the house. [Erminia] would make us sweet gravy and that's all we had to eat. I remember going to bed hungry and waking up hungry." The family's poor economic circumstances produced a rift between the spouses. Erminia believed that Audenago was living the high life in Nevada, attending parties and dances like a single man. Jose Bill recalled that the Great Depression forced a showdown between his parents. "Our mom became desperate. She wrote a letter to dad, telling him to either come back and take care of the family or to give her a divorce to see what she could do for us. To his credit, he came back. He didn't abandon us."[14] In the family's memory, Audenago chose to do the honorable thing and returned to his family when he could have very easily agreed to a divorce. Quite clearly, the Great Depression threatened to undermine the Vigil family and the viability of the region's regional community.[15]

When Audenago returned to New Mexico, he found new ways to support his family. He cut wood to sell or exchange for goods. Furthermore, Jose Bill remembered that his father was a prolific hunter. "Poverty in New Mexico was everywhere. I remember dad hunting rabbits to feed us. He had a single shot .410-gauge shotgun and one box of shells. He would put six shells in his pocket and come back with six rabbits. Poorness did not make him a good shot; it just made him a calculating one." Sometimes he brought home larger game. "He would tell us that he had killed a deer and that he and Nick would go in the dead of night and bring the meat in. It was much later that I found out it was not a deer that he had killed. It was someone's steer [on] the open rangeland. The people and relatives who had come to dinner kept saying that it was the best deer that they had ever tasted."[16] As with many families in the United States, Audenago and Erminia did anything they could, even poaching a steer, to stave off starvation during the Great Depression.

In the mid-1930s, Audenago found work offered by the Works Progress Administration (WPA), which presaged later labor arrangements he created for his family. In 1935, the WPA funded several road-building projects to improve life in Hispanic villages in New Mexico. Audenago worked on a road-building project in Valdez, north of Taos. Jose Bill accompanied him to Valdez and was in charge of cooking dinner for his father. After spending the work week sleeping in their car, Audenago and Jose Bill returned to their family in Pilar. As the children became older, they contributed to the family's labor arrangements. Jose Bill did not work on the roads but supported his father by making meals at the end of the day.[17]

At the start of the 1940s, the WPA took workers off relief rolls during harvest time to encourage their participation in agricultural labor in New Mexico and Colorado. War had broken out in Europe, and the United States had increased its agricultural production to help with the war effort. The agriculture boom produced an exodus from New Mexico. Reports that Colorado beet farmers paid considerably higher wages than could be found in New Mexico encouraged many people to leave the state. In Taos County, almost 50 percent of adult Hispanic men left to work in Colorado.[18] Audenago was among those who left New Mexico in search of better employment and a better life. In 1941, Colorado farmers sent representatives to New Mexico to recruit families for farm labor. Audenago went to speak with a labor recruiter in Taos and, after returning home, discussed his options with his father, Pilar, who encouraged him to move his family to Colorado. Following this advice, Audenago signed with the labor recruiter representing the Great Western Sugar Company and, in April 1942, took Nick and Jose Bill on a bus for Denver.[19]

The trip to Denver caused much trepidation among the trio. Jose Bill, who was ten at the time, remembered, "The first night we slept in Denver with people that were from New Mexico but my dad didn't know them, they weren't related. I didn't know where he met them but we slept in their apartment on the floor. [We were s]cared to death because there were people fighting up on top, or on the next floor, they had a big fight or argument."[20] After their restless night in Denver, the Vigils returned to the bus station and caught a bus for Berthoud, where they met Guyhart Miller, a young farmer who had just begun farming sugar beets.[21]

Sugar beet work required intensive manual labor, and Miller's equipment was broken down and horse-driven. Despite lacking the latest equipment, he still required an exact and speedy planting and harvesting of the beets. After plowing the field, he dug rows of furrows in the ground, and then the Vigils placed seeds in the grooves and covered them with dirt. In May, Miller expected Audenago and his sons to "thin" twenty acres of beets. The object of thinning was to make sure that each beet was about twelve inches apart and that two beets did not occupy the same hole. Some workers skillfully maneuvered a hand hoe to knock all the beets too close to each other out of the ground, whereas others scooted along on their knees and removed twin beets by hand. Weeding followed thinning, which required workers to remove weeds from the beet rows at least three times in the summer. In October, the Vigils "topped" the sugar beets. Sugar beets grow similar to turnips in that the bulb or meaty part of the plant grows under the ground and the top or green leafy part is above ground. The farmer went through each row with a plow and raised the beets out of the ground. Then the laborers followed with a large knife that resembled a machete with a spike extending out of the top. The workers used the spike to stick a beet and bring it up off the ground to their hand. Then, with the blade of the knife, they chopped the top of the beet off and put the bulb in a pile for others to gather. By the end of the harvest, workers had handled each beet several times.[22] Beet farming became the major source of employment for Audenago's family for many years.

When Audenago and his two boys started to work, Miller advanced some money to them for food and to bring the rest of the family from New Mexico. In May, Erminia and six Vigil children (one of whom, Esther, was only one month old) took a bus from Taos to Denver. The journey was quite challenging because Erminia could not speak English and had to rely on others to help her. The family had only one bag of cinnamon rolls to eat for the entire trip. Moreover, Erminia left behind a community of women and relatives who provided economic, social, and cultural support. The Vigils arrived in Denver at midnight, but no one was there to pick them up. Audenago was supposed to meet his family at the bus station, but Miller would not give him a ride. Instead, Audenago called the train station and asked them to tell Erminia to take a bus to Loveland the next morning. That night, hungry and afraid, the children depended on their mother's courage and patience to see them through to the morning. The next day, the Vigils boarded a bus and met Audenago in Loveland. Miller drove them to the farm in Berthoud about five miles away.[23]

Shortly after Erminia and the children arrived in Berthoud, the family settled into a domestic and work routine. On the Miller farm, Audenago and his family lived in a small three-room house, which they called "the beet shack." The house was located about one-fourth of a mile from Miller's farmhouse. The beet shack had an outhouse and a wood stove, but no other furnishings. For water, the Vigils walked to the main farmhouse, pumped water out of a well in the front yard, and hauled it to the shack. Each day, the family worked for Miller. Audenago and his oldest boys (Nick, Jose Bill, and Thomas) spent twelve hours a day working the beets and then gathered wood and hauled water for the family's use.[24]

By fall 1942, all of the family's effort in the beet fields had been for naught, and they needed a miracle to survive the coming winter. During the first season, Audenago was inexperienced in the sugar beet harvest and failed to plant and thin to Miller's expectations. He and his children spent the entire season attempting to meet his employer's high standards and the Vigils had no time to do any other work. Additionally, Miller had advanced money to the Vigils equal to their year's wages. Therefore, the family had no money to see them through the winter, when work was scarce in northern Colorado. Miller allowed the Vigils to stay in the beet shack, but they faced a harrowing winter.[25]

What happened next was truly amazing. Jose Bill explained,

> [Miller] had planted about 20 acres of pinto beans by the beet shack, and he had a tremendous crop. As was customary, at a given stage of ripeness, the bean plants were wind-rowed so the combine could thresh the beans from the pods. The bean plants would stay wind-rowed for a few days to allow the beans to ripen more. The night before the beans were to be combined a super high wind hit the area. The wind tumbled the bean plants all over the field and shelled all the beans out of the pods. The ground was covered with pinto beans and no economical way for Miller to salvage them. Miller came to my dad and told him that if we wanted to glean the bean field to help ourselves. The family went out and gathered many sacks of beans; without that wind, we probably would have starved, but we ate beans all winter and survived to do beets another year.[26]

If it were not for a high wind at the right moment and the destruction of the bean crop, Audenago and his family would have had serious problems that winter.

As soon as winter ended, Audenago tired of the working conditions on Miller's farm. He moved the family to the Betz farm, where living circumstances were far more favorable. The Betz farm, also in Berthoud, had a larger beet shack and a cistern for water, so the family did not have to carry water. At the Betz farm, the Vigils became more efficient at planting, thinning, and weeding beets. Carol Scott (née Vigil) recalled,

> I started out in the beet fields, and I was about seven or eight. I was daddy's thinner, he worked the hoe and I was the thinner. And I enjoyed thinning for daddy versus mother because mother would finish hoeing her row and she would sit at the end of the row and wait till the thinner caught up with her. On the other hand, dad would finish the row and turn around and go back and thin, and then he would take me and we'd both sit at the end of the row and drink coffee.[27]

Audenago used the labor of all his children, which allowed them to finish their acreage of beets with enough time left to harvest other crops. Depending on the season, the Vigil family augmented their income by picking cherries and green beans. Eleanor Vigil (née Ramos) remembered, "[In] Loveland, over where [Hewlett Packard] is [now], that was a prime area for cherry orchards. You could just see the miles and miles of white blossoms and that fragrance would just fill the . . . it was a beautiful sight."[28] During the cherry season, the Vigils often worked beets and picked cherries on the same day. Juan said, "We would wake up about four o'clock in the morning, or dad would wake us up, and we would go out and hoe beets till it got hot, and then from there we would go pick cherries till about three or four o'clock in the evening, then we'd come home, eat, and then we'd hit the [beet] fields again tell it was too dark to see."[29] By combining jobs, the family earned a decent wage. The Vigils made $7.50 an acre for hoeing beets and $0.50 a crate for cherries. When the family arrived at the cherry orchards, they acquired ladders and crates from the farmer, claimed a row of trees, and joined other families picking cherries. Sarah Chamberlain (née Vigil) remembered, "I was five, picking cherries I had a little bucket, a belt around my waist, and we picked the bottom while the older kids picked the top on ladders."[30]

In beet fields and cherry orchards, Audenago controlled the tempo of farm labor. He threw dirt clods at children who were off task or worked inefficiently and set daily goal for each of his children. Audenago Jr. stated,

> My dad had a quota for us. We all had to pick at least ten crates of cherries a day—each individual member of the family. And my dad was a pretty good general because he had my brother Nick, and my brother Bill, and my brother Thomas, they would take the top part of the trees with ladders and the rest of us were smaller, we'd pick the bottom of the trees.[31]

The quota engendered friendly competition between migrant worker families. Eleanor Vigil remembered, "Our parents, our father decided that we had to have a quota of forty crates a day. The Vigils, there were more of them, they could do fifty, sixty. Our parents were rivals to each other. The Ramoses are over there, the Vigils are over there."[32] Families competed with each other to see who secured the most ladders, crates, and cherries. Through their labor in the cherry orchards, Audenago and his family averaged nearly $50 a day.

After the cherry season, the Vigils harvested green beans when beet work allowed. They woke early in the morning and weeded the beet fields, then went to pick green beans. Vigil family members chose a row of green beans and picked enough to fill a bucket. When their bucket filled, they emptied it into a large sack. After the Vigils filled the sack, one of them carried it to the scales located near the trucks and the road. After the farmer weighed the sack, he paid the family two cents per pound. The children took the money to Erminia, who was always in the field working alongside her family and kept the money, usually coins, in a sock.[33]

The Vigils pooled the wages they earned in the fields of Colorado, and Audenago kept the money for the family's everyday needs. Planting and harvesting income had to see the family through the winter, when there were very few jobs available. Wages also purchased clothing. Each year every child received two pairs of clothing sets: two shirts, two bib overalls, two pair of socks, two pairs of underwear, and one pair of boots. The scarce wages required frugality and imagination with the Vigil family's resources. Audenago nailed metal taps into the toe and heel of each boot to make it last longer. Although he never paid his children, once in a while he treated them to a soda pop or an ice cream.[34]

Still, the Vigil children found ways to spend their wages as they saw fit. When Audenago Jr. and Juan were in the fifth or sixth grade, they wanted a basketball and hoop. The boys tired of playing basketball with a ball made from old socks and a coffee can with both ends cut out. They knew that their father would never give them the money for the sports equipment, so they skimmed money from the family's bean earnings. Juan said,

> We kept a quarter, a nickel or you know something out of the . . . And I would tell Daryl [Audenago Jr.] to tell dad that the bag weighed this much, that way we could keep some change. So that went on, oh I don't know, probably through the whole bean season. You know we would keep a little bit and then my mom one day was changing the bed . . . and she found all this money underneath the mattress. She found our stash. We had something like three hundred dollars, and of course we got a whippin', but we also got our basket goal and basketball.[35]

Although they earned their basketball, there was little time to play. The Vigils always had chores to do around the house. Usually one of the older children stayed at the house to tend the little kids while everyone else was out in the fields. There were many children to watch, too. Between 1942 and 1956, Audenago and Erminia had ten more children: Becky, Carolina, Robert, Sarah, David, Alexander, Ruth, Roger, Deborah, and Gilbert. In total, the fertile couple had nineteen children. Jose Thomas said, "Mom was always busy with the little ones. Mom had a child every year. It seemed like she was always raising a kid, always breastfeeding one."[36]

Although Erminia took the youngest child with her to the fields, there were still many toddlers in the house requiring care. Juan said, "I remember at three and four years of age having to, if I didn't go out into the fields, [Audenago, Jr.] and I would have to stay home and cook, clean the house, and take care of the little ones. Change their diapers; keep them clean and what have you."[37] Audenago Jr. had a difficult time watching his younger brothers and sisters.

> I didn't do very good in taking care of the family, I got promoted to the fields really quick and then my brother Thomas would take care of the kids and he could do a better job of taking care of the little ones. Of course he was probably two years older than I was or a year and a half older than I was . . . and I was working probably at the age of seven, at the age of six, I was probably working out in the fields.[38]

After Audenago Jr. moved to the fields, Jose Thomas took care of the little children and the house. He fed the children, played with them outside, made sure they did not put anything in their mouths, and changed diapers. Since the family had cloth diapers, he had to haul water to wash them every day. When the rest of the family came home from the field, Jose Thomas had dinner ready for them. Audenago often complemented his son for his work at the house.[39]

Aside from watching their siblings, the Vigil children had several household chores to complete. Audenago and his boys gathered firewood in the mountains or alongside roads. The family used wood to cook, warm the house, and heat water for baths. Audenago Jr. said, "Once a week we used to fill a tub with water, and we'd start out with the littlest one and my mom would give a bath to the littlest one and then the next one, then the next one, so when the last one got to take a bath there was about that much dirt in it [motions about an inch with his fingers] from the rest of the family."[40] They took a bath once a week because there was little time for it after they finished their work. These weekly baths, of course, required a lot of work. Juan recalled how important it was for the family to haul water.

> People probably wouldn't realize this but now everything is at your fingertip, but then you had to haul water in to cook. You had to haul water in to wash, you had to haul water in for

mom to do the washing, and you had to haul water in to take a bath and you had to haul wood in to put in the wood stove and in the furnace to heat the water, to cook. I mean you cooked out of a wood stove.[41]

As with other working people in the United States, the Vigil family remembered conflict with their employers. Yet they did not recall problems with the workplace. Instead, they noted that their employers attempted to interfere with their household economy and kinship ties. While living on the Betz farm, Audenago and his family planted a large garden. Audenago Jr. explained that Betz saw and coveted their garden. "Our family planted a really nice garden. We had everything in there, and the garden grew really good. So when it was harvest time the farmer seen how nice our garden looked and he wanted it, so he told us to get out and we had to move."[42]

After losing the garden and employment, Audenago searched for more work and a place to shelter his family. A farmer named Julius Carlson and his wife hired the Vigil family. At first, the Carlsons were fair people and the Vigils stayed with them for about a year. However, relations between the families soured. Carlson and his wife were childless and wanted to adopt Jose Bill.[43] Audenago Jr. remembered,

> We worked for Carlson for about a year and then because my dad had so many kids and Mr. and Mrs. Carlson they didn't have any kids at all and they couldn't have any. They wanted my dad to sell them one of my brothers. They wanted my brother Bill, and my dad said "No," he wouldn't do it. So because of that he [Carlson] told us to get out.[44]

Jose Bill also remembered the incident.

> [The Carlsons] wanted to adopt me in particular. They asked my dad if they could adopt me. They would put me to school and all that good stuff. Both my dad and my mom said that the children were not cats, to be thrown away or to be given away. That we were their children and they would raise us the best way that they could.[45]

After they left the Carlsons, Audenago found an evangelist preacher named Mrs. McCormick who believed that it was her mission to help Spanish-speaking people. She invited the family to stay on her land in a little house that was next to hers. While living on McCormick's land, Audenago found work with Fred Keihn, another beet farmer in the area.[46] Fred and his wife, Dolly, differed from the other farmers for whom the Vigils worked; they treated the family fairly and compassionately. The Keihns helped Audenago make chicken coops and pig pens so that family could raise chickens and hogs for meat. They sold the Vigils eggs and milk at reduced prices and gave the children odd jobs around the farm for extra money for school supplies. Fred found Audenago winter work, and his two boys, Neal and Gene, encouraged the Vigil boys to participate in sports. Audenago and his son also worked for Edmund Grip and his brother. This extra work enabled the family to save enough money to buy a house on Fifth Street in Berthoud. For many immigrants, especially Hispanics, homeownership created a sense of freedom and permanence in their new communities.[47]

Despite the security that the Vigils established with homeownership, the family once more picked up their belongings and moved to a new area. Esther remembered, "The [five oldest] boys were grown up." Nick and Audenago Jr. lived elsewhere in Colorado and Bill, Thomas, and Juan had enlisted in the military. Esther continued, "It was hard for my dad to be able to make a living out in the fields, and he knew he wasn't able to do what he did before with the girls."[48] Audenago depended on the five oldest girls—Delores, Mary, Ester, Becky, and Carol—to help with the beet harvest, but the girls were not as productive as the boys had been. In addition, changes in the workplace reduced the number of jobs in Colorado. Bob Vigil remembered, "there was still beet work to do but mostly it was getting turned over to machines."[49]

Audenago started looking for work that provided a more stable income. As with many people in postwar America, his gaze settled on California.[50] Family ties helped convince him to move there. Esther recalled, "My brother Bill was in the air force and he was stationed at Edwards [Air Force Base, near Lancaster, California], and he mentioned to my dad that, you know, we could probably find jobs out here [in California] that girls could do."[51] In addition to his son's advice, Audenago used kinship ties to ease the move. Bob remembered that the family relocated to Santa Maria, California, because two of Erminia's sisters already lived there and could help the family find work.[52]

In the summer of 1956, sixteen members of the Vigil family loaded up in a Chevy Bel Air and headed to Santa Maria. Bob said, "The way it was, was mom and dad and sister Delores, which was the eldest daughter, and Gilbert was the baby. So there was four in the front and the rest in the back. So that left twelve kids in the back, all jammed packed like sardines, and that's how we went. It was hot, it was muggy, it was miserable, and my dad would only go fifty-five miles an hour."[53] They traveled from Berthoud to Denver, down to New Mexico, and then took the famous Highway 66 to California. As the Vigils traveled along Highway 66, Audenago stopped for potty breaks whenever it was possible. While in the car, the kids had to be quiet. Bob remembered one morning when they stopped at a restaurant for breakfast,

> we all piled out of [the car] and went in to have breakfast one time, and brother Alex was sick, and dad was really upset because we all had to be in our perfect behavior. Because, you know, there is a lot of us in there, anyway Alex threw up all over the place. So a lot of us didn't get to finish eating, he kicked us out of there, told us to get back into the car, that he couldn't take us any place without somebody messing up. So we really got it, we were crying, we wanted to stay and finish eating.[54]

When they finally arrived in Santa Maria, they stayed with Erminia's sister Emma for about a week until they found a house on Western Street. During the time they lived in Santa Maria, the Vigils picked strawberries and green beans. Although they worked for several farmers, the family did not find any steady employment until Audenago met Domingo Masanga, a Filipino strawberry farmer. Esther remembered, "He was very nice to the family." Whenever Masanga took the strawberries to market, he returned "with ice-cream sticks, or something for us, or soda, you know, he was very nice." Many Vigils recalled that Masanga treated the family well because he had taken a fancy to their oldest girl, Delores. Esther added, "I think he wanted, at one point, he wanted to marry my sister, but he was much older and she didn't like him."[55] Despite Delores's protests, many Vigils liked Masanga and pushed for the union. Sarah said, "He even took us on a picnic, ride in a boat, some in front some in back, we had a good time, we said, 'Dodo [Delores] marry this guy!'"[56] Soon Masanga's courtship of Delores intensified. Carol recalled, "He bought a ring for her, because he wanted her to marry him."[57] Masanga asked Audenago for Delores's hand in marriage, but Audenago refused. Carol remembered, "When dad said no, [Masanga] stopped everything."[58] This led to some hard feelings, and the Vigils had to find work elsewhere. Sarah said, "We were poor again." Carol added, "We just got fired, because Dodo wouldn't marry him."[59]

Within the first six months of arriving in California, Audenago found a small, run-down house in Casmalia, approximately twelve miles south of Santa Maria. Carol remembered, "[We] moved to Casmalia because [dad] figured that it was far away enough from the city that the kids wouldn't be getting into trouble as much."[60] The Vigil family found abundant work in the fields near Casmalia. In February and March, they picked peas in Nipomo (twenty miles north of Casmalia), a new job for the Vigils. David remembered that picking peas was difficult because they grew on the side of the hill and the farmers placed the scales on the top of the hill. He packed bags of peas uphill to weigh them, and the farmers at the scales paid cash on the spot. Lorraine, Audenago's youngest daughter, said, "My [earliest] memories are in the pea fields, and I had a little red banket, but mine had little goodies in it so I just . . . I got to watch everybody else work, I must have been about three."[61] To secure enough work during the pea season, Audenago pulled his kids out of school to work. David said that when they returned to school, "[school officials] always asked me where I was at. I'd tell them I was sick. I lied because I was embarrassed I worked out in the fields."[62]

In April, May, and June, the Vigils picked strawberries, the family's primary occupation in California. David remembered that they earned fifty cents a crate.[63] Although not as difficult as beets, picking strawberries was still labor-intensive and tiring. Delores stated,

"It wasn't any easier, you still had to drag yourself on your hands and knees picking strawberries up and down the row." She continued, "[The farmers] had a little cart, that you would push, with a crate . . . you fill up the crate, then you fill up the cart, then take it down to wherever the stand was at."[64] Mary remembered, "You had to get up early in the morning; the farmers would like you to be there early so the strawberries wouldn't wilt during the day because it would get so hot. But in the morning it was so dog-gone foggy! I hated it!"[65] Mary was not the only one who disliked picking strawberries in the fog and on the wet ground. Carol said,

> I hated picking strawberries, because the plants were all wet, the rows were muddy sometimes, and the plants were down on the ground so you would have to get down on your knees, or bend over. If you bent over your back would hurt a lot, so you would have to get on your knees and drag yourself along the rows. And you would pick the strawberries with one hand and with the other nail pick the stem out. They had little carts with a wheel in front and two in the back, and then you would put your crate on top of the [cart] then you would just push it with your hand as you went. Then when your crate was full you would take it to the end of the row. And for market you would pick them the same way except you would leave the stem on. And you had to be careful not to smash them. They had to be pretty, bright, the biggest ones.[66]

After they took their cart full of strawberries to the end of the row the farmer punched a card to keep tally. At the end of the week, the Vigil family received a check for the work they had done.

The Vigils finished the summer picking carrots and string beans. In the carrot fields the farmer loosened the earth around the carrots with a plow, and the laborers came and snapped the tops off and put the carrots into bags. David said that when topping carrots they filled 100-pound sacks and the farmers paid fifteen cents per sack.[67] Mary remembered, "They had a lot of carrots over there, and we used to have to go pick carrots, put them in sacks and they would take them away."[68] After carrots, the Vigils picked string beans. Audenago wanted the family to pick more than 2,000 pounds of beans a day. The farmers paid two cents a pound and the Vigils could average around $25 a day if they met Audenago's quota. David remembered this difficult task.

> We'd pick them off the vine, sometimes they were good some-times they were bad. When they were really good we would, sometimes we would even pick way over 2,000 pounds, some-times we would pick over 3,000 pounds or more a day. And brother Bob and I would have to carry the sacks. I remember brother Bob, he used to sometimes, he would pack 130 pounds on his back, out of the rows to the scales. I'd pack, and I only carrying my own weight, I was carrying sometimes eighty, eighty-five pounds of beans on my back for over a quarter of a mile to the scales. And we did that for six days out of the week . . . so all day long we were the pack mules, we would pack all day long.[69]

Bob and David were not yet teenagers when they hauled sacks of string beans to the scales. Deborah also remembered Bob, David, and Alex packing bags of string beans to the scales. She said that the family piled beans into a "huge burlap sack that daddy would knee down and get as many pounds in those sacks as possible." As the boys packed the beans to the scales the rest of the family worked fast to finish their rows. When the family arrived at the field, Aude-nago claimed a large area. Deborah said, "Daddy would take, I don't know how many rows. I mean because we were such a big family, and he would section out a huge, umpteen rows for us. He expected us to be done by lunch time." This was difficult because the string bean vines grew up a fence made of string that was about four feet high, and each row went the length of the field. Deborah said, "Ruth picked the top and I'd pick the bottom, then we would switch."[70] Sarah recalled picking string beans: "I remember being dad's helper. I picked the bottom and he picked the top and then he went . . . and he'd get a clod of dirt and threw it at you and say, 'get to work!' I didn't like working for dad, I always wanted to be mom's partner."[71] Audenago and Erminia kept all the money earned by the family for the expenses of living, such as housing, food, and clothing. As in Colorado, then, Audenago continued to use family labor in California to make a living. He used the labor power of his entire family in the fields and pooled their wages for the family to make ends meet.

For years, the Vigils labored in the fields near Casmalia, but the children found new job opportunities in southern California. Esther, for instance, secured work through a youth employment agency.

> Fortunately for me, when we came in 1956 and the summer of my sophomore year, dad had indicated that if we find a job, we didn't have to go out and work in the field anymore. So they had this youth employment office set up, and Delores and Mary and I went down there, you had to be a certain age, so we went down there and filled out an application.

Esther had experience taking care of her siblings, so she emphasized her child care and domestic work skills. She found a job working for the McNeil family and their three children. Mrs. McNeil worked at Vandenberg Air Force base, and Esther took care of the children. Esther and the McNeil family developed a friendly relationship, and she worked for them for several years.[72] When school started, Esther lived with an aunt who lived near the McNeil family so she could continue working for them. Esther took the McNeil kids to school, then she went to her high school. After school, she picked up the McNeil kids and stayed with them at their house until their parents came home.[73]

Some of the other Vigil children also had jobs after school and chores at home. When they came home from school, the girls had to clean inside the house, and the boys had to take care of the yard and the animals. David remembered selling newspapers, shining shoes, and doing other odd jobs. He said, "Whatever I made I gave to my mother to help the family."[74] Bob also sold newspapers.

> As young men, one job we did have after school, but it was for our own, was we got to sell papers, at Vandenberg Air Force base—it was called Camp Cook at the time. And Alex, brother Dave, brother Ben and myself, and brother Gilbert, we got to go to Vandenberg Air Force base and sell the *Santa Maria*

Times for a dime. And we would get half of that, for every
paper we sold for a dime we would get a nickel.[75]

The *Santa Maria Times* sent a person, usually a college student,
with a van to pick up eight to ten kids at the Casmalia store, and
then they went on base to sell newspapers. This happened every
weekday night and during the day on Saturday. One time, a student
named Frank was driving the van and as they were heading toward
base, one of the rambunctious kids shot him in the back of the head
with a rubber band. Bob said, "Somebody shot him, and I don't
know if it was Mike Díaz or Alex that shot him, but he thought I
did it. So he came back there, parked the van, and he started whal-
ing on us. So we all jumped on him and we started beating this
dude up." After this incident Bob said, the *Santa Maria Times*
"started sending bigger guys to us, but we got along with them."[76]
    When reflecting on his life and the hard work required of him as
a young man, David remarked,

> Now that I am older and I look back, and I heard the stories
> of some of my brothers and sisters about their struggle. I say
> to myself they did the best they could, but when you're young
> you cannot see that because you're looking for better, and you
> want better because you see others having better. But it was a
> struggle. All I can say is that those hard times polished me,
> they made me, they strengthened me, they made me the man
> who I am today, and it makes me appreciate even more all that
> I have.[77]

Beginning in the early twentieth century, Audenago Vigil entered the ranks of the American West's migrant workforce. In Colorado, the Vigil family had a series of challenges and successes.
They left New Mexico in search of better opportunities and employment in Colorado and, although they struggled getting along
with several farmers, they persisted in providing and increasing their
labor until they found good employers. Through their labor and
the help of caring individuals, they saved enough to purchase a
house. Audenago's children contributed to the family income and
survival despite their many trials. Erminia assisted her husband in

the fields and cared for the children. In the 1950s, the family packed their bags for new job opportunities, this time in California. The Vigil children spent their young years picking strawberries, peas, and other crops in California's growing agricultural workforce.

Without oral history, however, we might lose sight of the Vigils and other family histories in the American West. Families rarely, if ever, appeared in the archival record. Yet the Vigil family and oral history contributes as much to the creation of the American West as more popularly known heroic and colorful characters, leaders, and politicians of American history. Their hard work and commitment to family steeled them during their two moves in the American West and against exploitive bosses. As David noted, these struggles, and those of other poor, migrant families in the twentieth century, helped form a sense of identity, gave them strength that sustained them through various travails, and populated the American West.

Notes

Judith Antell, William Bauer, Ned Blackhawk, Susan Johnson, Doug Kiel, and Philip Roberts helped in the development of his chapter. Vigil was writing a dissertation on Native peoples in nineteenth-century Colorado with Susan Johnson before passing away suddenly. This essay is dedicated to his wife, Janice, and his three children, Maccabeus, Douglas, and Cordelia. In his thesis, Vigil wrote, "I wish to express my appreciation to my wife, Janice. Thank you for typing many drafts of this thesis and for your help transcribing interviews. You have been with me every step of the way and have comforted me during frustrating times and have celebrated with me during times of great joy. Thank you for sharing this amazing journey with me."

1. The quote is from educator Riki Van Voeschoten, "Public Memory as Arena of Contested Meanings: A Student Project on Migration," in *Oral History and Public Memories*, ed. Paula Hamilton and Linda Shopes (Philadelphia: Temple University Press, 2008), 226, which reports a student project about Albanian immigrants to Greece.

2. Ingrid Scobie, "Family and Community History through Oral History," *Public Historian* 1 (Summer 1979): 38. See also James B. Rhoads, "The Importance of Family History to Our Society," *Public Historian* 1 (Spring 1979): 6–16; Allan Lichtman, "Personal Family History: A Bridge to Your Past," *Prologue* 16 (Spring 1984): 41–48; Kimberly Porter, "Oral History as an Ap-

proach to State History," *Journal of American History* 87 (September 2000): 606–10.

3. Here I am influenced by Walter Nugent, *Into the West: The Story of Its People* (New York: Vintage Books, 2001).

4. Skott Vigil, "'That's All We Knew': The Vigil Family History of the Southwest, 1807–1980," M.A. thesis, University of Wyoming, 2006, 12–38. There are family stories of Audenago's ancestors Geronimo and Pilar traveling with Utes, suggesting that the family retained ties with their Ute relatives on reservations in Colorado. For more on captivity in the American Southwest, see James Brooks, *Captives and Cousins: Slavery, Kinship and Community in the Southwest Borderlands* (Chapel Hill: University of North Carolina Press, 2002).

5. Audenago Vigil Jr., *Points of Interest* (Berthoud, CO: privately published, 2003); manuscript in author's possession.

6. Jose Belarmino Vigil, *Quien Eres?* (Blackhawk, SD: privately published, n.d.), 5.

7. Sarah Deutsch, *No Separate Refuge: Culture, Class, and Gender on an Anglo-Hispanic Frontier in the American Southwest, 1880–1940* (New York: Oxford University Press, 1987), 13–40. For a discussion of modernity in New Mexico, see also Pablo Mitchell, *Coyote Nation: Sexuality, Race, and Conquest in Modernizing New Mexico, 1880–1920* (Chicago: University of Chicago Press, 2005).

8. Jose Belarmino Vigil, interview by author, August 21, 2005, Blackhawk, South Dakota.

9. Ibid.

10. Ibid. For illegitimate children in northern New Mexico, see Deutsch, *No Separate Refuge*, 58.

11. J. B. Vigil interview.

12. Deutsch, *No Separate Refuge*, 41–62.

13. Ibid., 44.

14. J. B. Vigil interview.

15. Vigil, *Quien Eres?*, 6.

16. J. B. Vigil interview.

17. Suzanne Forrest, *The Preservation of the Village: New Mexico's Hispanics and the New Deal* (Albuquerque: University of New Mexico Press, 1989), 101–7; Jose Belarmino Vigil, interview by author, December 14, 2005.

18. Forrest, *Preservation of the Village*, 127, 169.

19. Vigil, *Quien Eres?*, 6; Audenago Vigil Jr., *Autobiography* (Berthoud, CO: privately printed, n.d.).

20. J. B. Vigil interview, August 21, 2005.

21. Vigil, *Quien Eres?*, 7.

22. Juan Vigil, interview by author, May 26, 2005, Longmont, Colorado; J. B. Vigil interview, August 21, 2005; Audenago Vigil Jr., interview by author, May 12, 2005, Berthoud, Colorado.

23. Vigil, *Autobiography*.
24. Juan Vigil interview.
25. Ibid.
26. Vigil, *Quien Eres?*, 7.
27. Carol Scott, sisters reunion, interview by author, June 30, 2005, Rio Rancho, New Mexico.
28. Eleanor Ramos Vigil, interview by author, May 11, 2005, Berthoud, Colorado.
29. Juan Vigil interview.
30. Sarah Chamberlin, sisters reunion, interview by author, June 30, 2005, Rio Rancho, New Mexico.
31. A. Vigil Jr. interview.
32. Eleanor Ramos Vigil interview.
33. A. Vigil Jr. interview; Juan Vigil interview.
34. Juan Vigil interview.
35. Ibid.
36. Jose Thomas Vigil, interview by author, June 16, 2005, Merced, California.
37. Juan Vigil interview.
38. A. Vigil Jr. interview.
39. J. T. Vigil interview.
40. A. Vigil Jr. interview.
41. Juan Vigil interview.
42. A. Vigil Jr. interview.
43. Vigil, *Autobiography*.
44. A. Vigil Jr. interview.
45. J. B. Vigil, interview, August 21, 2005.
46. A. Vigil Jr. interview; J. B. Vigil interview, August 21, 2005.
47. Vigil, *Autobiography*. Historian George Sanchez explains that Mexican American immigrants strived to purchase a home rather than rent in Los Angeles to maintain and create strong communities. George Sanchez, *Becoming Mexican American: Ethnicity, Culture and Identity in Chicano Los Angeles, 1900–1945* (Berkeley: University of California Press, 1995), 80–81.
48. Esther Brown, interview by author, June 19, 2005, Santa Maria, California, recording in possession of author.
49. Bob Vigil, interview by author, March 27, 2006, Berthoud, Colorado, recording in possession of author.
50. For postwar immigration to California, see Nugent, *Into the West*, 274–86.
51. Esther Brown interview.
52. Bob Vigil, interview.
53. Ibid.
54. Ibid.
55. Esther Brown interview.

56. Sarah Chamberlin, sisters reunion, interview.

57. Carol Scott, interview by author, June 17, 2005, Dublin, California, recording in possession of author.

58. Carol Scott, sisters reunion, interview, June 30, 2005.

59. Sarah Chamberlin and Carol Scott, sisters reunion, interview, June 30, 2005.

60. Carol Scott interview.

61. Lorraine Pilarcita Snowden, sisters reunion, interview by author, June 30, 2005, Rio Rancho, New Mexico, recording in possession of author.

62. David Vigil, interview, June 20, 2005.

63. Ibid.

64. Delores Flores, interview, June 17, 2005.

65. Mary Romero, interview by author, May 14, 2005, Rio Rancho, New Mexico, tape recording in possession of author.

66. Carol Scott interview.

67. David Vigil interview.

68. Mary Romero interview.

69. David Vigil interview.

70. Deborah Vigil, sisters reunion, interview by author, June 30, 2005.

71. Sarah Chamberlin, sisters reunion, interview.

72. Esther Brown interview.

73. Ibid.

74. David Vigil interview.

75. Bob Vigil interview.

76. Ibid.

77. David Vigil interview.

7

"Colorado Has Been Real Good to Us"

An Oral History Project with Japanese Americans in Weld County, Colorado

GEORGIA WIER

Folklorist Georgia Wier uses oral histories to show how stereotypes over-simplify complex experiences. Many studies of Japanese Americans have focused on World War II. Wier points out that Japanese Americans had moved to Weld County, Colorado, before the war and created a community that was very different from the one created by those forced to leave their homes and live in camps. There were limited stories about the Weld County Japanese Americans, and oral history was an excellent way to document their experiences. Following a pattern she learned in graduate school, Wier shared her paper with her interviewees during her research to make sure she was representing their lives correctly. This demonstrates how oral history can be revised, providing an opportunity to avoid misinterpretations in a way not available to those using only written sources. Her narrators not only told their own stories but also discussed their parents' immigration to Colorado.

IN 1905, GEORGE Matazo Tateyama left Japan, stopped in Hawaii to work in the sugarcane fields, and then made his way to Colorado to join his two brothers. The young men worked in packing houses, on construction, and on farms between Denver and Fort Platte, Nebraska. After one brother died in a horse accident and the other returned to Japan to assume family responsibilities, George started farming on his own in the Platteville area of Weld County. During an oral history interview I conducted in 2000, George's son Hiroshi Tateyama explained how his father started the process that led to his marriage. "[As] was customary in those days," George wrote to his parents that he was ready to be married, and they arranged for a neighbor to become his wife. In July 1915, George picked up his new bride, Chitoye, in San Francisco.

With the encouragement of a banker, George purchased a farm in Ault, a town north of Greeley in Weld County. The Tateyama family (which eventually included six children) raised beets, potatoes, pickles, carrots, and other vegetables. Hail damage in 1921 forced George to travel to work in a mine in Wyoming and leave the farm work in the hands of Chitoye and the children. A few years later, George became an invalid and once again had to leave the farm to his family. At three or four in the morning, Hiroshi got up to help his mother feed and harness the horses; after that they cultivated and planted beets. In 1931, thanks to their backbreaking labor, Chitoye and Hiroshi were able to take the final payment on the farm to the bank. Sadly, a couple of days after that, Chitoye died in a car accident. George, who was still ill at the time, directed the Tateyama children in their long hours of farm work each day. Hiroshi had to leave his junior high studies to peddle produce in Nebraska, but as soon as possible he returned to school and graduated with his original class.

As a young adult, Hiroshi worked hard and planned carefully as he established his own farm in Ault, but he and his wife, Yoshiye, did not experience the "almost total hardship" his parents had faced. Eventually, Hiroshi specialized in raising purebred brown Swiss cattle and traveled internationally as president of the National Brown Swiss Association. Hiroshi looked back with pride on his accomplishments in the dairy industry as well as his ability to help his children obtain good educations and establish themselves in secure professions.

Besides chronicling three generations in Colorado for the Tateyama family, the oral history interview with Hiroshi includes his
vivid memories of life in Weld County during World War II. Once
he and his family were refused takeout hamburgers in a neighboring town, and in a few other instances he encountered discriminatory remarks. In general, however, "as long as you stayed home,
you were okay. . . . I'll tell you, people in the area really treated us
well."[1]

Part of the Tateyama family saga has appeared in a few local publications, but it has not been widely available to those outside the
region.[2] The stories of early rural Japanese Americans in Colorado
have rarely found their way to print until recently. Conducting
oral history interviews with the *Nisei* (second-generation Japanese
Americans) is one of the best ways to learn about the experiences of
this generation as well as of their first-generation immigrant parents
(Issei).

This chapter, based on eleven interviews conducted in Weld
County, demonstrates the importance of oral history in telling the
story of Japanese Americans in the area. The interviews include not
only stories of agricultural trials and successes but also accounts of
how families lived through World War II during a time when approximately 120,000 Japanese American citizens and their immigrant parents were forced into "incarceration camps"[3] located
throughout the United States.[4]

Background Sources

Published, unpublished, and online sources all offer critical background information for this study of Japanese Americans. Articles
printed in Weld County's newspapers as early as 1885 demonstrate
the themes that local journalists found noteworthy.[5] Peggy Ford
(Waldo) relied heavily on these newspaper accounts for her unpublished article, "From the Land of the Rising Sun to the Rocky
Mountains: The Japanese Heritage in Northern Colorado," a sum-
mary of Japanese American history in Weld County and surrounding areas.[6]

Especially useful for an overview of the Japanese American experience on both state and national levels are works by Bill Hosokawa, "the foremost reporter and historian of the Japanese Americans in Colorado"[7] and an editor for the *Denver Post* for thirty-eight years. Hosokawa's *Nisei: The Quiet Americans* provides a journalistic analysis of the history of Japanese Americans in the United States.[8] His *Colorado's Japanese Americans: From 1886 to the Present* adds much-needed regional treatment to the literature, including narratives of the history of five farm families.[9] Robert Harvey expands the printed record of Japanese Americans in the state with *Amache: The Story of Japanese Internment in Colorado during World War II.*[10] Yuji Ichioka's scholarly work, *The Issei: The World of the First Generation Japanese Immigrants, 1885–1924,* contributes valuable background for understanding Colorado's place in the national story, and Mei Nakano's *Japanese American Women: Three Generations: 1898–1990* offers commentary not only about women's experiences but about family dynamics.[11]

Unpublished scholarly papers have also added greatly to the record on Japanese Americans in Colorado and other parts of the Intermountain West and have also demonstrated the value of oral histories in expanding this record. In "Colorado's Nikkei Pioneers: Japanese Americans in Twentieth Century Colorado," Kara Mariko Miyagishima uses extensive print sources as well as interviews with her own grandparents for her excellent overview of Japanese American history in the state.[12] Eric Waltz's "Japanese Immigration and Community Building in the Interior West, 1882–1945" offers a rare look into five rural Japanese American communities in Utah, Nebraska, Idaho, Arizona, and Colorado. [13]

The value of online resources for studying this topic cannot be overstated. In 2009, Arthur A. Hansen uses his research and the work of many other published and unpublished scholars for a six-part article summarizing issues related to Japanese American history in the Interior West. Hansen's article and Daryl J. Maeda's "Enduring Communities: Japanese in Colorado" appear in the online journal *Discover Nikkei,* a project of the Japanese American National Museum.[14]

Over the past three decades, activists and historians, including oral historians, have successfully brought Japanese American incarceration during World War II to the public's awareness, reexamining a chapter of US history that had long been ignored. In "Contested Places in Public Memory: Reflections on Personal Testimony and Oral History in Japanese American Heritage," Gail Lee Dubrow traces the blossoming of projects to collect and record internees' accounts of incarceration history.[15] The Densho Digital Archives, a rich repository of materials that "document the Japanese American experience from immigration in the early 1900s through redress in the 1980s with a strong focus on the World War II mass incarceration," includes interviews with a few people who were in Weld County during the war—either as regular residents or as temporary farm workers. In his dissertation, "American Dreams Derailed: Japanese Railroad and Mine Communities of the Interior West," Andrew Benjamin Russell covers another and largely unknown story: the firings and subsequent hardships experienced by hundreds of Japanese Americans who had careers with western rail and mining companies before the war.[16]

Japanese Americans in Colorado

Japanese immigrants first ventured from the West Coast into Colorado because the state needed labor. Prejudice against Chinese workers and the anti-Chinese riot of 1882 had led to a decrease in the supply of cheap Chinese labor at a time when workers were greatly needed for mining, on the railroad, in steel mills, and on construction jobs. Japanese immigrants were ready to take on that work. By 1903, Japanese immigrants began entering the state to work in agriculture. Although they began their farm work primarily as sugar beet field laborers, eventually many of them operated or owned their own farms. In Colorado, in contrast to California and all other states in the Intermountain West, no laws restricted or prevented landownership by the noncitizen Issei.[17]

Six of the eleven Japanese Americans in this study had parents who arrived in Weld County between 1900 and 1920. By 1920, people of Japanese descent numbered 726 out of the total county population of 54,059.[18] This was a period of tremendous expansion in agriculture and population in the county. In the 1870s, the founding members of the experimental Union Colony developed the "scientific application of water to an arid land," allowing them to settle in the town they named Greeley. Expansion of this irrigation technology led to the development of sugar beet culture—both farming the beets and refining the sugar—all along the South Platte River.[19]

Three of the interviewees spent much of their childhoods in North Platte, Nebraska. In about 1935, after she graduated from high school, Hannah Sameshima moved to Greeley with her widowed father and five younger siblings. Sameshima explained that four other families also moved from Nebraska to Weld County in search of land with more water.[20] The final two interviewees in this study arrived in Weld County during or immediately after World War II.

All eleven interviewees were members of families who farmed irrigated areas that could sustain sugar beets and other produce. The farms where they lived—in or near the towns of Fort Lupton, Platteville, La Salle, Evans, Greeley, and Ault—were all on land in the Cache la Poudre and South Platte River valleys. They were located along both a railroad and a highway, giving the farmers easy access to supplies and markets for their produce.[21]

Local newspaper articles in Weld County give an idea of how Caucasian journalists regarded the Japanese Americans in their communities. From the period of early Issei settlement in Weld County through 1942, published articles included such topics as Japanese farmers in Fort Lupton joining the Colorado Cabbage Exchange, lectures criticizing Japanese exclusion policies (the Immigration Act of 1924 prevented further Japanese and Chinese immigration), a theatrical production designed to educate Americans about Japanese culture, and Japanese high school students being honored at the Fort Lupton Buddhist Church.[22] The *Greeley Tribune* also published arrest notices for men of Japanese descent for various crimes and a satirical editorial favoring Japanese exclusion, but in general the articles indicate that Japanese Americans in Weld County were allowed to conduct business and lead their lives with minimal prejudicial treatment.[23] As in the rest of the country, Issei were not allowed to apply for citizenship until 1952, but their American-born children automatically became citizens at birth.[24]

The bombing of Pearl Harbor by Japan on December 7, 1941, changed the world for most Americans, including Japanese Americans in Weld County. On February 19, 1942, President Franklin D. Roosevelt signed Executive Order No. 9066, an action that led to the evacuation from the West Coast of noncitizen Issei and their citizen children. For about two months, federal agencies encouraged Japanese Americans living on the West Coast to voluntarily relocate further east. Unlike several other governors of states in the Interior West, Governor Ralph Carr of Colorado announced that his state would welcome Japanese Americans who needed to move away from the coast. Citing data published by the US Department of the Interior, Miyagishima reports that "overall, several hundreds of voluntary evacuees settled on Colorado farms, including fifteen families who evacuated to Greeley during this period of 'voluntary evacuation.'"[25]

Because of Carr's stance, along with his assertion "that we have among us many of a new generation of Japanese people born in the United States—sincere, earnest, and loyal people."[26] Colorado's Japanese American community has honored Carr with a bust in Downtown Denver and in many other ways during his lifetime and after his death. In 1999, the *Denver Post* posthumously recognized Carr by naming him Colorado's Person of the Century. However, during the time he served as governor, anti-Japanese rhetoric from the press and a majority of the other leaders in the state, as well as opposition from the public, resulted in him losing an election to serve in the US Senate, and ultimately, in him losing his political career.[27]

Opposition from most politicians and much of the public in the states of the Interior West contributed to the federal government ending the voluntary relocation period on March 27, 1942. After that time, federal officials supervised the mandatory relocation of most West Coast Japanese Americans into temporary "assembly centers" and eventually into ten incarceration camps, including Amache in southeastern Colorado. In 1944, the federal government made plans to begin closing the camps and encouraged evacuees to find their own housing and employment. Many people from the West Coast had lost their property and most of their assets and feared the anti-Japanese attitudes in their old communities. Hundreds of them chose not to return to their old homes and resettled in Colorado either temporarily or permanently.[28]

The Interviews

Volunteers and staff of the City of Greeley Museums worked with me in conducting the interviews examined in this chapter between 2000 and 2006. Some interviews were among those recorded during two oral history collection days in Greeley and Fort Lupton.[29] The oral histories reveal ways that national and state policies and attitudes of local people affected the interviewees and their families. The narrators' stories also demonstrate how the experiences of this group of Japanese Americans in Weld County mirrored or occasionally diverged from those of Japanese Americans in other parts of the country.

All Nisei interviewees in this project told something about their parents' emigrating from Japan and beginning to work in America. Hosokawa's *Nisei* and Ichioka's *The Issei* give general descriptions of the work the Issei undertook on entering the United States in mining, on the railroads, and in agriculture. The two authors also describe the positions some men took as "schoolboys" in West Coast households. These men did chores for Caucasian housewives for a few hours a day in exchange for room and board and a small amount of money, and they spent the middle part of the day learning English.[30] When the Issei fathers of interviewees in this study told their children about their early lives in America, they frequently left out many specifics such as where they had worked and what they did.

Sometimes it is the brevity of what the parents revealed to their children that is most telling. Two sisters, Mary Jane Arakawa and May Yago, knew that their father arrived on the West Coast at the age of seventeen and worked as a schoolboy. They also knew that he used his English skills to do translation work in Wyoming, but they didn't know whether that work was for the railroads or in the mines. They knew their mother came as a "picture bride," but not the year she arrived.[31] Amy Numoto thought (but wasn't sure) that her father (Tokujioro Honda) worked on the railroads before he married and settled down. She explained, "They didn't talk about it and you didn't ask either. Nowadays, why, younger people want to know your ancestors, and you can't tell them about that."[32]

Although the Nisei interviewees may have known little about their elders' backgrounds, they did know that their parents had worked very hard and that they didn't talk much about the hardships they had faced. Amy Urano was amazed to think of Issei men and women coming to a foreign country without knowing the language and making do with the situations they landed in. "They made a living and raised big families. . . . And I didn't hear a lot of complaints or anything."[33] Similarly, Nakono writes about how Issei in general and Issei women in particular expressed feelings of satisfaction rather than bitterness as they looked on their difficult lives in the United States.[34]

Issei also tended to hold the attitude that children should help their parents whether in urban businesses or on the farm.[35] All the interviewees helped on their parents' farms, though some experienced more difficult circumstances than others. Hiroshi Tateyama skipped weeks of school to harvest the crops.[36] On the other hand, Daisy Kiyota and her six siblings were able to have some fun with the farm work. "We'd pile stacks of beets. Two of us would load by hand and my father would use a fork and load on the truck. So we'd always try to beat him."[37]

Education and Religion

Hosokawa writes, "Whatever the chief incentive might have been, the Nisei as a group did remarkably well in grade and high schools. A disproportionate number of them became valedictorians and salutatorians with straight A grades. Stubborn persistence had as much to do with their success as brilliance."[38] Even though they helped on their family farms, the Nisei interviewees valued education greatly and all finished high school.

May Yago's family lived several miles from Greeley High School, and May struggled to get to and from school. She worked out an arrangement to ride to school with the son of the family's landlord and then return home in the car of a friend's sister. During her senior year, Yago did not live at home but worked as a schoolgirl, helping around the house for the family with whom she boarded. That year, she used a bicycle to travel the several miles to high school from this family's house, except during the winter when she caught a ride with another student. Yago had school friends who were Caucasian and Hispanic as well as Japanese American. She couldn't join in on after-school activities, however, because of her responsibilities.[39]

Albert Watada expressed vivid memories of starting school in Platteville. "My parents put me on a bus not knowing one word of English. How I even got through I don't even know." He eventually learned English and particularly enjoyed mathematics, agriculture, and shop. He would have loved to continue his education past high school, but his duty to the rest of the family prevented that. "Being the eldest," Watada explained, "I took the responsibility [and helped with the other children's educations] although I got a scholarship to go to college."[40]

Religion also had importance in Weld County households headed by the interviewees and many of their Issei parents. Some interviewees grew up in Methodist families and some in Buddhist ones, and most retained the religious affiliation their parents established for their families.

In 1908, Japanese immigrants in Colorado founded their first religious institution, which became the Japanese Methodist Episcopal Church in Denver. This church grew and evolved in its mission and now is located in a Denver suburb and called the Arvada United Methodist Church.[41] Amy Urano's parents attended the Japanese Methodist Episcopal Church, but they raised their children in the Methodist church in Fort Lupton. "No matter how busy we were on the farm, they always made sure that we had time for Sunday school," she recalled. Until her death, Urano attended the church in which she was raised, while her sister Daisy Kiyota and Daisy's husband, John, joined the closer Platteville United Methodist Church.[42]

A Japanese priest came to Denver to provide spiritual guidance to Colorado Buddhists in 1916, and soon thereafter the Denver Buddhist Temple was established. In 1930 a new minister named Yoshitaka Tamai took Buddhism "like a circuit rider, to Japanese farm families in outlying areas where, despite a limited population, groups of Japanese were organizing modest facilities for practicing their faith."[43] Albert Watada explained, "This Denver Mother Church was head of Colorado, Wyoming, Nebraska, some of Montana, some of Utah, some of New Mexico."[44]

In some cases, Issei-headed families switched from attending Buddhist to Christian churches (or vice versa) according to the circumstances. Hannah Sameshima's family had been attending an Episcopal church in North Platte, Nebraska. When Reverend Tamai came from the Denver Buddhist Temple to serve Japanese Americans in Nebraska, her family joined the Buddhist church. "I think we joined because our friends did, you know," Sameshima explained. After they moved to Colorado, she and her family continued their Buddhist associations. "In the beginning we had service in someplace in Kersey. Then they built the little church in Greeley and they've remodeled it."[45]

Church was often a place for adults and youth to socialize with other Japanese Americans as well as worship.[46] Couples met and married, and community celebrations offered opportunities to celebrate with Japanese food and other forms of cultural expression. John Kiyota, whose family attended the Methodist congregation in Longmont and Denver, met Daisy Funakoshi at an Epworth League (Methodist) meeting for youth held in Fort Lupton. Japanese American Methodists had gathered there for a visit from the minister from Denver's Japanese Episcopal Methodist Church. John's and Daisy's families were already acquainted, and although the two young people had met on their own, John followed an old Japanese custom in asking another couple to act as a go-between and get the two of them together.[47]

May Yago's sister-in-law was the first bride to be married at Greeley's newly constructed Buddhist church.[48] Later, in 1951, Yago's sister Mary Jane married Norman Yoshi Arakawa there. For her wedding, "in those days they had a feast with fish and all the Japanese food. But they don't do that anymore. Everyone has gotten older." In a period when the Greeley Buddhist Temple had younger and more active members than it does today, Mary Jane remembered that the flower festival *(Hanamatsuri)*, celebrating the birth of the Buddha, was "quite a festival" there. Church members wore Japanese kimonos, danced, and acted in plays.[49]

World War II

Amy Numoto's comment, "I couldn't even believe it. It just came on the radio, that December 7,"[50] reflects the surprise expressed by many of this study's interviewees over the Japanese attack on Pearl Harbor. The World War II experiences recounted in the group's oral histories include those of a woman from Japan who married an American GI and traveled to the United States to join him on his family's farm, of another woman who relocated to rural Colorado from an incarceration camp in Arizona, of a man who served in the US military, and of several others who spent most of the war period in Weld County.

Interviewee Shigeko Yamaguchi has spent much of her adulthood farming with her husband in Weld County. She grew up in Oregon, met and married Frank Yamaguchi, and moved to the Yamaguchi family farm in Westminster, California. When Shigeko heard about Pearl Harbor, "everything just stopped. It was a shock." President Roosevelt's evacuation order meant that the Yamaguchis had to abandon their home and farm. Frank's parents and brother, along with Shigeko, Frank, and their two young children, were sent to Poston Camp (formally named Poston Relocation Center) in Parker, Arizona.

After the family had spent a year in the camp, government policy changed to "if you want to move out voluntarily, and have a sponsor, you can move out." Frank's parents stayed at Poston until the end of the war, but he and Shigeko decided to take advantage of an opportunity to move with their children to Brighton, Colorado. A friend's brother who lived there had offered to sponsor the young family. "Governor Carr was one of the governors that opened the door for us, and that's how we came to Colorado," Shigeko explained.

For their first season in Colorado, Frank drove trucks for wheat farmers and thinned sugar beets in the spring. Later, the Yamaguchis rented a farm in Fort Lupton, where they raised onions, potatoes, sugar beets, pickling beans, and later tomatoes for a cannery. Shigeko found that in general, people in Fort Lupton accepted them. Frank had his farm equipment shipped from California; later he sold the California farm and purchased one in Platteville. Shigeko and her husband never considered moving back to the West Coast. "Colorado has been real good to us."[51]

Chikako Murata began her life as wife and mother on a Greeley farm in 1948. She was born in 1926 to parents in Fukuoka, Japan. Her father manufactured silk sashes for kimonos, and her mother managed the household. After finishing high school, Murata attended a women's college, where she majored in Japanese classical literature. She selected her major not in preparation for a career but because "I like to read books."

Chikako had also studied enough English to be able to assist in a photographer's shop by interpreting for the GIs who were part of the American-led occupation of Japan that began at the end of World War II.[52] One of the men who came to develop film was Takeshi "Tak" Murata. He and Chikako were married in Japan in 1947. The next year they traveled by boat to Seattle and then by train and car to the Murata family's farm in Kuner, Colorado.

Chikako had no way of guessing what life on a Colorado farm would be like because even in Japan "I didn't know the farmers— what they did. So I just came and I looked and experienced. I did it bit by bit." She remembered that when she started going to work in the fields, "I didn't know how to do it. I didn't have experience. It was a sad time for me, because oh—I came this far and I was doing this kind of thing, and I cried." For a while, when Chikako saw the sun going down in the western sky, she became very sad and wanted to go home to Japan. But then her daughter was born, and a son five years later, and the young woman began to adjust to her new life. She eventually prepared roast beef and made stuffed mushroom appetizers as well as Japanese dishes. She also reported, "Now I'm a pretty good expert in gardening. . . . I learned by experience all these fifty years."[53]

Shigeko Yamaguchi and Chikako Murata adjusted to their new lives and they prospered in Weld County after the war. Many other Japanese Americans also regained their footings despite severe losses and the knowledge that they had, as a group, experienced treatment that was unjustified and unfair. Even when they had been born in the United States or had been living and working in America for thirty or forty years, immediately after Pearl Harbor many found themselves the target of suspicion and hostility from neighbors who previously had been their friends as well as from both local and federal officials. In literature and oral history collections, there are many accounts of horrific treatment of Issei and Nisei that occurred on the West Coast. Hosokawa theorizes that

> in an environment where anti-Oriental racism had been a seldom-questioned tradition . . . it was inevitable that the racial stereotype should be projected onto the Issei and Nisei and their loyalty loudly challenged. On the West Coast this was as predictable as a knee-jerk is to the stimulus of a rap with a rubber hammer. There were whites who honestly believed they were helping to win the war by throwing a brick through the window of a Japanese grocery store or firing a shot from a speeding car into the home of a Japanese farmer.[54]

From newspaper articles of the time and more recent literature, it is clear that substantial prejudice against Japanese American residents also existed in northern Colorado throughout World War II. In 1944, a delegation from the town of Brighton and Adams County (which adjoins Weld County), including farmers, businessmen, and Brighton's mayor, led a movement to prevent Japanese immigrants from owning land. Colorado voters defeated by a slim margin an Anti-Alien Land Law amendment to the state constitution that would have established this discriminatory policy.[55] Despite the prejudice toward people of Japanese descent, Robert Harvey writes, "Most citizens of Colorado were not guilty of direct racial or economic oppression. Most would never have dreamed of asking a Japanese American to leave a store. . . . Most, in fact, would have opted to just mind their own business instead of dealing with the complex issues brought by evacuation."[56] Nisei interviewees who grew up on or moved to Weld County farms expressed attitudes of relief and gratitude over being accepted or assisted by their neighbors. They encountered some prejudice from Caucasians in their communities, but they speak mainly of support from their neighbors during World War II.

Albert Watada was seventeen years old when the war started. Like others, his family was not allowed to travel more than twenty-five miles from home. "Yes, there was some discrimination, but as a whole the community accepted us. And classmates were all good to us. So we didn't have a whole lot of problems except for the fact that we couldn't go very far." Watada did end up traveling during the war because he was drafted into the army in 1942. Out of the ten boys in his family, eight served in the armed forces.[57]

Amy Urano contrasted the treatment she experienced in California after Pearl Harbor with her experiences in Weld County. She married Frank Urano in 1940, and the two of them moved from Colorado to California soon thereafter. They were in California when they experienced the shock of Pearl Harbor and the overt hostility from those who had previously treated them normally. "After the war started, why, it was just a different atmosphere. People would [say], 'Oh, there's Japs,' and, you know, shun. But . . . everybody here [in Fort Lupton] knew people and respected the Japanese people, and I don't know anyone that discriminated against." The Uranos made quick plans to return home from California to Colorado. Amy remembered, "We were going to drive back, and they advised us not to. We had bought a car for $25. . . . So we sold the car back for $25 and came back on the train."[58]

A story told by Amy Numoto demonstrates how one of the government regulations, though much less disruptive than incarceration, caused her and her husband to lose their livelihood and change the course of their lives. In 1939, Amy married John Yasuichi Numoto, a professional photographer, and moved from her family's farm in Evans to Pueblo, Colorado. Japanese Americans had to give up their cameras during World War II. Without a camera, there was no way for John to follow his profession, and the couple moved back to Weld County and began farming with Amy's father. Although her husband had never farmed before, "he was a hard worker and he really tried." Until very recently, Amy cultivated the land that the two of them farmed as they raised their three children.[59]

Along with sharing memories of how they were treated by their Weld County neighbors during the war, interviewees provided accounts of experiences with those Japanese Americans who resettled in the area during or after the war. Daisy Kiyota, attending high school in Fort Lupton during the war, enjoyed going to school with Japanese American students whose families had come from the

Figure 7.1 John and Daisy Kiyota (far left) and their young daughter Karen (seated with her uncle on right) with John's siblings and parents, posed on the Weld County land farmed by John's parents and later John and Daisy, ca. 1947.

West Coast to escape the camps (see figure 7.1). "It was kind of fun, because we met so many new people. Usually there [were] only four or five Japanese in a class. And when everybody evacuated, I graduated with fourteen Japanese in the class. So that was very different. . . . We met a lot of people and had lasting friendships with them. That was very good."[60]

For Hannah Sameshima (see figure 7.2), socializing with a man who had relocated led to more than friendship. Sam Isamu Sameshima left his trucking business in California and moved to Weld County, where he took up farming. He and Hannah got to know one another during baseball games and other social events. Hannah explained that because of government restrictions for Japanese Americans, "we couldn't go travel . . . so we couldn't go to Denver to see our reverend [and] he came over here." The Buddhist minister performed the marriage ceremony in a little house on the farm where Sam worked. As they raised their family, Sam and

Figure 7.2 Hannah (Ogada) Sameshima, right, with her parents and siblings in their home in North Platte, Nebraska, taken in the 1920s before the family's 1933 move to Weld County, Colorado.

Hannah farmed for several years then bought the grocery store in Kersey and ran it for sixteen years.[61]

Oral History Benefits

The Nisei interviewees' reflections on living through World War II in Weld County with relatively little discrimination from their neighbors, or of moving to the county from other places during and after the war, add a dimension to wartime narratives that has not yet been fully documented. Whether they were talking about their parents' immigration and work experiences; their farms, school, and church during their childhoods and as adults; or their experiences during and after World War II, the eleven interviewees in this study provide narratives that help round out the history of Japanese Americans in Colorado. Without these oral history recordings, there would be no public record of these vivid memories of how these interviewees and their families experienced personal, regional, and worldwide events that spanned the twentieth century.

Making otherwise unknown life histories available to documentarians, family researchers, students, and other historians is one of the positive outcomes of conducting oral history projects in our communities. A writer has already used one of these oral histories in this study.[62] I discovered that another potential benefit of projects like this one is providing interviewees with opportunities to participate in crafting the historical record that includes their own lives. During this project, the first opportunity came when the interviews were conducted; the second occurred when I contacted each still living interviewee during the course of writing this essay in an effort to make sure that I represented his or her viewpoints accurately. As I talked with them once more, some for the first time in several years, I discovered that many had new insights that gave the stories they had told even more meaning.

William Schneider explained an Alaskan Inupiaq woman's role in a family's hunt for moose and caribou and voiced clearly the value that an oral history can have: "Personal narratives often tell a part of a big story, filling in an important dimension that isn't commonly known or a part that just hasn't been highlighted."[63] Studies like this oral history project offer verbal images such as the one of Hiroshi Tateyama and his mother harnessing horses at three in the morning and that of Chikako Murata traveling from Japan to arrive at her new husband's family farm without any knowledge of agricultural life. In general, the events described and attitudes expressed in this study have much in common with findings made by scholars of Japanese American history and culture. The importance of this study lies more in the particulars, both of everyday life and of significant occurrences, in the lives of Issei and Nisei in a region that lacks major public records of Japanese American experiences. The interviews help fill the gap of information on and understanding of Japanese Americans in one portion of the Intermountain West. From a more local standpoint, the interviews supply new information and viewpoints on the agricultural, educational, religious, political, and social history of Weld County.

Appendix: Weld County Residents Interviewed

Mary Jane (Shinn) Arakawa. Born 1932, North Platte, Nebraska.

Daisy (Funakoshi) Kiyota. Born 1926, Fort Lupton, Colorado.

John Hisao Kiyota. Born 1917, Lafayette or Erie, Colorado. Died 2009.

Chikako (Nakashima) Murata. Born 1926, Fukuoka Prefecture, Japan. Died 2012.

Amy Fusaye (Honda) Numoto. Born 1917, Weld County, Colorado.

Hannah Hana (Ogata) Sameshima. Born 1917, North Platte, Nebraska.

Hiroshi Tateyama. Born 1916, Ault, Colorado. Died 2006.

Amy Chiyoko (Funakoshi) Urano. Born 1919, Fort Lupton, Colorado. Died 2011.

Albert Watada. Born 1924, Fort Lupton, Colorado. Died 2004.

May (Funakoshi) Yago. Born 1927, North Platte, Nebraska.

Shigeko (Ohashi) Yamaguchi. Born 1917, Gresham, Oregon.

Notes

1. Hiroshi Tateyama, interview by author, April 29, 2000, Greeley, Colorado; City of Greeley Museums, Permanent Collection.

2. Tommie Steele, "George M. Tateyama Leaves Japan to Find Riches in America," in "A Salute to Eaton's Centennial," supplement, *North Weld Herald*, October 29, 1992, 15. Copies of this and other articles on Hiroshi Tateyama and his family are available at the City of Greeley Museums, Permanent Collection.

3. The phrases "internment camps" or "relocation centers" were (until recently) commonly used to describe the compounds where Japanese Americans were forced to live under armed guard during World War II. The website of Densho: The Japanese American Legacy Project (http://www.densho.org/causes/default.asp) offers commentary that explains why these terms are euphemistic and misleading and suggests alternate phrases such as "concentration camp" or "incarceration camp" for today's researchers to more clearly express the harsh wartime experience. The website also notes, "At present there is no clear agreement about the most appropriate terminology for what Japanese Americans underwent during World War II." Most frequently, those interviewed for this study simply used the term "camps" without a descriptive adjective.

4. The statistics are from Brian Niiya (editor under the auspices of the Japanese American National Museum), *Encyclopedia of Japanese American History, Updated Edition: An A-to-Z Reference from 1868 to the Present* (New York: Facts on File, 2001), 142.

5. In 1995, Shirley Soenksen compiled "A Reference Guide to Race and Ethnicity in Weld County as found in Local Newspapers: Japanese." She revised the list in 2008. The unpublished guide is available at the City of Greeley Museums, Permanent Collection.

6. Peggy Ford, "From the Land of the Rising Sun to the Rocky Mountains: The Japanese Heritage in Northern Colorado" (1999), available at the City of Greeley Museums, Permanent Collection.

7. Stephen J. Leonard and Thomas J. Noel, foreword to Bill Hosokawa, *Colorado's Japanese Americans from 1886 to the Present* (Boulder: University Press of Colorado, 2005), xii.

8. Bill Hosokawa, *Nisei: The Quiet Americans*, rev. ed. (Boulder: University Press of Colorado, 2002).

9. Hosokawa, *Colorado's Japanese Americans.*

10. Robert Harvey, *Amache: The Story of Japanese Internment in Colorado during World War II* (Boulder, CO: Taylor Trade Publishing, 2003).

11. Yuji Ichioka, *The Issei: The World of the First Generation Japanese Immigrants, 1885–1924* (New York: Free Press, 1988); Mei Nakano, *Japanese American Women: Three Generations: 1890–1990* (Berkeley: Mina Press Publishing in partnership with National Japanese American Historical Society, 1990).

12. Kara Mariko Miyagishima, *Colorado's Nikkei Pioneers: Japanese Americans in Twentieth Century Colorado*, master's thesis, University of Colorado at Denver and Health Sciences Center, 2007.

13. Eric Waltz, "Japanese Immigration and Community Building in the Interior West, 1882–1945," PhD dissertation, Arizona State University, 1998.

14. Arthur A. Hansen, "Enduring Communities: Japanese Americans in the Interior West: A Regional Perspective on the Enduring Nikkei Historical Experience in Arizona, Colorado, New Mexico, Texas, and Utah (and Beyond)," *Discover Nikkei Journal*, a web project of the Japanese American National Museum (the six parts dated October 16, October 23, October 3, November 6, November 13, and November 20, 2009), http://www.discover nikkei.org/en/journal/series/enduring-communities/. Daryl J. Maeda's *Discover Nikkei Journal* article titled "Japanese Americans in Colorado," dated January 30, 2008, was part of the same "Enduring Communities" series.

15. Gail Lee Dubrow, "Contested Places in Public Memory: Reflections on Personal Testimony and Oral History in Japanese American Heritage," in *Oral History and Public Memories*, ed. Paula Hamilton and Linda Shopes (Philadelphia: Temple University Press, 2008), 128–38.

16. A component of Densho: The Japanese American Legacy Project, the Densho Digital Archives holds more than 600 videotaped interviews as well as photographic and print materials, see http://www.densho.org/archive/; Andrew Benjamin Russell, "American Dreams Derailed: Japanese Railroad and Mine Communities of the Interior West," PhD diss., Arizona State University, 2003.

17. Miyagishima, *Colorado's Nikkei Pioneers*, 35–60 and 71–80.

18. US Department of Commerce, Bureau of the Census, *Fourteenth Census of the United States Taken in the Year 1920, vol. 3, Population 1920: Composition and Characteristics of the Population by States* (Washington, DC: Government Printing Office, 1922), 139.

19. Peggy Ford, "A Thumbnail Sketch of Weld County's History," *Greeley Style Magazine,* special edition 1990, 10–14, available at the City of Greeley Museums, Permanent Collection.

20. Hannah Sameshima, interview by author, June 23, 2006, Kersey, Colorado. City of Greeley Museums, Permanent Collection.

21. For information about beet culture, irrigation, and Weld County immigration, see Ford, "A Thumbnail Sketch," 10–15, and Carl Abbott, Stephen J. Leonard, and Thomas J. Noel, *Colorado: A History of the Centennial State*, 4th ed. (Boulder: University Press of Colorado, 2005), 7–8, 154–60.

22. Harvey, *Amache*, 6.

23. Ford, "From the Land of the Rising Sun," and Soenksen, "A Reference Guide to Race and Ethnicity," both refer to these newspaper accounts.

24. Niiya, *Japanese American History*, 69.

25. Miyagishima, *Colorado's Nikkei Pioneers*, 109–19.

26. Adam Schrager, *The Principled Politician: The Ralph Carr Story* (Golden, CO: Fulcrum Publishing, 2008), 82. Schrager examines the reasons for and ramifications of Carr's historically rare stance.

27. Hosokawa, *Colorado's Japanese Americans*, 87–93, 97–99; Schrager, *The Principled Politician*, 315, 330–32.

28. Miyagishima, *Colorado's Nikkei Pioneers*, 113–19, 128, 161–78.

29. The Fort Lupton Museum collaborated on four of the interviews. The volunteers and Greeley Museums staff members conducting the interviews during oral history collection days were members of a group called the Weld County Oral History Collectors. The Colorado Council on the Arts was a sponsor of the Northeast Regional Folklorist Program and thus this oral history project.

30. Ichioka, *The Issei*, 22–28, 57–82; Hosokawa, *Nisei*, 59–78.

31. Mary Jane Arakawa, interview by Nancy D. Penfold, March 28, 2002, and interview by author, April 3, 2002, Greeley, Colorado; May Yago, interview by author, March 23, 2002, Greeley, Colorado. City of Greeley Museums, Permanent Collection.

32. Amy Numoto, interview by author, November 16, 2004, Greeley, Colorado.

33. Amy Urano, interview by Sheryl Kippen, December 16, 2000, Fort Lupton, Colorado.

34. Nakano, *Japanese American Women*, 37–41.

35. Ibid., 41.

36. Hiroshi Tateyama interview.

37. Daisy Kiyota, interview by author, December 16, 2000, Fort Lupton, Colorado. City of Greeley Museums, Permanent Collection.

38. Hosokawa, *Nisei*, 161.

39. May Yago interview.

40. Albert Watada, interview by author, December 16, 2000, Fort Lupton, Colorado. City of Greeley Museums, Permanent Collection.

41. Hosokawa, *Colorado's Japanese Americans*, 58–64; Miyagishima, *Colorado's Nikkei Pioneers*, 97–100.

42. Amy Urano interview, and telephone conversation with author, July 5, 2008.

43. Hosokawa, *Colorado's Japanese Americans*, 65–68.

44. Albert Watada interview.

45. Hannah Sameshima interview.

46. Miyagishima, *Colorado's Nikkei Pioneers*, 97.

47. John Kiyota, interview by Richard Gibboney, December 16, 2000, Fort Lupton, Colorado; Daisy Kiyota, telephone conversation with by author, July 5, 2008. City of Greeley Museums, Permanent Collection.

48. Interviewees and many other Japanese American Buddhists in Greeley refer to their house of workshop as the Greeley Buddhist Church rather than using its more formal name, Greeley Buddhist Temple.

49. May Yago interview; Mary Jane Arakawa interviews.

50. Amy Numoto interview.

51. Shigeko Yamaguchi, interview by author, May 21, 2005, Greeley, Colorado. City of Greeley Museums, Permanent Collection.

52. Hosokawa, *Nisei*, 399–400. Hosokawa discusses the part Nisei played in the occupation and reconstruction of Japan.

53. Chikako Murata, interview by author, March 23, 2002, Greeley, Colorado. City of Greeley Museums, Permanent Collection.

54. Hosokawa, *Nisei*, 248.

55. Hosokawa, *Colorado's Japanese Americans*, 115–18.

56. Harvey, *Amache*, 147.

57. Albert Watada interview.

58. Amy Urano interview.

59. Amy Numoto interview.

60. Daisy Kiyota interview.

61. Hannah Sameshima interview.

62. Jean Goodwin Messinger, *Same War; Different Battlefields: Inspiring Stories from Civilians Impacted by WWII* (Windsor, CO: White Pelican Press, 2008), includes material from Wier's interview with Chikako Murata.

63. William Schneider, . . . *So They Understand: Cultural Issues in Oral History* (Logan: Utah State University Press, 2002), 73.

8

Using Oral History to Record the Story of the Las Vegas African American Community

CLAYTEE WHITE

Historian Claytee D. White examines the African American community in Las Vegas, Nevada. Historically there have been few blacks in the West, and few scholars have attempted to document their experiences. When White moved to Las Vegas, she became part of a project to document the African American experiences there. She was not surprised that blacks came west for better economic opportunities— that is a very American pattern. However, she was surprised at how many came from the tiny towns of Fordyce, Arkansas, and Tallulah, Louisiana. The Las Vegas black community developed as friends and family followed the westward migration stream to an urban area with different industries than most places in the West and even the country. Oral history was the only way to learn the African American experience because there were no documents in public sources. Her oral histories have the added benefit of encouraging the interviewees to share their personal records with the archives at the University of Nevada, Las Vegas.

THE PURPOSE OF this essay is to illustrate the documentation of portions of the history of blacks in Las Vegas as a direct result of oral history methodology. As a black historian working in Las

Vegas, I wanted to explore the contributions of early African Americans to the development of the city. Only through oral history have I been able to delve into a heritage that was not often written. Interviewing also allowed a ground-up approach to gathering history. Deconstructing the history of the local black community uniquely showcases oral history, especially for a group that might not otherwise have appeared in the historical record in a significant manner. After explaining my experiences, I use interviews to add details to an incomplete history of blacks in Las Vegas.[1] The focus of this work is the migration process, work and labor framed by race and class, and some of the accomplishments of the integration process.

Fortunately, groundwork in local black history began in the mid-1970s. Dr. Ralph Roske taught his University of Nevada, Las Vegas (UNLV) history students to conduct interviews, and each semester they combed Las Vegas, interviewing the city's founding fathers. Those interviews included minimal sessions with early blacks. The Oral History Program for the state located at the University of Nevada, Reno (UNR), collected three major oral interviews with blacks in Las Vegas: Clarence Ray, Lubertha Johnson, and Woodrow Wilson. These were captured early enough to include stories and memories of black life in Las Vegas in the 1920s.

As Roske's interviews became well known and highly regarded near the end of the twentieth century, UNLV history department administrators expressed an interest in incorporating oral history as part of the curriculum. Staff and graduate students were invited to attend seminars, workshops, and eventually classes in the art and science of conducting oral history research. A segment of the small group decided to create a collection of local histories. Joyce Marshall, a graduate student, proposed collecting the history of women in Las Vegas because, as she explained, "Everything ever written about Las Vegas is about men." Joanne Goodwin, a women's historian for the department, served as the mentor and project advisor. It was decided that a focus on women in gaming and entertainment would allow a broad range of interviews with myriad female narrators. This project started my research with black women at all levels of the hotel casino industry. That work began with Hazel Gay and a long list of black maids and resulted in my master's thesis. In later years, the research expanded to capture the history of the Las Vegas black community as a whole.

This comprehensive research traced events, experiences, and advances in the African American community from Las Vegas's 1905 beginning through the 1970s. Conducting research as part of the Women in Gaming and Entertainment Oral History Project proved the value of the oral history method of interviewing. Themes captured and enhanced by this methodology sketched black life in Las Vegas as painful and triumphant, simple and complex, and isolated yet integrated into the whole of city history. Topics investigated included migration, class structure, economics, work and labor, racism and classism, the civil rights movement, the welfare rights movement, and other major historic episodes. The added privilege of meeting historical sources face to face brought the history of the community to a personal intellectual level. Additionally, oral history sessions conducted in private homes allowed for the acquisition of manuscript and photograph collections for Clark County and UNLV libraries.

At the intersection of race, culture, class, and gender are the two people in the interview room. I grew up as a sharecropper in the South and was enrolled in a master's degree program as the first person in my family to complete college. Across the microphone from me were women at points on that same continuum who had migrated from the South. Many, just like me, had worked in fields that they and their families did not own. Narrators enjoyed some schooling; many were entrepreneurs; and some had earned undergraduate and graduate degrees. The playing field was level with interviewer and interviewee sharing similar cultural and historical backgrounds as well as a common grounding in religious theology, whether African Methodist, Baptist, or Pentecostal. We understood the same method of analyzing social problems because the structure of our lives, family lives, and communal relationships had much in common. The home, the school, and the church taught blacks throughout the South the value of safety, the importance of place, and generational knowledge that tied age groups together, acknowledging an unstated understanding in worldview.

This is not to say that only black women can interview each other. However, if the combination of culture, race, class, and gender makes a difference in discourse, then oral history is one of those places where the evidence can be significant. The discussion or dialogue was like that of a gospel choir that moves into and out of rhythmic patterns in an elegant design. I believe that is exactly what happened as interview gathering began and progressed over the vast era that marked the uncovering of Las Vegas black history.

I faced two challenges before my choir could sing. First, my academic training insisted that I find all available sources. These included newspapers, manuscript collections, books, a few interviews already mentioned, and a documentary film, *The Road to Las Vegas: A Black Perspective* that explored the World War II migration of blacks to Las Vegas from small towns in the South.[2] Thus facts about several periods in African American history appeared, but many more questions than answers emerged. I needed to find people who could answer my questions.

My second problem was finding one early African American migrant to share memories and introduce me to others. The black community's networking mechanism helped me locate the first narrator and that opened the floodgates. During my then-weekly appointment at a black beauty parlor, Clonie Gay had an appointment right after me. I told her I wanted to talk to someone who knew about the World War II migration of blacks to Las Vegas. Clonie shared the story of her mother and father and gave me their phone number.

I called and made an appointment. Hazel Gay shared her story and that of her husband, Jimmy, about the "great migration" to Las Vegas from Fordyce, Arkansas. Jimmy Gay had recently suffered a series of mini-strokes and could not speak, but Hazel agreed to the request of an interview. They had moved West in the early 1940s. *The Road to Las Vegas* addressed this migration from towns like Tallulah, Louisiana, and Fordyce, Arkansas, but Hazel Gay was the first of many travelers who allowed the journey to come alive one mile at a time.

Hazel was a gracious hostess and put me at ease on the initial outing, my very first interview. She began the interview by talking about her early childhood and that of Jimmy in the small town of 5,000 people. Jimmy was reared by a white family who owned Fordyce's mortuary, bank, furniture store, and many other enterprises. Having no son, the family taught Jimmy their business acumen and operational and management techniques and educated him to be a mortician by sending him to college to secure a bachelor's degree.[3] Hazel, too, was an entrepreneur who owned a restaurant. She assumed the role of prodding Jimmy to move to Las Vegas once the idea was broached. Like many migratory women, she originally stayed behind while Jimmy blazed the family's trail to the West.

The influence of small Southern towns proved pivotal in the history of blacks in Las Vegas. Those towns functioned as the conveyance mechanism of a fundamental idea of protest brought to Las Vegas via the migration stream. Residents from Fordyce, Tallulah, and other small towns brought with them a hunger for a better life that included economic opportunities, good schooling for their children, and a little fun for themselves.[4] The racial divide in Fordyce was not as firm or severe as that in Las Vegas, so Jimmy Gay ignored the imposed racial barriers. He could defy prejudices because his background sanctioned a different response when faced with white expectations of black stereotypical behavior. He arrived in Las Vegas as a licensed mortician, but in Nevada he was not allowed to test for a license in his chosen occupation. He waited nine years, until 1962, to be allowed to become a licensed mortician.

Women and men assumed typical gendered roles in the migration process. Men blazed the trail in many cases, and women prepared food for the trip, communicated with other female travelers for advice, and cared for children along the way. Judge Lee Gates's mother acted as the trailblazer. In 1959 or 1960, the Gates family moved from Tallulah, Louisiana, when Lee was eight years of age. Uncharacteristically, his mother not only provided the push to get the family out of the South but conducted scouting expeditions as well. First she went to Chicago, where several brothers lived, and then to Los Angeles, but neither place provided the atmosphere she sought for her family. She remained in those cities long enough to test the workforce and the lifestyle of the black communities. Finally, she tried Las Vegas and liked it because of the small size, not a lot of traffic, "the housing looked pretty good and of course she could work. After having worked in the fields picking cotton and then working in houses as a maid being paid nothing, and then to come here and make ten bucks a day or $12 or $13. And they had the union; they felt they had some rights."[5]

In the beginning, securing a job, living in housing reserved for blacks, and finding kinship groups were not challenging tasks. The most arduous undertaking was simply getting to Las Vegas. Essie Jacobs left Fordyce on Monday and arrived in Las Vegas on Wednesday. "We never slept in a hotel. We just kept driving because there were two drivers."[6] Viola Johnson, also from Fordyce, remembered arriving by car and not stopping along the way except for gasoline. "When we left home everyone in the car had food with them—big boxes of food, cakes and chicken. We did our sleeping in the car."[7] Blacks stayed in the place set aside for them by the system of Jim Crow. Staying in a motel or eating in restaurants in unfamiliar territory could be unsafe. In 1961, when Henrietta Pace came out with three other adults, they decided to stop for breakfast somewhere in Texas. They sat at the counter in a small diner and placed their orders. The waitress informed them that they would have to eat the food in the back room. They left without eating.[8] Shoeboxes filled with fried chicken and other Southern staples provided the sufficiency of the migration to the promised land.

The first phase of uncovering the Las Vegas African American story extended beyond the Women in Gaming and Entertainment Oral History Project. Viola Johnson, Jackie Brantley, Lucille Bryant, Hattie Canty, Rachel Coleman, Faye Duncan Daniels, Pat Feaster, Ruby Garland, D. D. Cotton, Inez Harper, Cathren Holder, Essie Jacobs, Alice Key, Sarann Knight Preddy, Juanita and Bubba Simmons, Barbara Kirkland, Esther Langston, Corine Tisdale, Faye Todd, Ida Webb, Alma Whitney, Coleen Wilson, and Anna Bailey along with Hazel Gay and Judge Lee Gates shared their migratory experiences, work and labor memories, community development strategies, and family life anecdotes experienced in a desert terrain very unlike the towns and cities that pushed blacks out of the South. Gradually the story, the timeline, and the understanding of the importance of the black World War II migration emerged. A steady flow of migrants continued into the 1970s from origins that spanned the country. Spoken primary source accounts proved to be powerful, added meaningful historical content, and contained colorful stories.

Interviews provided new insights into the migration story, especially pertaining to work. Families and friends formed chains to pull relatives and neighbors out of the South. Fordyce and Tallulah kinship and social groups prodded those "back home" to move west, where jobs were plentiful. Economics proved to be the driving force of the migratory wave. Narrators contrasted the financial situation in the South to that of Las Vegas. Lucille Bryant from Tallulah explained it well. Employment opportunities for black women consisted of field work or domestic chores in homes of whites. Lucille earned $2.50 a day chopping cotton on hot summer days or $5 a week in homes where the work included cooking, taking care of children, cleaning, washing clothes, and ironing. Black men worked in agricultural pursuits or at local lumber mills.[9] From these interviews and many others, the historical origins of the Las Vegas black community fell into place. Oral history provided the human story and intricacies behind the pushes and pulls of the migratory process. Previous thinking, in a very general sense, was that most people left the South because of the prevalent and widespread racial discrimination. Instead, economic well-being proved to be the reason that topped the list of why families joined the migration. Naturally, the unspoken cause of poor financial standing can be linked to discriminatory institutional practices.

These early interviews led to the investigation of racism and classism in Las Vegas. The Gay interviews, along with others, spoke of a racism that was different from that in the South. It was unexpected in the West. Migrants did not know that Nevada was built on a racial divide just as the South was.

The fight for equality reignited in Las Vegas in the next century with an element of classism added to racism. Lucille Bryant's experience and that of Jimmy Gay were different, leading to evidence of the obvious class differences in the small-town South and Las Vegas. Jimmy Gay was a college graduate who intended to become the first black mortician in southern Nevada, and he did just that, but his wait to acquire credentials was lengthened by racism.

> The day that I came to Las Vegas I applied at a funeral home and they looked at me like I was crazy. I immediately took my credentials to Carson City to the State Board of Embalmers

and I didn't hear anything at all from them so I started writing them letters and asking when the board would meet and eventually I did have a letter from the secretary who said, "we will notify you when we will have an examination." Well, this went on and on and I realized there weren't a lot of embalmers who came to the state, but there were a few who were given the examination without my knowing about it. This went on for nine years. Eventually, I became connected with Palm Mortuary and the president of Palm Mortuary was on the board of directors and this is the sole reason why I ever had a chance to take it [the exam]. Prior to that, there had not been a black in the state that had taken any state examination before I took this.[10]

Lucille Bryant's first day in Las Vegas was the complete opposite. It occurred about ten years later, and it reflected how workers were shielded by the back-of-the-house structure in hotels. The Culinary Union Local 226 made this protection possible while Jimmy Gay faced the employment sector without any safeguards.

I got here on the fourth of October of 1953 and I got a job the very first day at the Algiers Hotel. When I got here that morning, my cousin Gladys was getting ready to go out to the Algiers Hotel where she had been working and was going to quit her job because she had found a better one. So, she said, "You want to go with me?" I said, "Okay." We got out there and I asked the housekeeper [black woman from Fordyce] if she needed someone to work today. She said, "Yes" and took me upstairs to show me the rooms and what I was supposed to do to clean seven or eight rooms and she said it paid $8 per day. When the lady left the room, I got on my knees and gave God thanks: Eight dollars per day and working in the shade![11]

The combination of classism and racism worked as a double-edges sword, cutting workers in the back of the house and the middle class with equally broad strokes. The initial interviews offered me a window into the class structure within the black community and also how blacks were juxtaposed with other groups citywide.

The class system kept workers on the lower employment rungs, and discriminatory practices held the middle class at a certain mediocre place, never at or near the top. Class can be identified through occupation, social and public actions, education, and family ties, among other criteria. Barbara Kirkland worked as schoolteacher and helped found La Femme Douze, an organization that introduced black debutantes into society from 1954 to today.[12] Another La Femme Douze founder, Esther Langston, became one of the first black professors at UNLV. Sarann Knight Preddy owned the first gaming license of probably any black person in the country and influenced the social structure of the community.

While racism reigned, it appeared to be a less prohibitive force against middle-class advancement; the class structure combined with racism held back progress by those in the working class, especially the working poor. Class constraints changed slowly over time. Laws could not be instituted to lift one from the working poor to the middle class. Education was the main equalizer. Blue-collar workers had little and in most cases could not pass on the benefits of a good education to their children. Unfortunately, jobs that produced an adequate living wage in the back of the house passed on to immigrants of different ethnicities and races within two generations. Class was a place keeper.

The public school system in the South added to the difficulties of many migrants. Many did not pass on the love of academic learning to the next generation because they were educated poorly at best and possibly only through the eighth grade. The school term for blacks in Fordyce and Tallulah was determined by crop cycles. Classes started later in the fall than those of white students. Henrietta Pace told of attending school as a child in Fordyce later in the school year or when the weather was too inclement to allow work in the fields.[13] My queries about their children attending college was met with disinterest by most parents.

Racism was different. It was the force that maintained the glass ceiling above the middle and professional classes. Therefore blacks used the law, civil disobedience, and an arsenal of other tools to fight against it. Those tools included their life experiences, education, etiquette, connections, golf skills, and attitude, often called "juice" in Las Vegas, their "juice." One of the reasons hotels began to allow Sammy Davis Jr. to stay at Strip properties was probably because of actions by Frank Sinatra. Jimmy Gay moved into management at The Sands partly because of his golf expertise. Dr. Charles I. West, Sarann Preddy, Bob Bailey, Jimmy Gay, Alice Key, and others, because of their backgrounds, knew great numbers of entertainers and could sometimes go to their shows before they were permitted to do so by the city's racial restrictions. Racism crossed class boundaries but seemed more harsh as the arsenal of tools diminished. The poorer and less educated traced the effects of racial discrimination from birth in inferior hospital wings to homes with poor financial prospects continuing to schools with substandard supplies. Dr. Charles I. West was a fifth-generation medical doctor with connections, knowledge, and "juice" that spanned decades and extended throughout the country.[14]

Jimmy Gay, a member of the middle or professional class, used unique tools to combat racism. He learned golf from the white family that reared him, and golfing made it possible for Jimmy to open other doors for the black community. He was the first black person to hold an executive position at The Sands as the director of communications and later personnel consultant in the gaming industry and taught many of his white co-workers to play the game. Additionally, he helped found a black golf club that played at the city's municipal golf course (see figure 8.1). Gay was known as the "Father of Fordyce" because he put so many blacks to work. He worked tirelessly and knew everyone in town. When a black person needed assistance of any sort, Gay had a ready referral. His broad base of acquaintances allowed him to be the key NAACP fundraiser, chairing the annual Freedom Fund Banquet for many years. Banquets such as these across the country were the organization's largest source of revenue, both locally and nationally. In later years, he was appointed as the first black person to the Nevada Athletic Commission by Governor Grant Sawyer. Gay enjoyed political clout as well. When Sarann Knight ran for the Las Vegas City Council, Alice Key served as her campaign manager. Whenever Alice needed to speak with, secure campaign funds from, or get information from hotel casino owners or other influential city denizens, she called Jimmy Gay. He never failed to get Knight and Key the audience they requested.[15]

Figure 8.1 Valley View golf members. Standing (left to right): Uvalda Caperton, Q. B. Bush, A. T. McCoy, Loyd Mayfield, Calvin Washington, John Winters, J. Guran, E. Moore, Willie Hughes, Larry Wilborn. Kneeling (left to right): James Gay, R. Sheppard, F. Cobbs, James Roberts, Henry Moore, M. Branch, A. Sanders.

The benefit of a good oral history interview proved invaluable in the documentation of this early period in Las Vegas history. Clarence Ray's memories and newspaper accounts allowed research of the black community to reach back before construction of the Hoover Dam, to a point just five years after the beginning of the town. Because community members who knew him in the recent past marveled at his capacity to recall names, dates, and events, his contributions became invaluable to those examining Las Vegas history. Ray moved to Las Vegas in 1925, helped organize the NAACP, worked in the gaming industry on the West Side and downtown, and was friends with other movers and shakers in the community.[16] The NAACP served somewhat as an equaling force for the middle class, and the Culinary Union Local 226 served as the leveling devise for service workers.

Learning about the Culinary Union was an obscure endeavor because no records were available to the public.[17] Maids interviewed for the Women in Gaming and Entertainment Oral History Project in the 1990s reported that the then-president of the Culinary Union was a black woman. Hattie Canty scheduled an interview and answered questions about her trajectory from a maid to the second most important position in the union. Nineteenth-century labor unions denied membership privileges to blacks. This behavior continued into the twentieth century but began to diminish. Though the Culinary Union Local 226 allowed black membership, the 1971 consent decree stated that only certain positions had been open to nonwhite workers.[18]

Absorbing the history of the Culinary Union Local 226 was necessary for thorough research of the black community. Facts gathered made the union sound mysterious and a bit secretive but a positive place for blacks. Historically, blacks had been barred from labor union membership but the culinary union represented all the jobs in the back of the house that were almost exclusively reserved for blacks as the gaming industry expanded in the late 1940s and 1950s. These invisible positions included maids, linen room workers, and some kitchen help. The name Al Bramlet was synonymous with Local 226, and his murder made this an intriguing story. The Local 226 began in 1948, and in 1954 Bramlet was elected secretary-treasurer, the most powerful position. All interviewees respected Bramlet, believed that he was fair in his dealing with employees, and followed him if he declared a strike. The union held a three-day strike in 1967, a twenty-four-hour strike in 1971, and a serious ten-day strike in 1976.[19] In 1977, Bramlet's body was found in a shallow grave just outside the city.

Black women found a measure of power in union activism. Hattie Canty followed in the footsteps of another black woman, Sarah Hughes, a union representative who had worked with Bramlet. The benefits offered by the union put Canty on the path to become the Local 226 president after her husband died, leaving her with ten children, eight still in the home.

> In working for the Maxim Hotel, I began to learn what kind of organization [Culinary Union] that had all of these great benefits that I had gotten. One of my boys had a cancerous growth removed from the nerve near his ear. If I had not belonged to the union and if I had not had that culinary insur-

ance, I wouldn't have been able to get that operation. . . . I
am living proof that a maid can own at home, buy cars, pay
property taxes. and send her kids to college.[20]

Canty began picketing on her days off at any site that needed pro-
testers, then she became a committee leader, a union trustee, and
finally president of the union in May 1990, again in 1993, and by a
landslide vote in 1996.[21] She linked the labor movement with the
civil rights movement in a very profound way. There were not
enough blacks in certain positions that paid well. "And I'm concerned because when I started most of the maids were black. Now
that maids are being paid a decent salary, blacks are not there anymore."[22] The joy of financial well-being expressed by Lucille Bryant
in 1953 was short-lived. The black back-of-the-house working class
had been moved. Black men fared somewhat better.

Interviews with many women seemed to indicate that the World
War II migration was fueled by the fledgling casino industry, but
when men's voices and stories are added, greater evidence point to
the war complex. The Las Vegas area was one of the places singled
out by the federal government as a recipient of projects that provided numerous jobs. In the 1940s, one of the most profound
federal installations was Basic Magnesium, Inc. (BMI), which processed the magnesium used to build aircraft and ammunition for
the war effort. Many jobs were grueling and the work was dirty, so
black men were recruited from small towns in the South. Franklin D. Roosevelt's Executive Order 8802 paved the way for black
recruitment.[23] The migration floodgates opened offering jobs to
men.

Migration can be broadly defined as an act of protest. Men and
women traveled hundreds of miles to gain a better life that proved
to be more elusive than expected. Dissent began to appear in the
form of black men's union protests similar to those of women in
the Culinary Union. Joe Neal from Tallulah worked as a compliance person for the 1964 Civil Rights Act He was looking for civil
rights violation and there were no blacks in the old boys' club.

See, what was happening, the unions would have this list, kind
of a family thing and it was most peculiar to the plumbers.

They would have this long list and they kept adding their relatives. So I had a friend who had gone to work for the Equal
Rights Commission. I asked him if he could get me a copy of
the list and he did. We watched that list for about a year and
saw what was happening. Then I filed a complaint with the
State Apprenticeship Council which oversees the apprenticeship programs and the labor unions.[24]

In the early 1970s, the list system was eliminated and blacks entered the building trades unions as apprentices and skilled workers.

This action eventually led to the ability and the right to engage
in organized protest. Black workers at BMI faced not just the 110°F
temperature, desert sand and dust, poisonous fumes, and molten
metal but also racial discrimination, segregated amenities, lower pay
for the same job classifications as whites, and at least initially poor
housing. Furthermore, management let them know that they would
have no opportunity to advance beyond certain lower levels of various jobs.[25] There were additional complaints as well; one concerned
segregated changing facilities that had been integrated in the beginning and another centered on the issue of promotions as black
men became more competent at their low-skilled positions. Black
workers were routinely given the most menial work in the hottest,
most filthy areas of the plant. Although the unjust treatment of
black workers continued unabated, it was only a matter of time before they reached their breaking point.

Conditions finally boiled over. In October 1943, 200 black men
angrily walked out of the plant in protest. The walkout was not a
spontaneous act. Rather, it resulted from careful planning. Lubertha Johnson had assisted the residents of Carver Park with forming
a Tenants Council that held meetings sometimes attended by labor
union representatives from Los Angeles, particularly James Anderson, a black organizer with the Congress of Industrial Organizations (CIO).[26] In addition to Anderson, Elsie and Leslie Dobbins
led the men in this protest effort.[27]

Woodrow Wilson's description of labor union activity probably
affected his move into politics. He became involved with the American Federation of Labor (AFL) when most black men at BMI
turned to the CIO. When the CIO-led strike occurred, Wilson

tried to encourage the leaders of the protest to halt the action or at least have the strikers relinquish their company badges. His pleas were ignored, but his instincts proved correct. "After the walkout they [management] gave them a certain deadline to return to work and then terminated them. The walkout was a failure."[28] According to Johnson, only minor changes resulted, such as the reintegration of bathrooms and changing facilities.[29]

Even though BMI proved less attractive than at the beginning of the great Las Vegas migration, the salaries were still more than most of the men had ever earned. Moreover, the living conditions were different—some much more attractive and some less so than those in the South. While the West Side was crowded with few amenities, BMI provided homes that were convenient, newly constructed, and structurally sound. Nevertheless, new black residents opted for community over nice surroundings, one of the pushes that propelled them out of the South. Additionally, the majority of black women worked but had no occupational outlets in the Basic Town site. Their work was downtown and on the Strip. At the end of BMI employment, men entered the gaming industry through the backdoor, but many accepted positions at the Nevada Test Site, the Cold War–era location where nuclear bombs were tested, just sixty-five miles north of Las Vegas. Male strides were clearly seen in the political arena; men who worked at BMI claimed the first black seats in the state assembly, ran the NAACP branch, and founded churches of all denominations that reflected life in the South.

The spirit of protest led directly to the initial victories of the push for integration. The opening of the Moulin Rouge Hotel Casino introduced blacks to the upscale entertainment environs that whites took for granted. It was the first integrated posh venue that rivaled those on the Strip. Before that, Jackson Street was the West Side Strip. Small nightclubs/casinos peppered the thoroughfare where Sammy Davis Jr., Count Basie, the Teniers, Nat King Cole, and Pearl Bailey returned to have fun after performing on the Strip. In general, blacks were not allowed to stay where they performed unless the circumstances were unusual. In 1952, Josephine Baker would only perform if she stayed on the grounds of the Last Frontier Hotel Casino and have a reserved table down front for her guests.[30] The Moulin Rouge served as an early ray of hope as well and was a solid, substantial reminder of its purpose.

The Moulin Rouge was located on Bonanza Boulevard, just across the railroad tracks that divided the city along racial lines. Although its heyday lasted only six months, the meaning still lingers for African Americans. On May 15, 1955, the Moulin Rouge opened with a standing-room-only crowd and operated with this capacity audience for six months. It closed because the bills were not paid, but the myth is that it closed because it was more popular than equal venues on the Strip. Anna Bailey, one of the house dancers, talked about the Rouge.

> The employees were all black. The uniforms were beautiful and the service was the best in town. And we were the only ones doing a late show. I think it was two o'clock in the morning. So all of the Strip would empty out and they would all come over to the Moulin Rouge. You've never seen so many stars. Tallulah Bankhead and Belafonte and Sammy, just all the stars would hang out there. I really in my heart believe that's why it was closed, because we closed to standing room only.[31]

She also described opening night. "Opening night was exciting. Edward G. Robinson was there and I remember so many stars and all the flowers that were sent to us backstage by almost all of Hollywood. We made the cover of *Life* magazine."[32]

The white-owned Moulin Rouge was a showplace. Deauville Room waiters served an international gourmet cuisine while wearing tuxedos and white gloves. The dress shop was stocked to capacity with the finest clothes available and was operated by Hazel Gay. The bar was huge and constructed of the most elegantly polished wood. The audience was filled with politicians, celebrities, and high rollers every night. The entertainment was the best in the city because after the paid acts completed their shows, other entertainers who were there as customers would give impromptu performances. The dancers were the crowning glory of the Moulin Rouge. They were the first African American house line in the city and were hand-picked for their beauty and talent. Joe Louis served as the greeter,[33] and I located the *Life* magazine that Anna Bailey mentioned.

The Moulin Rouge was the spark that probably led to integration of the Strip. In 1960, the local NAACP president and first black dentist, James B. McMillan, sent a letter to the mayor of the city threatening a march on the Strip on a Saturday afternoon if the city did not allow blacks to enter casinos, hotels, and restaurants on an equal footing with whites. On March 26, 1960, the morning of the proposed march, after weeks of negotiations, the governor, mayor, publisher of the *Las Vegas Sun Newspaper*, and leaders in the black community met at the Moulin Rouge to talk about integrating downtown and the Strip. The verbal Moulin Rouge agreement reached that morning allowed blacks to become full citizens of the city.[34] The meeting made the headlines of the newspapers, but it was a series of oral interviews with McMillan that allowed historians to learn the intimate details of the march that never happened.

The watershed era for blacks in Las Vegas occurred in the 1970s. Protest ideals instilled by migrants from small towns, union affiliations, and middle-class customs combined and spilled over. Demonstrations of this spillover appeared as management positions on the Strip, rights for welfare mothers, and a school desegregation plan. Though downtown and Strip casinos and hotels began to allow blacks to enter the front doors in 1960, integrated housing, school desegregation, and desirable employment opportunities did not occur until the following decade. Newspaper articles chronicled housing and school integration, but very little can be documented about raising the glass ceiling in the employment arena and the welfare rights movement. Again, oral interviews saved the day.

In 1971 the NAACP, along with many newly arrived attorneys, filed a consent decree enforced by the Federal District Court that mandated 12.5 percent of the total number of employees in each listed job category in the gaming industry being set aside for blacks. These job classifications included dealers, casino cashiers, secretaries, bellmen, cocktail waitresses, waiters and waitresses, security officers, PBX operators, doormen/parking attendants, captains, bartenders, and keno writers.[35] Three black women who entered midlevel management positions at major Strip properties as a result of this order were contacted and invited to add their stories to the growing oral history of the black community. Jackie Brantley worked as a maid and as a secretary for the Clark County School District; in 1975 she became a secretary at the Desert Inn. This position was not the typical clerical job. Brantley remembered, "Thirty women had flown in from around the country, from Los Angeles and various other places, who were interested in that position. It was considered a stepping-stone position; a glamorous type of position but at the same time you would have the opportunity to learn firsthand about entertainment, public relations, and how hotels operate."[36] Brantley soon moved into management and became advertising and publicity manager.

Faye Todd climbed even higher. After five years as special events coordinator at the Desert Inn, she became entertainment director and corporate executive assistant at the Landmark. "The owners, Ted and Zula Wolfram, came to town about once a month and appreciated her work so much that she was given a bonus on each visit and on one occasion, a new car. After six glorious years, Todd's dream job ended when Ted was accused and convicted of fraud in his stock brokerage firm in Ohio."[37]

The last of the three women interviewed was Faye Duncan Daniels, who became an assistant hotel manager at the Plaza in downtown Las Vegas. In that position, she put together the Hotel Manager's Association, which allowed managers across the city to share goals and experiences. She felt her major accomplishment was the creation of job training and English programs for Mexican Americans as well as a literacy program for all employees.[38]

These midlevel management achievements can be juxtaposed against the plight of the working poor. To attain these positions, the Las Vegas black middle class used the court system, and almost simultaneously, poor mothers took to the streets to ensure fairness. Ruby Duncan and other mothers led a welfare rights movement that closed the Strip on a Saturday morning in 1972. Of course, that march with Ralph Albernathy and Jane Fonda was on national television, but who were those women with the nerves of steel who dared close the Las Vegas Strip? Oral interviews permit us to look into their lives, and Duncan's stands as a good example of the information that was uncovered.

Duncan suffered an injury when she slipped on a puddle of oil in the kitchen of the Sahara Hotel where she worked. Additionally, while working, she encountered unacceptable behavior from supervisors and witnessed how the power of organized workers could remedy situations. Duncan's manager at the Flamingo often ordered overtime at the last minute without giving the maids the opportunity to make arrangements for additional child care. One day, Duncan's response to the request was different: "You ladies cannot leave because there are more beds that have to be made up." "I'm not going to make any more beds." The boss said, "Well you have to." Duncan responded, "I'm going home to my kids." The next morning, Duncan was called in and fired, but the Culinary Union Local 226 negotiated her reinstatement and secured overtime pay.[39]

The lessons learned by similar experiences lived by women who worked as maids prepared them to be pushed into the forefront of the campaign waged by welfare mothers. Battles began when benefits to dependent children were severely cut by the state of Nevada. Without a high school education, Ruby left Tallulah, Louisiana, and moved to Las Vegas, where she and her family lived for months in an abandoned motel with no running water. Left with little financial support for her family after a divorce and getting hurt on the job, Ruby applied for Aid to Dependent Children (ADC) at a time when funds could be cut off if a late-night search of a recipient's home resulted in evidence of a man's presence. This lack of respect coupled with a sudden drastic reduction in benefits led white, black, and Latina women to organize.

Welfare rights movement leaders made their own decisions but had assistance from several fronts. The fledgling group was trained by George Wiley of the National Welfare Rights Organization and given legal assistance by a group of young attorneys working for legal aid. Ruby Duncan, Mary Wesley, Alversa Beals, Emma Stampley, and Essie Henderson, among others, were arrested many times for protest activities such as the eat-in at the Stardust Hotel and Casino, where children who had not eaten meat in a while enjoyed steak, lobster, and prime rib. The well-known Shell Oil heiress, Maya Miller, funded many of the organization's trips to Carson City, the state capital, where Duncan learned to lobby the state legislature and became active in Democratic Party politics. Duncan eventually traveled as far as Russia espousing women's rights.[40]

This movement was never stagnant. From just advocating for welfare rights, it morphed into Operation Life, a nonprofit group that provided food for children, established the first library on the West Side, opened a medical clinic for children, and provided job placement services. These women, like many others in the back of the house three decades earlier, were undereducated and from small towns in the South, but they created the group to provide for their greater good. First the Culinary Union Local 226 and then Operation Life helped shape a brighter future when class and discriminatory issues had to be overcome.

Migrants pulled together and shaped the story of the West Side, strongly influencing and staging the history of Las Vegas. A clear picture of the black community's work, protest, and ordinary lives could not have been seen without the oral history discipline. The migration story was different from earlier movements out of the South to the North and Midwest. The Southwest was new and wild. Historian Frederick Jackson Turner believed that the earlier white migration to the West defined Americanism. Immigrants put their stamp on a new land as they simultaneously flung off the Old World culture. "For the first time," Turner states, "This country became the United States of American bearing traits of individualism."[41] At the turn of the nineteenth century, customary Jim Crow practices controlled behavior patterns between and among racial groups in new industrial cities as well as the South. The West was no exception. Turner forgot these practices in his famous essay, which guided historical thought in the writing of American history for decades. The rugged individualism granted by his thesis does not shape the story of blacks in the West. Black actions and opportunities were curtailed by their skin color. The black-owned Boston Saloon in Virginia City was popular and prosperous, but what measure of success would have been seen by archaeologists in 2003 if the entire community had congregated there? A reshaping of the Turner thesis is necessary to write the black history of the West and especially Nevada. Oral history made that possible.

The realization of this African American oral history project was also made possible by the wave of feminist researchers who began to include those on the margins into the writing of mainstream history. Although individual blacks received places of prominence in history books, never did maids, porters, community organizers, farmers, miners, dealers, and cocktail waitresses have a say. This subjugated knowledge, thought to be forever silent, was unearthed.[42] The new feminists created some of the initial modes for theorizing the field of oral history through the constructs of race, class, gender, and culture. They sought social change and got both social and historical change.[43] Oral history became a real discipline as valid as newspapers, diaries, manuscript collections, and photographs. Once again, those who made and experienced history find themselves speaking it in their own words from a center place in the narrative.[44]

Oral history allowed the Las Vegas story to become more than a tale with two sides but a chronicling of events from a multiplicity of standpoints.[45] Both the narrator and interviewer have a side; one tells the story through discourse and the other with questions. Even more telling are the follow-up queries that are entirely off-the-cuff inquiries submitted as a response to answers given by the narrator. Indeed, oral history, like all forms of historic primary source material, is slanted. Therefore, the project-based ventures into oral history are significantly effective forms of collecting history. A project-based approach (versus one that is individual-based) provides a significant number of interviews to be collected regarding a central topic with one set of questions. This technique allows researchers to investigate each person's responses and to write history from numerous multifaceted answers about the same sets of historical events. Faye Todd, Faye Daniels, Jackie Brantley, D. D. Cotton, and Anna Bailey tell the story of black women securing jobs in positions other than those in the back of the house. Oral history captured these new frontiers.

Historian Alan Govenar introduced the concept of African American frontiers and oral history. Migratory movements engendered new ways of thinking and involved many frontiers that offered the promise of new opportunities.[46] This idea held true for the Las Vegas black community. The migratory process, the West Side environment, work, labor unions, the fights for integration and welfare rights, and the mini-migration of blacks within Clark County provided opportunities in economics (higher paying jobs in the casino industry, at BMI, and the Nevada Test Site), politics (blacks ran for political office and operated Operation Life) society (black men and women organized the Jolly Club and La Femme Douze), cultural affairs (Masonic organizations, the Fordyce Club), and fashion shows that allowed the community to have fun, engage in charity drives, and introduce intellectual discourse.

Oral history reveals that blacks participated in the complete story of the city. Though these interviews are readily accessible, they not the sole collection site of black conversations. Historical integrity is ensured because additional projects are under way and/or completed by the West Las Vegas Library; the Westside School Alumni Foundation; a College of Southern Nevada political science professor; Sonya Horsford, senior resident scholar with the Lincy Institute at UNLV; Stan Armstrong, local filmmaker; and several other individuals and entities. All of these groups and individuals have conducted focused oral history research in various aspects of the African American saga. In some instances, this work has gone beyond the academy and has become the people's history. Thus by 2011, that inclusive history was verbalized from numerous projects throughout the city, eliminating any taint of the slant that one interviewer or one institution might impose.

Notes

1. The terms "African American" and "black" are used interchangeably throughout this chapter. Currently, both are considered politically correct. Early interviews and some older narrators still use "Negro," "colored," and "Afro-American," all terms that were accepted during periods within the twentieth century.

2. Lee Winston and Greg Morris, *The Road to Las Vegas: A Black Perspective*, 30 minutes, co-produced in association with KLVX, Ch. 10, Las Vegas, NV, Ark. Educational TV Network, Louisiana Public Broadcasting, 1984.

3. "Pioneering Civic Leader, Hotel Executive Gay Dies at 83," *Las Vegas Sun Newspaper*, September 13; Hazel Gay, interview by author, December 2, 1995, Women in Gaming and Entertainment Oral History Project, Las Vegas.

4. Essie Jacobs, interview by author, February 1, 1996, Women in Gaming and Entertainment Oral History Project; Lucille Bryant, interview by author, December 13, 1995, Women in Gaming and Entertainment Oral History

Project; and Trish Geran, *Beyond the Glimmering Lights: The Pride and Perseverance of African Americans in Las Vegas* (Las Vegas: Stephens Press, 2006). One of the key themes of Geran's book is why blacks moved to Las Vegas.

5. Judge Lee Gates, interview by author, December 5, 1996, Boyer Early Las Vegas Oral History Project, 4.

6. Essie Jacobs interview, 6–7.

7. Viola Johnson, interview by author, Women in Gaming and Entertainment Oral History Project, March 12, 1996, 16–17.

8. Henrietta Pace, interview by author, June 15, 1996, University of Nevada, Las Vegas.

9. Lucille Bryant interview.

10. James A. Gay III, interview by Elizabeth Nelson Patrick, December 1978, Black Experience in Nevada Oral History Project, Donated Tapes Collection, James R. Dickinson Library, University of Nevada, Las Vegas.

11. Lucille Bryant, interview by author, 1997.

12. Barbara Kirkland, interview by author, November 12, 2004, Boyer Early Las Vegas Oral History Project.

13. Henrietta Pace, interview by author, 1995, Women in Gaming and Entertainment Oral History Project.

14. Alice Key, interview by author, 1998, Women in Gaming and Entertainment Oral History Project, University of Nevada, Las Vegas.

15. Ibid.; "Pioneering Civic Leader, Hotel Executive Gay Dies at 83"; Hazel Gay interview; Elizabeth Nelson Patrick interview. The "Father of Fordyce" moniker is found in almost all interviews conducted with Fordyce migrants. Other members of the black golf club were Uvalda Caperton, Q. B. Bush, A. T. McCoy, Lloyd Mayfield, Calvin Washington, John Winters, J. Geran, E. Moore, Willie Hughes, Larry Wilborn, R. Sheppard, F. Cobbs, James Roberts, Henry Moore, M. Branch, and A. Sanders.

16. Helen M. Blue and Jamie Coughtry, *Clarence Ray: Black Politics and Gaming in Las Vegas, 1920s–1980* (Reno: University of Nevada Oral History, 1991).

17. Siti Zabedah Amri and April Leilani Aloiau for the Hospitality Research and Development Center, *Labor-Union Training Workshop,* Kim Beach, "Hotel Employees and Restaurant Employees International Union Culinary Local 226," student paper, University of Nevada, Las Vegas, June 30, 1993.

18. Civil Action No. LV1645 Consent Decree, US District Court of Nevada, June 4, 1971, *United States of America v. Nevada Resort Association, an employer association*; Prell Hotel Corp., dba Aladdin Hotel, Hughes Tool Co., dba Castaways Hotel, Desert Palace, Inc., dba Caesara Palace, Hughes Tool Co., dba Desert Inn Hotel & Country Club, M & R Investment Co., Inc. dba Dunes Hotel and Country Club, Flamingo Resort, Inc., dba Flamingo Hotel, Hughes Tool Co., dba Frontier Hotel, Las Vegas Hacienda, Inc. and Casino Operations, Inc., dba Hacienda Hotel, Las Vegas International Hotel, Inc., dba International Hotel, Hotel Properties, Inc., dba Landmark Hotel and Ca-

sino, Hotel Riviera, Inc. dba Riviera Hotel, Sahara Nevada Corporation and Consolidated Casinos Corp., dba Sahara Hotel, Hughes Tool Co., dba Sands Hotel, Silver Slipper, United Resort Hotels, Inc. and Karat, Inc., dba Stardust Hotel, Dewso Services Inc., and Consolidated Casinos Corp., dba Thunderbird Hotel, Hotel Conquistador, Inc. and Tropicana Casino, Inc., dba Hotel Tropicana, Local Union No. 995, Professional, Clerical, Ground Maintenance, Parking Lot Attendants Car rental Employees, Warehousemen and Helpers; Local Union No. 720, International Alliance of Theatrical State Employees and Moving Picture Machine Operators of the United States and Canada; Local Union No. 226, Culinary Workers Union; Local Union No. 165, Bartenders Union; Local Joint Executive Board of Las Vegas, Culinary Worker Union, Local No. 226, and Bartenders Union, Local No. 165. Available in pan files in Special Collections, Lied Library, UNLV.

19. Beach, "Hotel Employees and Restaurant Employees International Union Culinary Local 226," 8.

20. Hattie Canty, interview by author, February 27, 1998, Women in Gaming and Entertainment Oral History Project, 8.

21. Ibid., 31.

22. Ibid., 22.

23. Executive Order 8802, signed in June 1941, was also known as the Fair Employment Act. The order declared it to be the policy of the United States "that there shall be no discrimination the employment of works in defense industries or government because of race, creed, color, or national origin." To oversee the policy, Roosevelt established the Fair Employment Practices Committee. A. Philip Randolph (president, Brotherhood of Sleeping Car Porters), Walter White (NAACP executive secretary), and Mary McLeod Bethune (Minority Affairs director) urged Roosevelt to address the issue. See Fair Employment Practices Committee, *Teaching Eleanor Roosevelt Glossary,* http://www .gwu.edu/~erpapers/teachinger/glossary/fepc.cfm (accessed June 6, 2012); James A. Henretta, W. Elliot Brownlee, David Brody, Susan Ware, Marilynn S. Johnson, *America's History,* 3rd ed. (New York: Worth Publishers, 1997), 840.

24. Joe Neal, interview by author, February 7, 2006, Boyer Early Las Vegas Oral History Project, 6.

25. William T. Dobbs, "Working for BMI. Reflections on Life and Labor at America's Largest World War II Magnesium Plant," student paper, University of Nevada Las Vegas, spring 1984; A. D. Hopkins, *The First 100: Portraits of the Men and Women Who Shaped Las Vegas,* ed. A. D. Hopkins and K. J. Evans (Las Vegas: Huntington Press, 1999), entry for Howard Eells, 93.

26. Jamie Coughtry, *Lubertha Johnson: Civil Rights Efforts in Las Vegas: 1940s–1960s* (Reno: Oral History Program at the University Nevada, Reno, 1988), 16–17.

27. Ibid., and Jamie Coughtry, *Woodrow Wilson: Race, Community and Politics in Las Vegas, 1940s–1980s* (Reno: Oral History Program, University of Nevada, Reno, 1990).

28. Coughtry, *Woodrow Wilson*, 38–39.

29. Coughtry, *Lubertha Johnson*, 18.

30. Ibid., 39, and Coughtry, *Woodrow Wilson*, 81.

31. Anna Bailey, interview by author, March 3, 1997, Women in Gaming and Entertainment Oral History Project, 35.

32. Ibid.

33. Claytee D. White, "The Roles of African American Women in the Las Vegas Gaming Industry, 1940–1980," master's thesis, University of Nevada Las Vegas, 1997, 52.

34. James B. McMillan, *Fighting Back: A Life in the Struggle for Civil Rights* (Reno: University of Nevada Oral History Program, 1997).

35. Civil Action No. LV1645 Consent Decree.

36. Jackie Brantley, interview by author, October 27, 1996, Women in Gaming and Entertainment Oral History Project.

37. White, "The Roles of African American Women in the Las Vegas Gaming Industry," 62; Homer Brickley Jr., *Master Manipulator* (New York: Amacom Books, 1985).

38. White, "The Roles of African American Women in the Las Vegas Gaming Industry," 63.

39. Annelise Orleck, *Storming Caesars Palace: How Black Mothers Fought Their Own War on Poverty* (Boston: Beacon Press, 2005), 57–58.

40. Ruby Duncan, interview by author, February 12, 2007; Orleck, *Storming Caesar's Palace*.

41. Frederick Jackson Turner, *The Turner Thesis Concerning the Role of the Frontier in American History*, ed. George Rogers Taylor (Boston: D. C. Heath, 1956).

42. Patricia Leavy, *Oral History: Understanding Qualitative Research* (Oxford: Oxford University Press, 2011), 4.

43. Ibid.

44. Paul Thompson, *The Voice of the Past: Oral History* (Oxford: Oxford University Press, 1988), 2.

45. Ibid., 5.

46. Alan Govenar, *African American Frontiers: Slave Narratives and Oral Histories* (Santa Barbara, CA: ABC-CLIO, 2000) xi–xiii.

9

Women at Work in Las Vegas, 1940–1980

JOANNE L. GOODWIN

Historian Joanne Goodwin shows how oral history is important to understanding women's history. The old western history—and to some degree even the new western history—has neglected women's role in the West. Goodwin's chapter shows how women no longer fit the Victorian cult of true womanhood stereotype, especially after World War II. Historian Betsy Jameson explained this stereotype "assum[ed] . . . that men's and women's worlds were separate, that men were public and women were private, that men were active and women were passive."[1] For Jameson and Goodwin, oral history shows that western women "did not see themselves as passive civilizers or as uniquely oppressed, as wholly private or public. They understood that they performed valuable work for their families and their communities whose interests were intertwined."[2] Goodwin demonstrates that well in her interviews showing Las Vegas women actively involved in unions and improving work conditions. Goodwin also shows the kernels of truth that give rise to stereotypes. Some work, as historian Sue Armitage puts it, "has always been gendered."[3] That is especially true in Las Vegas where many women work as part of the sex industry. Goodwin's oral histories go beyond the stereotypes and show how Las Vegas showgirls view their work. After using all the available sources, Goodwin concludes her oral history took her further than any other historical source.

FLORENCE SCHILLING LOVED learning, but she forfeited her opportunity to attend the University of Illinois and instead took secretarial

175

classes as a concession to her family. Like many women of her generation, her family told her that skills in office work would provide her with job opportunities until she married. This proved true for the Illinois native when World War II broke out. She moved to Ypsilanti, Michigan, to work for the war effort and later in the war she moved to Miami, Florida, where she used her secretarial skills for the military in the Security and Intelligence Division. Two things happened in Florida that set the course of her life and ended up bringing her to Las Vegas. She met her future husband, and she worked at the Fontainebleau Hotel. Years later, after moving around with the military and raising two children, Florence Schilling McClure again took a job using her executive secretary skills at the International Hotel in Los Angeles. When her boss moved to Las Vegas in 1966 to open the Frontier Hotel and Casino, he wanted McClure to join him. She agreed and moved with her husband to the desert. She worked in the executive suite of the Frontier Hotel and the Desert Inn Hotel and Casino during the heyday of Las Vegas gaming. A few years later, she left office work to finish her college education and start the civic work she always dreamed of doing. McClure's story captures several themes in the lives of women who entered the workforce between 1940 and 1980 in Las Vegas. She came to the city from somewhere else, she blended wage earning with raising a family, and she became involved in the larger community of the city that she made home.[4]

Las Vegas has drawn the attention of scholars in the recent past, yet little is known about women in the city during its period of greatest expansion following World War II. Historians have written about the history of the area, but they have asked about the accomplishments and milestones of men in business and politics. Popular characterizations of the city focused on gamblers, mobsters, mavericks, and mavens. Women in these scenarios were glamorous appendages or marginal to the story. Yet as social historians have shown, the histories of ordinary people provide significant alternative perspectives from those who have the power—perspectives that help us rethink what we know. Western women's history has helped us better understand the impact of gender on the settlement and development of the West, yet only a small (but growing) part of that published scholarship addresses women's involvement in the urban West after 1945.[5] This chapter illustrates how essential oral histories are in understanding women's experiences. It compares the utility of traditional sources with oral narratives in an exploration of women's work in one of the largest tourist economies in the West. Oral histories provided a rich and essential source from which to understand Las Vegas as a city of workers and families in the Sun Belt, not simply of mobsters and mavens on the make.

Finding Women in the Sources

Since 1996, the Las Vegas Women Oral History Project has collected oral narratives to better understand the lives of women in Sin City. The portrayals of women in the city's tourism industry offered a limited and commercially constructed image. Yet the history of women in other parts of the western United States revealed a more complicated picture of women's lives and motivated the author to seek a fuller understanding of women's experiences in Las Vegas. The oral history project evolved from the creation of the Nevada Women's Archives at the University of Nevada, Las Vegas (UNLV). In our efforts to collect sources on women's lives, it became clear that traditional archival material would not include a large segment of the city's population—working women. The project originated from the author's work with three UNLV graduate students who were working on their master's theses. Their interests centered on women who worked in the city's gaming and entertainment industries. Together, we devised a research design and an outline of questions that could be compared across groups. These questions filled out the narrators' experiences: (1) with family, school, and early influences; (2) migrating to Las Vegas and their observations about the area at the time; (3) at work, including their daily routines, comparisons with work "back home," networks of employment, obstacles, and opportunities; and (4) balancing the challenges of combining work and family. Over the years, the original participants graduated and new ones arrived. The project continued and expanded to include women as community builders. To date, fifty-one oral histories have been completed or are near completion.[6]

Several themes emerged from the completed oral histories. First among these themes was that the narrators, like millions of other Americans, moved during and after the war. Our narrators moved within the West and to the Southwest from other parts of the country and the world. Their reasons corresponded with the second theme: pursuit of employment opportunities in the rapidly expanding tourist economy of Las Vegas. Whether an African American housekeeper from Louisiana, a native-born Texan entertainer, or a performer who emigrated from Korea, they found an abundance of work in Las Vegas. The third theme was a desire to be part of a larger community. The value of these findings derived from oral histories reaches beyond Las Vegas. These themes suggest new perspectives on women's lives in the second half of the twentieth century as well as ways in which tourism in the West served the national economy during the deindustrialization process.

Women workers have made up an increasingly large part of the US labor force since 1945. During those postwar decades, the national economy transitioned from a position of global dominance in manufacturing and industrial production to a wide range of service industries. Tourism (one of those service industries) developed rapidly in the postwar era as Americans had more leisure time and more discretionary income. Tourist businesses cultivated the importance of consumers in the postwar economy and provided municipalities that lacked a manufacturing base with another way to develop revenue.

To better understand the paid work of women in Las Vegas, I initially consulted the US Census between 1940 and 1980. The census data documented the number of women who worked, the types of work in which they engaged, and their demographic differences across a span of forty years. Two significant findings emerged from this analysis. First, more women in Las Vegas worked outside the home than in the nation as a whole.[7] Historically, such patterns existed for single women before they married; however, the workforce in Las Vegas included higher percentages of women in every marital status (single, married, with or without children, and widowed) than at the national level.[8] Since Las Vegas expanded its population through in-migration during those decades, one can reasonably assume that many women came to the resort city to find work. The second difference between Las Vegas and the country as a whole was that the city lacked significant manufacturing jobs, yet had a higher proportion of workers in professional and service occupations than found across the country.[9]

The census data provided a skeletal framework from which to understand the basic outlines of women's employment as well as its growth and change over four decades. Yet it left so much unknown. Why did women leave the familiarity of "back home" and move to Las Vegas? Did they come alone or with family? For those who took a job, what did Las Vegas offer that other places did not? Why did they stay? Traditional sources such as archival manuscripts or newspapers offered little evidence for answering these questions. Working women rarely leave written accounts, diaries, or letters. Newspapers offered limited information on women's lives because their coverage tended to focus on a particular event such as women's club news or a crisis such as criminal acts.

The answers to these questions about women in Las Vegas would not exist without oral histories. No other sources could provide the detail and texture of these gendered lives at mid-century. While the census provided the proportion of women that worked, oral histories explained who they were, where they came from, and why they worked outside the home. The census defined the occupational type of jobs women held and the change or continuity over time. Oral histories elaborated on why they took that job, what the job was like, and why they moved into other fields. The census provided aggregate data on women's family status, and oral histories offered explanations by individuals on how they combined family life with wage earning. The oral histories filled in the outlines of women's lives drawn from the census data. This is not to say that an individual narrative accurately represents all women. Nor would I argue that the themes culled from the interviews of the project completely describe the experiences of Las Vegas working women of the era. The oral histories take us further than any other historical source, however. They provided the texture of social history with their information about narrators' influences—planned or unplanned choices, interactions with cultural practices such as discrimination by race and sex, and the gendered perspectives on life, labor, and family.

A Period of Change for
Women in the Workplace

The landscape of work opportunities for women and racial-ethnic minorities changed dramatically with World War II as the demand for workers increased in war industries. The Rosie the Riveter Revisited oral history project (1980–82) documented this crucial mobilization of women for war work during World War II. Single and married women worked in war industries across the country, yet their migration to western and southwestern states for jobs continued after the war.[10] Historians originally suggested that women left the workplace to care for homes and children when veterans returned to claim their jobs. However, the extent of women's disengagement from paid employment has been overstated. Both historians and economists have shown a definitive increase in the proportion of women entering and remaining in the workplace over the second half of the twentieth century. Since the 1950s, a higher proportion of married women has joined the labor force. Women may have changed the type of work they did, but they stayed in the workforce in full- and part-time employment.[11]

Choice and need intertwined for many working women. The consumer culture of the 1950s and 1960s motivated some women, and simple economic need motivated other families who tried to compete in an economy that discriminated by race and sex. By the end of the 1970s, barriers to jobs, equal pay, and cultural prohibitions shifted as the workplace began to reflect the changes in antidiscrimination laws. Whether pursuing professions, supporting families, or simply earning a living, women appeared firmly entrenched within the workplace by the 1980s.

The western states shared these characteristics of the national economy. The mobility of workers had a notable impact, especially on the Pacific slope and in the Southwest. Employment sectors of the military-industrial complex expanded after 1945 and created economic booms in cities from Seattle to San Diego. The expansion of service industries, specifically tourism, provided numerous jobs in the consumer-driven postwar economy; jobs that had tips made low-wage positions more appealing. No place epitomized the rise of the tourism industry in postwar America better than Las Vegas. The city had been a boomtown for most of its history until the Great Recession. Unlike the boomtowns of the early twentieth century, which relied on mining, the Las Vegas boom centered on entertainment.[12] Nevada's legal gambling and the phenomenal transition of gambling into gaming turned Las Vegas from a remote desert hangout into a world-class tourist destination. From the Mob-run beginnings through the corporate reorganization, the businesses drew tourists, investment capital, as well as women and men from around the country (and the world) to live and work in Las Vegas. Most of the narrators in the Las Vegas Women Oral History Project described the city as the land of opportunity—one with ceilings, but not walls. They came to the city looking for work or to pursue a professional opportunity and they stayed because work was plentiful.

Coming to Las Vegas

Betty Bunch, a native of Texas, moved to Los Angeles, where dancers found plentiful work. She auditioned for George Moro in Los Angeles and joined the Moro-Landis Dancers. That job brought her to Las Vegas for the first time in 1956. She continued to live in Los Angeles for several years and danced at the famed Moulin Rouge nightclub. All the while, she frequently took entertainment jobs that brought her to Las Vegas. At the end of one engagement, Bunch recounted a job offer that came on her way out of town.

> I was sitting in the coffee shop at the Dunes with my suitcase by my side. . . . A choreographer I knew walked over and said, "What on earth are you girls doing here?" and we told him and he said, "You mean you're out of a job Betty?" and I said, "Yes, I am, I'll go back and look for work starting tomorrow, you know, we're all meeting here. We're going to get in the car and drive back." He said, "You want to go to work?" I said, "Well, sure." He said, "Hold on." He walked to a booth, like three booths away and I'm watching him, like that, and when he got down there, he talked for a few minutes and then this

woman stuck her head out and looked at me. And then, he walked back over and he said, "O.K., you're hired."[13]

In 1961, she moved permanently to the city when she realized "that all the work was in Las Vegas."

The place grew on the newcomers. Another dancer, Rosemary Tall DeHart, found the employment opportunities irresistible and unlike anything she knew in England. "I wanted to have a nice style of living. I think if you're a blue-collar worker in England, you're always going to be a blue-collar worker, whereas over here you can come over with $50 on you and if you work really, really hard I think you've got a chance of improving your standard of living. There's an opportunity for the future that I believe is greater over here than people realize."[14]

Janet Kravenko, a native of Great Britain, began touring internationally with the Bluebell Dancers at age seventeen. This dance company, known for its tall and professionally trained showroom dancers, had a base in Paris and approximately four troupes that toured the world from the 1950s through the 1980s. Kravenko recalled her arrival in 1959 by airplane for the second Lido de Paris company under contract at the Stardust Hotel and Casino. The troupe flew from Paris, stopped in New York City, and then arrived in Las Vegas.

> So we arrive and they open up the door and of course the hot air hit us and it was like, "Oh my God, how are we going to survive this?" So we're out on the tarmac and we all go down the steps looking our best in our heels and—what a way to travel, heels and big skirts, can you imagine? And the photographers were waiting for us at the bottom and we had to wait while they pulled out the skiffs with the costumes so they could pose the showgirls on the skiffs. Fully clothed, of course. . . . [Then] they put us in buses and started off down the Strip. Well of course, in those days there were great gaps between hotels and it was desert, you know, and it got very quiet on that bus. We'd just come from Paris; you can imagine, you know. Very civilized, very small, busy city. Got very quiet. . . . But we were like, "Oh my God, we're here. Oh well, I'm not

staying here. I'm not gonna pick up my contract. Six months, I'm back to Paris," you know.[15]

Despite her first impressions, Kravenko stayed in the city, raised a family, and opened a school of dance when she could no longer perform.

The earliest traveler included in the oral histories was Sarann Preddy, who arrived in Las Vegas in 1942. She came from Oklahoma with her husband and her father, who had war industry jobs at the magnesium plant in Henderson, a small neighboring community. At the time, Las Vegas had de facto racial segregation in housing, public accommodations, and employment. Blacks were not welcome as customers on the casino floors or in the showrooms downtown or on the Strip. Segregation created a business opportunity as a separate area of clubs developed on the old West Side. Sarann Preddy worked as a dealer in several of those clubs before she decided to open her own.

> I remember when I first came, the only club on the West Side was the Harlem Club. It was owned by a white person. Then the Cotton Club came and it was owned by a white man but it wasn't long before he turned it over to a black man and then he formed a little group. There was two or three of them that owned it. And then a black man originally owned the El Morocco and then black people owned the Town Tavern. People only stay in gaming for so long and they start selling out or turn it over to somebody else. . . . I went to work at the El Morocco and I can't remember exactly, but it didn't stay open very long, maybe a year. I worked there until it closed. When it closed I went to work at the Louisiana Club, working for the Chinese people who had [it]. Then Chinese people bought the Town Tavern and it was a little nicer club so migrated over there—went to work over there. I worked there for maybe a year and then they stopped the women from dealing.[16]

Preddy referred to a city ordinance that prohibited women from dealing in Las Vegas in 1958. This resourceful entrepreneur ran her own clubs before she and her family began the massive effort to renovate and reopen the Moulin Rouge Hotel and Casino, the city's first interracial casino.

Many of the city's African American residents moved to Las Vegas from two Southern towns. Lucille Bryant arrived in 1953 following the path of many of her townspeople from Tallulah, Louisiana. Like many African Americans who left the Deep South during the postwar years, she came to Las Vegas for better work opportunities.

> I started in the cotton fields when I was like twelve years old, eleven or twelve years old, working in the cotton fields and I did it every summer until I left and came to Las Vegas. In the winter I would do domestic work. You got paid more in the fields because you got paid by the day. I could make $2 a day or $2.50 a day. . . . I decided to come to Las Vegas to get work for myself because, at that time, I wasn't married. I came in 1953 and I decided to come here because there was no jobs in Tallulah, just domestic work. . . . I worked in the kitchen of the white lady's house. . . . And, I did everything in her house except slept with her husband. I mean, you did all the work. You washed, you ironed, you cooked, you took care of the baby and the highest I ever got was $5 a week for that.[17]

Bryant found a job as a maid at the Algiers Hotel on her first day in Las Vegas. She recalled that she earned $8 a day for cleaning about eight rooms. She said, "$8 a day and working in the shade. You know, not back-breaking in the sun. $8 a day, all this money. I wrote back [home] and I said, 'everybody come on out here. White folks gone crazy. They're giving us $8 a day for making a bed and cleaning a bathroom.'"[18]

Las Vegas had another type of migration unique to the city. During the 1960s, law enforcement cracked down on illegal gambling across the United States. Areas that previously allowed gambling in private clubs, particularly where local law enforcement received pay-offs, changed their policies and closed those clubs' doors. Las Vegas became the destination for anyone who wanted to work legitimately in gambling. Dealers of card or dice games began to move their families to the only legal place to work. Bernice Jaeger recounted her family's transition to Las Vegas.

Well, they closed gaming in Kentucky. Gaming had been in northern Kentucky for years and years. It was underground, but everyone knew it was there. Cincinnati was a very conservative city, and all the fun and entertainment was across the river in northern Kentucky. When that closed down in 1961, actually we were one of the first families to come out. I just had a feeling [that] it wasn't going to open again, and where else would you go but Las Vegas, if that's the kind of business you were in.

So we packed up and came out here, and then after a few weeks more and more people came. That whole summer they started to come out, and into the fall. There was a real colony of us. The fellows helped each other find jobs and the women helped each other. We had this box that we kind of circulated through the crowd. When we came, we didn't bring anything. We brought the kids, [the] electric skillet, my sewing machine, four dishes, and some silverware. That was it. We all had to start over, and so we had this box we'd circulate. It had some linens and some pots and pans and a couple of dishes and some old cups and things like that. I know that sounds crazy, but so many of us came without an awful lot until our things got here. So we all helped each other.[19]

Jaeger moved into hotel administration after raising her children and later returned to school for a counseling degree. She became a substance abuse counselor in Las Vegas.

Women at Work

The narrative detail found in oral history provided information about work life that was unavailable in any other source. Las Vegas jobs offered better pay (including tips) or exciting opportunities that countered the long hours, minimal flexibility, and in some cases outright job discrimination faced by our narrators. The twenty-four-hour town meant that dealers and cocktail waitresses might work any one of three daily shifts. Schedules varied until one had some seniority. Bosses frequently took the attitude that if a worker could not meet the scheduling needs, that worker must not want the job. In addition, the hotel-casinos, like most industries of the period, organized jobs by race and gender. The service work in the back of the house was reserved for African Americans in the 1940s through the 1960s. Latinas gradually moved into those jobs, as did a smaller proportion of Southeast Asian immigrants, by 1990. On the casino floor, women could take jobs such as cocktail servers, food servers, and change girls. By the 1990s, positions as dealers had opened up on the Strip.

Although historians have discussed the post-1945 era as one in which women either stayed at home and raised a family or worked out of need, the Las Vegas stories from working women indicate that combining wage earning with family life occurred often. This certainly has been historically true for lower-income working mothers. Yet the Las Vegas case suggests that blending work with family responsibilities happened across occupations and economic class. Many women said they worked shifts that allowed them to be home before or after school to oversee their children. When that did not work, they asked family or neighbors to watch their kids. Some, like dancer and performer Betty Bunch, planned her performance jobs to fit around the early years of her two sons.

> I was in *Bottoms Up* at the Thunderbird by that time and we had a rare day off. . . . [Joel] and I drove up to Tonopah and got married and then very shortly, like three months later, I got pregnant. That's the reason I got married is that I had an attack of baby fever. Then, I stayed in *Bottoms Up*, pregnant, until I was six months along. I danced until I was six months along. Well, that was 1965 and the chemise was the heavy-duty fashion at the time, so, it hid nearly everything. I wore a leotard in the finale, but I had a prop that I could hold over my stomach, and besides, I was a dancer and in marvelous shape, you know, I just looked a little thick.[20]

When her son was six months old, she decided to go on tour with her former company:

> I said, Joel quit your job there at the Desert Inn, dealing, take full time to study real estate to get prepared to take your bro-

ker's license, come with me to the Bahamas to baby-sit Ricky at night so that I can do the show. You need a vacation, you haven't been off in a long time. So, that's what we did. We went with *Bottoms Up*, taking Ricky with us. He was six months old in his little carriage and we worked and we came back and [then] . . . I have a contract for one year at Caesars Palace. Well, I didn't want to miss that. That was the juice job of the world.[21]

When she became pregnant with her second child, she stopped dancing to raise her children. Years later, Bunch returned to stage performance.

Hattie Canty did not enter the workforce when she first came to Las Vegas in the 1960s. She had a big job raising her ten children. She remembered that when she decided to go to work, it was to get a break from all the work at home.

I didn't go to work right away. And when I did decide to go to work, it was in the early 1970s. But I was a homemaker. I took care of my family. I took care of my husband. And by this time, when I did decide to go to work, I was taking care of so many people until I was trying to get out from under all of that. I really didn't know how. The only way I could get out from under it, I thought, if I got myself a job as a maid. I did not know of anything else to do. I had not gone to college for anything. I wasn't trained. Had not taken any kind of course to do anything else. But cleaning a house, I knew I could do that. . . . With the family, I needed something that didn't require a lot of thinking to do. I wanted to relax a little bit because when I get home at night, I didn't want to be so uptight that I couldn't be mom. I had to be mom once I walked into that house. Then for the next four to six hours, I was really mom because I was cleaning and cooking. Maybe by twelve o'clock, I got to bed.[22]

When her husband became very ill and died in 1975, she became the sole support for eight of her ten children who still lived at home. She took a job doing what she knew she could do—cleaning.

I didn't think that I would ever be able to do that because my
husband was the type of husband who had always taken care
of me and the kids. . . . But now the table turns, where I'm
taking care of him and I got everything to worry about. I
stayed home and I took care of him and then when he died,
that's when reality is setting in. The amount of money that he
was bringing home, I had to live off of like a fourth of that
amount of money. . . . So then I didn't go back to the Thunderbird [working as a maid], I went to the school district because I needed to work a shift that I thought that I could take
care of my kids even better. That was a straight swing shift. At
the hotel, I couldn't get a straight swing shift. I worked for
the school district for one year as custodian.[23]

She returned to hotel housekeeping a short time later and gradually
became involved in union organizing. Canty developed her commitment to the labor struggle through that work. She eventually led the
powerful Culinary Union (Local 226 of the Hotel Employees and
Restaurant Employees union) in the 1990s during Las Vegas's longest and most contentious strike.

In the showroom, the glamour obscured the heavy work schedules of performers who worked three shows a night every day of the
week. As Rosemary Tall DeHart recalled, management finally introduced a "swing girl" to give dancers one day off.

Now the singers got a day off a week because there were seven
singers for six spots. So they got a day off a week at that point,
but we didn't. . . . So what they did is they hired a couple of
extra dancers and every six weeks we got four days off. That's
how they worked it. Six weeks, four days off. And then they
had a girl come in for those four days. She did your spot. And
then the next girl goes off and she did that spot.[24]

Dancers and showgirls also provided time and talent as models or
ambassadors for the resort city. They frequently posed for public
relations photos or appeared at special events. According to the narrators, they did it because it was "fun," and they never thought of
being paid. The glamour of entertainment jobs and the opportunity

to work in one's chosen field made up for sometimes demanding work settings.

Job discrimination on the basis of sex and race existed until Congress passed Title VII of the Civil Rights Act in 1964. During the 1950s, women of color performance artists might work as a solo act, such as Lena Horne, or in a single-ethnic group, like the Kim Sisters. Racial integration of acts including the chorus lines of showrooms did not take place until the mid-1970s when legal challenges to race discrimination began to gradually influence hiring patterns throughout the hotel-casino. Also during the late 1970s, women of various racial-ethnic backgrounds began to find work alongside white women in administrative positions.

Jackie Brantley, a Las Vegas native who grew up in the neighborhoods of West Las Vegas, began working as a housekeeper, moved into clerical jobs, then kept moving up to middle management in casino public relations. "The West Side was our village and it was a town where everyone knew everybody," she recounted. "The teachers intertwined with the parents and the neighbors intertwined with the parents and the teachers. And the church had a role. It was just one wonderful place to grow up in—here in Las Vegas."[25] After graduating from high school, Brantley entered the workforce and within a short time became the first African American woman to work in public relations for the Desert Inn Hotel and Casino. She had a high-visibility job and obviously the talent to do it well. In 1998, she recalled, "My position was to represent the hotel, in as much as possible, for any affairs that went on. . . . I pride myself in the fact that I never had to sleep with anyone to keep my job or to get my job. Because I've had people, even Alex Haley ask me, 'How did you get here?' And I told him, 'I got here because I was talented and I'm staying here because I'm talented.'"[26]

Most of the working women interviewed for the project worked across their life span. Some may have left the workforce temporarily to raise children or heal from injuries, but they returned. Rosemary Tall DeHart recounts her shift from showroom entertainer to dealer and then to dance teacher.

> I didn't want to be a cocktail waitress so I decided I'd go to dealing school. So I learned how to deal blackjack and within

ten days I was working at some hokey-pokey downtown joint
called the Lady Luck. . . . I dealt out of a shoe, face up, pick
and pay, let them lay. . . . And all of the crooks used to come
down, because you were what's called a "break-in dealer." . . .
So I was there about three weeks, two days, two swing, and
one grave, which was really hard work. . . . And then I went to
the El Cortez after I got off one day and there was a man that
I knew from dealer school that was dealing at the El Cortez,
and he says to his boss, "You gotta have some girls dealing?
Pick that one. She's sharp." . . . I then went to the Stardust
and I auditioned back at the Stardust with Frank Rosenthal. . . . And then I quit dealing and started teaching [dance]
full-time.[27]

Many entertainers (dancers, singers, and showgirls) found a second career when age or disability took them off the stage. Some
moved into production roles, some opened dance schools, and others sold real estate. Those in service jobs frequently relied on unions
for job protection and transfers.

As civil rights laws opened up new opportunities in some areas,
the casino floor (aside from the aforementioned jobs) remained off-
limits to women dealers and supervisors for another decade. In
1981, the US Equal Employment Opportunity Commission filed a
suit against the Nevada Resort Association to prohibit sex discrimination in employment in casinos on the Las Vegas Strip. Two weeks
later, a consent decree ordered an end to discrimination in hiring.[28]

Building a Better Community

Las Vegas will not be remembered by most historians as the site of
social activism like other western cities, such as San Francisco or
Seattle. The social movements of the 1960s and 1970s appear to
have passed over the resort town with a few notable exceptions.[29]
On a smaller scale, however, narrators talked about their involvement in groups with the design to improve their own lives as well as
benefit the community: movements such as labor organizations,
civil rights, women's rights, combating violence against women and

children, and antipoverty. To paraphrase Margaret Mead, we must not underestimate the ability of a small group of committed individuals; their efforts are responsible for change in the world.[30] The sentiment of these words ring true for the efforts of these Las Vegas community builders. The engagement of ordinary women in public life also refutes the notion that Las Vegas is a city without a soul or conscience. Florence Shilling McClure, whose story opened this chapter, offers a fine example of such a resident.

A few years after leaving the hotel business, McClure became the foremost advocate for rape victims in Las Vegas and the state. In 1973, she attended the first community meeting about the lack of services for women who had been raped and the harsh repercussions of the legal system. Although she had no personal experience of rape, the injustice of the survivors' treatment by hospitals, police, and court systems riled McClure and led her to commit her energies to improve the situation. She learned the ropes of city governance and the state's legislative process through the League of Women Voters. She worked with a handful of concerned citizens to start Community Action Against Rape and volunteered her living room for the organization's office. She and her co-workers began a rape hotline, put rape kits in hospital emergency rooms, and provided counseling services. McClure did not counsel but served as an advocate for victims. Sitting in court, she witnessed attorneys assassinate the character of those who had been raped, watched the accused get off with the flimsiest of defense, and recognized that Nevada's rape laws needed to be changed. She was relentless in her pursuit of justice for rape victims. She studied other states' laws and worked with allies to adapt them to Nevada. She slowly gained the support of elected officials as she lobbied to reform Nevada's statutes.[31]

For McClure and others who took on the work of improving their community in Las Vegas, activism came as a result of their life experiences. They did not set out to be agents of change, but saw a problem that needed a solution and worked to make it happen. How would a historian learn about these community builders without oral history? Newspapers might cover milestones in an organization's history. State legislative records would describe the result of action, but not the process. Although oral histories must be contextualized and not taken at face value, their content gives not only historical detail but glimpses into the hearts and minds of historical actors.

Conclusion

The narrators of the Las Vegas Women Oral History Project make a major contribution to our understanding of the development of Las Vegas, its hotel-casino industry, and the building of the greater community. As workers who moved to the "resort city in the sun," we better understand the mobility of *all* Americans during the postwar expansion, but particularly of women, single or married, as they undertook new ventures and looked for greater opportunities. As wage earners, professionals, or intermittent workers, the experiences of women in Las Vegas indicate a far greater continuity of earning in women's lives than has been previously understood. They describe an environment of plenty of jobs and a tip economy that made the work much more lucrative than in other places. Women blended paid work with family life as part of one whole, not as two separate worlds, to the extent that their jobs allowed. Most of our narrators worked to retirement age, and several professionals continued beyond that. Several who stayed became active in the community. Some improved labor conditions for hotel and restaurant employees. Some worked with the National Association for the Advancement of Colored People to improve civil rights in a town nicknamed "the Mississippi of the West." A few made a commitment to improve the conditions for women and children by changing laws and developing social services. In a city where tourists wondered "does anyone really live in Las Vegas?" the oral histories begin to offer not only an affirmative "yes," but the substance of "why."

Notes

1. Elizabeth Jameson, "Women as Workers, Women as Civilizers: True Womanhood in the American West," *Frontiers: A Journal of Women Studies* 7, no. 3 (1984): 1.

2. Ibid., 7.

3. Susan H. Armitage, "From the Inside Out: Rewriting Regional History," *Frontiers: A Journal of Women Studies* 22, no. 3 (2001): 44.

4. Florence Alberta Schilling McClure, interview by the author [transcript], January 24 and February 6, 1996, Las Vegas Women Oral History Project, Women's Research Institute of Nevada, University of Nevada, Las Vegas, 2006.

5. The scholarship on women in the western states is most fully developed for the period of Euro-American settlement through the early twentieth-century mining booms and Progressive Era reforms. Farming, ranching, and mining dominated the economic life of that period. We know less about urban women in the West, although recent scholarship is changing that. For work on western urban women, see John C. Putman, *Class and Gender Politics in Progressive-Era Seattle* (Reno: University of Nevada Press, 2008); Douglas Flamming, *Bound for Freedom: Black Los Angeles in Jim Crow America* (Berkeley: University of California Press, 2005); Gordon Morris Bakken and Brenda Farrington, eds., *The Gendered West* (New York: Garland, 2001); Gayle Gullet, *Becoming Citizens: The Emergence and Development of the California Women's Movement, 1880–1911* (Urbana: University of Illinois Press, 2000); and a classic in the field of western women's history, Susan H. Armitage and Elizabeth Jameson, eds., *Writing the Range: Race, Class, and Culture in the Women's West* (Norman: University of Oklahoma Press, 1997). See also Quintard Taylor and Shirley Ann Wilson Moore, eds., *African American Women Confront the West, 1600–2000* (Norman: University of Oklahoma Press, 2003). Classic works in US women's labor history offer important characteristics of women's wage-earning experiences, such as occupational segregation, intermittent wage earning, professionalization, and the challenges to unionize women workers. See Alice Kessler-Harris, *Out to Work: A History of Wage-Earning Women in the United States* (New York: Oxford University Press, 1982). In addition to synthetic works, histories of urban working women cover the major areas of employment open to women workers *before* antidiscrimination legislation was passed. These areas included domestic service, manufacturing, retail, and professions like teaching, nursing, and social work. For example, see Dorothy Sue Cobble, *Dishing it Out: Waitresses and Their Unions in the Twentieth Century* (Urbana: University of Illinois Press, 1991); and Vicki Ruiz, *Cannery Women, Cannery Lives: Mexican Women, Unionization, and the California Food Processing Industry, 1930–1950* (Albuquerque: University of New Mexico Press, 1987). On the development of tourism in the American West, see Hal K. Rothman, *Devil's Bargains: Tourism in the Twentieth-Century American West* (Lawrence: University of Kansas Press, 2007).

6. The original project members included the author, Myoung-ja Lee Kwon, Joyce Marshall, and Claytee White. Caryll Dziedziak joined the project later and expanded the interviews with community builders. The process of

creating the Nevada Women's Archives and the origins of the Las Vegas Women Oral History Project may be found in Joanne L. Goodwin, "From the Ground Up: Building Archival Sources for the History of Women in Las Vegas," *Nevada Historical Society Quarterly* (Winter 2006): 263–76; and "Revealing New Narratives of Women in Las Vegas: An Archive of mid-20th Century Experiences," in *Finding Women in the Sources,* ed. Nupur Chaudhuri, Sherry Katz, and Elizabeth Perry (Champaign: University of Illinois Press, 2009).

7. The analysis used census data from four decades, 1940 to 1980. The figures are for the Las Vegas urbanized area, which included the city as well as many unincorporated areas that developed as the city grew. The higher rates of employment by women in Las Vegas when compared to the nation as a whole is clear for 1960 (44 percent versus 35 percent, respectively) and 1970 (47 percent versus 43 percent). By 1980, the gap had closed as national rates increased. Joanne L. Goodwin, "'She Works Hard for Her Money': A Reassessment of Las Vegas Women Workers, 1945–1985," in *The Grit Beneath the Glitter: Tales from the Real Las Vegas,* ed. Hal K. Rothman and Mike Davis (Berkeley: University of California Press), 243–59.

8. For example, married women with a husband present had higher employment rates in Las Vegas than in the United States for 1960 (40 percent versus 31 percent, respectively). The rates remained higher for women with children under age six (28.4 percent versus 18.6 percent) during the same period. "Marital Status of Women in the Civilian Labor Force," *Historical Statistics of the United States, Colonial Times to 1970* (Washington, DC: Government Printing Office, 1975), 133.

9. Goodwin, "'She Works Hard for Her Money'," 251.

10. Sherna Berger Gluck, *Rosie the Riveter Revisited: Women, the War, and Social Change* (Boston: Twayne, 1987).

11. Some, such as African American women and in some economies Latinas, already had long histories of employment during marriage. For the lasting impact of this wartime mobilization, see Claudia D. Goldin, "The Role of World War II in the Rise of Women's Employment," *American Economic Review* 81, no. 4 (1991): 741–56; Shirley Ann Wilson Moore, "'Not in Somebody's Kitchen': African American Women Workers in Richmond, California, and the Impact of World War II," in *Writing the Range: Race, Class, and Culture in the Women's West,* ed. Susan H. Armitage and Elizabeth Jameson (Norman: University of Oklahoma Press, 1997); Joanne Meyerowitz, ed., *Not June Cleaver: Women and Gender in Postwar America, 1945–1960* (Philadelphia: Temple University Press, 1994).

12. Located in the Mojave Desert, roughly halfway between Salt Lake City and Los Angeles, Las Vegas had one abundant resource that made it the choice for a railway stop—water. While the railroad and the springs gave the town its start, federal funds kept it alive with a variety of projects. From the construction of the Hoover Dam during the 1930s, the wartime industries and devel-

opment of Nellis Air Force Base during the 1940s, and the postwar construction of the Nevada Test Site, federal funds greatly assisted the region. By the 1970s and 1980s, the Bureau of Land Management began releasing acreage for development that led to the area's second largest local economy—construction.

13. Betty Bunch, interview by Joyce Marshall [transcript], January 9 and February 7, 1996, Las Vegas Women Oral History Project, Women's Research Institute of Nevada, UNLV, 2006, 7.

14. Rosemary Tall DeHart, interview by Brigid Kelly, November 14, 2002, Las Vegas Women Oral History Project, Women's Research Institute of Nevada, UNLV.

15. Janet Kravenko, interview by Brigid Kelly [transcript], August 7, 2002, Las Vegas Women Oral History Project, Women's Research Institute of Nevada, UNLV, 2006, 7–8.

16. Sarann Preddy, interview by Claytee D. White [transcript], June 5, 1997, and March 11, 1998, Las Vegas Women in Gaming and Entertainment Oral History Project, Women's Research Institute of Nevada, UNLV, 1998, 57, 25. Prior to 1958, a few women worked as card dealers in casinos in the city of Las Vegas. However, job competition became so stiff that a group of male dealers successfully persuaded the city commissioners to prohibit women's employment as dealers. This mandate stayed in effect until 1970, when the city lifted the ban. Women did not deal cards or dice in casinos on the Las Vegas Strip until later. Las Vegas City Commission, Minutes, XI, November 5, 1958, 233–35, Special Collections, Lied Library, UNLV.

17. Lucille Bryant, interview by Claytee D. White, December 13, 1995, Las Vegas Women in Gaming and Entertainment Oral History Project, Women's Research Institute of Nevada, UNLV, 2–3.

18. Ibid., 14–15.

19. Bernice Jaeger, interview by author [transcript], July 25 and 30, 1997, February 3, 1998, Las Vegas Women in Gaming and Entertainment Oral History Project, Women's Research Institute of Nevada, UNLV, 2003, 15–16.

20. Betty Bunch interview, 35–36.

21. Ibid., 36. The term *juice* refers to a connection or relationship that pays off handily for the recipient; in this case, it was a great job.

22. Hattie Canty, interview by Claytee D. White [transcript], February 27 and June 17, 1998, Las Vegas Women in Gaming and Entertainment Oral History Project, Women's Research Institute of Nevada, UNLV, 2000, 4–5.

23. Ibid., 7–8.

24. Rosemary Tall DeHart interview.

25. Jackie Brantley, interview by Claytee D. White [transcript], October 27, 1996, Las Vegas Women in Gaming and Entertainment Oral History Project, Women's Research Institute of Nevada, 1998, 2.

26. Ibid., 17, 20.

27. Rosemary Tall DeHart interview.

28. For a discussion of antidiscrimination reforms by sex and race see, Eugene P. Moehring, *Resort City in the Sunbelt: Las Vegas, 1930–2000*, 2nd ed. (Reno: University of Nevada Press), chap. 6, esp. 201–2.

29. One such exception is the antipoverty movement and the community organizing of Ruby Duncan. Both are discussed in Annelise Orleck, *Storming Caesars Palace: How Black Mothers Fought Their Own War on Poverty* (Boston: Beacon Press, 2005).

30. Cultural anthropologist Margaret Mead is widely attributed with having said "never underestimate the ability of a small group of committed individuals to change the world," but I am aware of no citation in print.

31. Florence Alberta Schilling McClure interview.

10

"Every Woman Has a Story"

Donna Joy McGladrey's Alaskan Adventure

SANDRA K. MATHEWS

Historian Sandra Mathews titles her article "Every Woman Has a Story" and describes how she uncovered the story of her aunt, Donna Joy McGladrey, an extraordinary woman who sought adventure in Alaska but went searching for it as a teacher, a traditional female role. In Alaska, she developed a community with fellow teachers and other local people. McGladrey died in a plane crash, but when Mathews went to Alaska, she found a community that still remembered her aunt and the work she had done there. Through her research, Mathews shows how oral history can re-create the social and community context in which people live their lives. She also shows that oral history gives a voice to ordinary women and provides a context for understanding, as historian Susan Armitage explain, "their coping strategies."[1]

IN 1991, NOTED historian Elizabeth Jameson declared to her Western Women's History students, "Every woman has a story." She then encouraged her students to look for letters, journals, or diaries of our female relatives. As I listened, I remembered some letters that my grandmother had copied and sent to me in the mid-1980s written by her daughter, Donna Joy McGladrey. In the letters from the 1960s, Donna had meticulously described what she perceived as a unique experience that needed to be recorded for posterity: a young white woman from south Chicago moving to the "last frontier"—Territorial Alaska—to teach music in the remote village of Dillingham in the late 1950s. Donna expressed to her mother emphatically: "Please save my letters in your chest . . . I want to write a book someday."[2] Verna diligently saved all of Donna's letters and, after Donna's death, transcribed and copied them for family members. Because Verna had removed some of Donna's descriptions during transcription, I located all of the original handwritten letters and transcribed them in their entirety, and a story began to emerge. Women's history tells historians that sometimes women tend to filter their story to their parents, so after much research, I located Donna's former best friend from high school, June (Swatosh) Delahanty, hoping that she had kept letters as well. Fortunately, June had saved all of the letters Donna had sent to her (as well as the envelopes in which they arrived). Finally, Donna's sisters discovered letters that their father had sent home from Alaska in 1960. Once all of the letters were completely transcribed and assembled chronologically, Donna's story became captivating. Conducting archival research and oral history interviews to fill gaps in her story provided the next logical step to corroborate the information that Donna had shared about living in Alaska and as the first band instructor in Dillingham during the 1958–59 school year.

Donna was born in Mora, Minnesota, twin to Dorothy and sister to Joan. Her older sister, Joan Eik (then Engelsen), told about the conditions in which their parents raised their daughters. Donna's sisters explained the difficulties of living in south Chicago during the Depression, during World War II, and as impoverished daughters of a Methodist minister who worked as an insurance adjuster on the side to make ends meet. They remembered car trips to visit relatives before the war:

DOROTHY: The old-time cars, the electrical equipment or the batteries weren't as good as they are now so when it was raining . . . the windshield wipers would go slow or fast depending on whether you're going uphill or downhill so we would sing, ah, with the windshield wipers being the metronome and we'd be singing really slow and the windshield wipers were going slow 'cause we're going uphill then we'd go real fast 'cause we were going downhill. And we'd just laugh and laugh, laugh so we couldn't hardly sing.

JOAN: I remember one occasion we were traveling . . . anyhow, we were singing hymns . . . one of dad's favorites was, what? [I think?] Earl Marlott's "Are Ye Able" . . . "Are ye able said the master," and uh, there's a part where it says . . .

DOROTHY AND JOAN [*singing*]: Yea the sturdy dreamers answer.

JOAN: And he sang out . . .

DOROTHY AND JOAN [*singing*]: Yea the dirty streamers . . .

JOAN: We laughed all the way to the next state.[3]

The girls obviously enjoyed a fun childhood. But Dorothy and Joan also explained that in the family dynamics, Donna seemed to be the favored child for a variety of reasons—not the least of which was her quiet demeanor, pleasing nature, beautiful singing voice, blonde curly hair (which fraternal twin Dorothy did not share), showmanship qualities, and big dimples on her cheeks like her father. In one long interview, Dorothy revealed which daughter was their mother's favorite: "Donna, Donna was her favorite."[4] Joan said, "I'll tell you what, my, my things was, Donna would do the, the crime and I'd . . . get the time. . . . I know one time I, I confronted mother and I said . . . I didn't do that, whatever it was, Donna did it. She says, I know, but you're here. So, um, we had some bad feelings occasionally, though in retrospect one forgets those things pretty much."[5]

Dorothy and Joan understood that Donna received most of the attention from their parents, so as many children did, they acted out:

DOROTHY: Oh, we had some really good knockdown, drag out fights.

JOAN: I can't remember getting into that kind of a thing with Donna. What we would do, oh, yes, [*laughter*] we had, we had, we had the car rides, lots of car rides. Mom and Dad would sit up front and the three of us were there [Joan, Donna, Dorothy]. Usually we had bare feet and we stuck it around dad's head or out the window or something, but the elbows would start to go as we grew up, and it got worse and worse and then somehow, when it was time for us to be separated we managed, thankfully, that Donna had to sit up front with mother.

DOROTHY: It was the, uh, to sit up front with mother was . . . punishment. . . . But, but there was certain ways you would poke your sisters so that the sister was the one that got in trouble, not you.

JOAN: I'd view Donna as an outsider. She was an independent . . . there was always separate and special about her. Now, I don't know if that's because of the way she was treated, I mean, she was cute. She had her picture taken on the pony, oh gosh, that is one cute picture [see figure 10.1] . . . and we didn't get to . . . I said, can't we have our pictures? No, so. . . . They could only afford one picture, I'm sure.[6]

As the girls recalled their later years, they talked about how they viewed relationships with boys (and how their mother attempted to discourage them by telling them stories that left the girls thinking boys were "smarmy").

DOROTHY: She had a way of warning you about these things that, that made you . . .

JOAN: squirm. . . . Our stomach would churn sometimes. . . . Smarmy, real smarmy.[7]

They explained that, perhaps as a result, Donna never really dated boys (which was relevant in understanding her later life). Dorothy recalled in one interview, "I don't remember her ever dating except the, that one boyfriend tried to take her out and she wouldn't go 'cause he was supposedly mine. But she did ask Jimmy Swatosh to take her to the prom, which he did, so that's the only date I'm aware of in high school that I can remember."[8] Furthermore, their interviews explained Donna's propensity for very high standards, love of music, and their parents' special attention to her.[9] They explained what life was like as a preacher's kid (a PK), with the internal and external pressures that came as a result—many of which influenced Donna's behaviors and likely desire to live far away from watching eyes. The children were scrutinized any time they stepped

Figure 10.1 Donna McGladrey on pony in south Chicago. Photograph courtesy of Dorothy Mathews.

outside their home. For example, they described how the local community watched them carefully:

JOAN: Mother told one story where she was uh, out in the garden, behind the house, and a parishioner came up and chastised her. You're a minister's wife, what are you doing back here? As if she should be above that. . . . Yeah, we were under the microscope.

DOROTHY: Of course, smoking and drinking were totally taboo.

JOAN: We were expected to perform better.

DOROTHY: You had to behave better than than anybody else.

JOAN: But not be snooty.

DOROTHY: Yeah, and not, not feel that you were better than them because you were behaving better than them.[10]

It was a difficult balance that even young girls understood. The community held the family to higher standards than the rest of the parishioners, and Donna seems to have carried this with her, internalized it, and been consumed by it by the time she arrived at all-women's MacMurray College in Jacksonville, Illinois, to work on her music education degree.

When asked about why Donna became a teacher, Joan's immediate response was that "mother was a teacher." Dorothy elaborated, "Well in those days you were either a teacher, a nurse or secretary. That was it. Um, as far as performance, she, she was good, but she wasn't that extra quality . . . and she knew that . . . and many people appreciated the level of quality she was and that's why it was so wonderful in . . . Alaska because they did. She was better than anyone else who lived in the town so that was good for her self-image. And uh, they really appreciated her skills."[11]

After graduating from college, Donna had a one-year teaching position at Meadowbrook Elementary School in Northbrook, Illinois (a more affluent suburb of Chicago). Unfortunately, she encountered issues with attempting to find funding and found herself in conflict with the school board very quickly. As a music instructor, according to Joan, "she thought kids learning music should have something to do music with." Dorothy added, "she sent letters home to the parents asking them to buy . . . recorders, you know, it's the flute-like thing but quite inexpensive. . . . And so she had all [of] the parents' permission and the parents did it, but then she got in trouble with the board of education for doing that." Joan continued, "It was a real unhappy situation and I don't know if she had been fired or if she voluntarily wanted to go, I think she, maybe a little of each." As a final note, Dorothy added, "she felt that the kids were coddled and spoiled. . . . The ones in Alaska were more interested in what she was trying to do and the spoiled ones weren't."[12] By the end of the summer, she found a teaching job in a state where her parents were spending a summer camping. Their descriptions in letter after letter home described the pristine beauty of the waters, forests, and mountains, causing Donna to write them back asking them to find her a job before they returned.

Donna was the first band instructor in the salmon fishing village of Dillingham on the Nushagak River in Bristol Bay, during the 1958–59 school year. In her letters home, she thoroughly shared details about her life, her physical surroundings, and—with the eye of an anthropologist—the town and its people during her year in Dillingham. She wrote her parents, her sisters, and best friend, June Swatosh, about the town and its people, as well as her accomplishments, frustrations, love life, and annoyances. She shared stories about her students, their successes, and foibles, as well as her continued hunt for a place to live and her nonteaching life as a volunteer musician (pianist, organist, and singer). She described crime and subsequent punishment, the economy, the fishing industry and even reported on Russians who had snuck a submarine into Bristol Bay—indeed a scary prospect during the cold war years. She wrote about the poor sanitary conditions and having to haul her own drinking and cooking water from a community well, even in the dead of winter. She announced proudly that she planned to reinvent herself anew in this vast and far-flung frontier. Even more, she delighted in the prospect of living her own life without depending on another person financially or otherwise. She found the latter to be very difficult—especially since she found out in late September that her first paycheck would not arrive until the end of October, a month later than she expected. As difficult as conditions were, she had the "training" to deal with them:

> Our family went camping and when you go camping you carry your own water, you go to the outhouse, you, you do a lot of things from scratch that you don't do in an apartment with all the automatic things and I think that training helped Donna

in Alaska because she was able to, to cope with some things that if you've never done outside, do-it-yourself things that uh, a city girl might not have been able to cope with as well as she did.[13]

Regardless of her plucky attitude, Donna still complained about the children and the people in the community on occasion. Using rather judgmental words describing the children, Joan explained very easily that "you saw that in the letters that she, she used words like spoiled brats and she was judgmental uh, in some ways that, that was very peculiarly characteristic of her language, she didn't have much tolerance for things she didn't agree with so she was a little bit like mother in some, but more outspoken than mother ever was."[14] Years later during interviews, when first asked to describe Donna, almost all of the members of the Dillingham community remembered that she was "beautiful" and "vivacious."

A nice person indeed, but many of the residents also remember her as "sickly" or in poor health. Indeed, she suffered a significant number of ailments while in Dillingham. Some were caused by the poor quality of water hauled from at least two wells in town. She took her water from a community well just below the cemetery that was literally ten feet from the cemetery fence at the bottom of a small hill. Some of her illnesses likely were caused by simply being under stress and teaching children who bring in a variety of ailments. Besides teaching, she found more and more tasks piled onto her already heavy load, such as hosting events and raffles to try to raise money to buy instruments and hand-copying sheet music for every band and choir member. This occupied her time well into the evenings, sometimes until midnight, and she also established friendships that took up some of her time.

One of those friendships included one of the men in Dillingham whose interest she had piqued. From October 1958 until her letters from Alaska stopped in 1959, plumber and student pilot Richard Newton somewhat relentlessly pursued a relationship with her. Richard worked with his brothers, Charles and Royce Newton, for the family business—Matanuska Heating and Plumbing Company. Richard's sister, Mary Anne Mateson, expressed Richard's tendency to smother a girl too much. If Richard took an interest in a woman, she explained, he would always want to be with her or know where she was. Donna wrote, "Sometimes I'm mad about him and other times I can't stand him."[15] She had learned very early in their acquaintance that Richard tended toward jealousy. Even his younger sister, Mary Anne, recalled, "I was thinking about [when] he was jealous of Donna when she wanted to go with that Steve guy and got mad about it . . . I [think] that's what he was like with these girls," adding that sometimes situations in a person's life makes a person "hang on to someone maybe a little too tight."[16]

Donna continued to try to wiggle in some freedom for herself to explore her new independence, but Richard was not going anywhere, for his company had the contract to help construct Dillingham's new high school, slated to open the first week of January 1960. While working on the school, Richard lived in Dillingham, with his brothers flying supplies to him from Anchorage (350 miles east) in their four-seater company plane, a white and silver Cessna 175. When Richard met Donna, he found her very attractive and gave her more attention than she had ever received from a man. According to Donna, Richard's family, and Dillingham locals, he pursued her with much gusto. She quickly became frustrated with his constant interruptions in her life. Richard, however, was very insistent and showed up at her apartment during all hours of the day and night. She described being torn between establishing her own independence and trying not to hurt Richard's feelings by distancing herself from him. Her adventurous side seems to have superseded her need for independence, however, for on numerous occasions she flew with Richard and his brothers and sometimes their hired hand Hermann Kroener in planes[17] to go visit other bush villages like Bethel to bid a plumbing job, or to visit the Newtons' mother who, in her sixties, had taken out a homestead near Willow on the original Iditarod Trail and was proving up on the homestead alone.[18] Even though they spent a lot of time together, Donna and Richard never appeared at the bars or dancehall. In fact, Hilda Kroener, one of Donna's eighth-grade students, asked about Donna's upbringing. When told it was strict and with high expectations, she responded, "I gathered that. I've seen a lot of teachers come to town and they just dated and drank and danced and went out partying and Donna didn't do that. Donna was a church-going girl. And she had good morals. I didn't see anything wild or she didn't use bad language. I mean, she was very prim and proper. . . . She really was."[19] Interviews with Donna's best friend in Dillingham, Tressie Vander Hoek, former students, townspeople, a landlord, neighbors, teacher colleagues, members of the churches that she attended or performed at, elders at the Senior Center, a public health nurse who had lived in Dillingham since the 1950s, various members of the Federal Aviation Administration and local pilots (who flew in the search for her or knew the area), a daily journal kept by town booster David Carlson,[20] and Richard Newton's sister, sisters-in-law, friends, and colleagues, corroborated her participation in the local churches and lack of appearance at bars and the dancehall. Therefore, Donna's circle of friends likely did not include the itinerant workers who participated in the largest salmon fishery in the world, Bristol Bay.

Donna often wrote in her letters about the salmon industry (fishing and canning), the only large employer in the region, and if the fish ran in good numbers, people had money for the entire year. If not, they had to make do—not an easy task on the arctic frontier. People had yearly dry goods and other supplies shipped in by barge from Anchorage between May and September, when the Nushagak River was not frozen, and had to depend on the wholly undependable weather for small aircraft to bring supplies and mail otherwise—a very expensive proposition. Though seemingly isolated, depressed economically, and in Donna's words "uncivilized," other bush villages were even more so—as Donna learned the day after her arrival in Dillingham. Interviews with locals provided context for Donna's commentary about the town and explained the reasons behind her perception of it. So many years later, Dillingham residents (and former residents) filled in many gaps about Donna's experience in Alaska, her interaction with townspeople and schoolchildren, and her relationship with Richard.

One key informant in Dillingham was Verna Lee Heyano, who in 1958 was in Donna's sixth-grade class and remembered her well. A beautiful woman in her fifties when I interviewed her, Verna Lee has an infectious laugh and positive personality. She immediately began telling stories about what it was like to grow up in Dillingham. She described people's livelihood being directly connected with the salmon industry; whether they fished with set nets or on boats or worked in the cannery with the itinerant summer laborers who came in from bush villages, the town lived and died by the salmon run. Because the salmon industry occurred for only a few weeks in the summer, the economy rose and fell with the fishing industry.

The community had few resources for public improvement in the early days. Therefore, children had few opportunities for fun. Verna's father raised money and built a youth center, but with the arrival of water and sewer lines in the 1960s, the building was turned into a fire house, and once again there were no places for the kids to play. While some children had tended toward mischief and horseplay, others practiced musical instruments for hours or borrowed books from the library and rode their bikes. She described how most young teachers came to Dillingham and were gone within a year or two because of the lack of opportunities. Some teachers frequented bars and pool halls, but she and the other kids (who sometimes snuck in to play pool) never saw Donna at those places. She vividly remembered Donna's time in Dillingham, as well as her death. Her memories about life in Dillingham provided great context about Dillingham's local history. She pointed me to an extant diary collection at the Samuel K. Fox Museum, located at the library (which her dad built), written by David Carlson, an early town founder.

She described the beginning of electrification in Dillingham (that her father helped bring), and how before electrification, the town's residents used windmills for power. She introduced me to many locals who expanded Donna's description of Dillingham in the late 1950s, including Lyle Smith, JoAnne Armstrong, V. I. Braswell, Wayne Schroeder, Dorothy Erickson, and many others. Verna insisted that I interview Hilda Kroener and her husband, Hermann, who used to live in Dillingham but had since moved to Chugiak.

She laughed as she began telling me story after story about life as a child in Dillingham during the 1940s and 1950s. One of her stories involved recess breaks and children as young as the sixth grade going into the cemetery just up the hill behind the school to hide in the high weeds and smoke cigarettes. They smoked until a cloud formed in the air above the weeds and a neighbor came out of her house and shooed them back to the playground. I burst out laughing, retrieved the transcripts of Donna's letters, and read to Verna Lee from one of them: "Smoking as low as the 6th grade is common."[21]

Hilda Kroener told me that when Donna arrived, "no one played even an instrument at school when she came to town."[22] This corroborated what Donna had written in a letter on arriving, "The school had had no music program previously. Therefore, I have to start with nothing—no music except for a few [picture] books."[23] This provides another example of the importance of pursuing interviews to corroborate what researchers can learn from journals, letters, or diaries. Donna's former students' stories continued and provided a far better understanding of the community from a child's point of view—a point of view that proved valuable to understanding Donna's life and the frustrations she faced as a teacher.

Another important informant about Dillingham's history was JoAnne Armstrong, another longtime resident. Armstrong was a public health nurse who also owned an air cargo company with her husband, Richard (Dick) Armstrong. JoAnne shared stories about public health, local politics, development of sanitation and public power, and many other incidentals about living in Dillingham. Perhaps the most interesting stories that she shared had to do with two issues: public health and Ann Carr (Donna's roommate). She recalled that when Donna lived in Dillingham, no public sewage or water system existed. She and Mary Newton, Richard's sister-in-law, described how the springtime yielded melting fecal matter from sled dogs as well as humans. Armstrong explained her son sank into the leach pond from the Dillingham Hotel when he was walking just up the street from their home. She campaigned tirelessly for a city sewer system that was finally completed in the 1960s.

Hilda Kroener also provided recollections about Ann Carr that illustrated her demanding nature, but reiterated that she must have been a good teacher because, as Hilda said, "we learned a lot."[24] Hilda, Verna Lee, and JoAnne all provided several stories about Ann Carr that perfectly corroborated Donna's descriptions of her roommate: an overbearing, self-centered, yet talented teacher. Every conversation had to be directed by Ann, even if she entered

late into an existing conversation. It therefore came as no surprise
that Donna and Ann had periodic disagreements.

Like JoAnne, longtime Dillingham resident Lyle Smith was second only to Verna Lee in telling wonderful and detailed stories
about the village in a highly energetic and engaging way. Lyle had
many stories about growing up in Dillingham during the 1940s
and 1950s, providing information about windmills, power generation for the school and surrounding buildings, being hired by
teachers to run errands (such as hauling water from the wells), what
businesses people seemed to frequent in town, and what people did
for fun. He provided an interesting explanation of the tower not
readily identifiable in an early photograph of the school. It was, in
fact, a windmill—but Lyle knew the story about why the windmill
had no blades.[25]

Another fascinating character was Wayne Schroeder, a local me-
chanic whose shop used to belong to his father, the former Dillingham school bus driver Hermann Schroeder. He proved very forth-
right with information, I discovered. Wayne admitted he remembered
Donna's dimples and pretty blonde hair. He was one of those boys
who whistled at Donna during recess and had written, "Gee, you're
pretty!" on his homework for her to see—something that Donna
had written home about as both flattering and later annoying.
Wayne never owned up to it directly, but he always had a big grin on
his face, revealing his complicity. His wife confirmed my suspicions.
Many other residents I interviewed in Dillingham filled in important
information about the town and its fascinating history, its depen-
dence on salmon, its multicultural population, and how people interacted. They were sad to see Donna leave Dillingham—especially
the boys.

In the summer of 1959, Donna distanced herself from Richard
and returned to Illinois to attend Northern Illinois University and
work toward her master's in music education. During that summer,
Joan and Donna spent a great deal of time together, talking about
life. Joan's husband, Malvin, had gone home to Norway to be with
his ailing mother, so Joan had more time to spend in conversations
with Donna:

> So I was down there and Donna was in Waterman [Illinois]
> for the summer and she was taking some classes at, at North-

ern Illinois University. So in the evening . . . Donna would
frequently come over and we would, we would chat . . . she
shared some of her confusion about Richard. . . . this is something that, that we didn't talk about frankly in those days but
she was approaching confusions about her sexual progressions
and stuff and I don't know to what point she'd gotten but she
felt a great danger about going beyond what we were supposed to have done and at that point because their relationship was pretty intense and she really didn't know. She, she felt
as if she, she would go over the edge, you see, if she stuck with
him any longer. . . . I was there and it was really kind of a nice
summer in that respect because it was one of the few times I
got to know her as an adult. . . . And that's the time that we
were the most, the closest as grown-ups, the only time, really. . . . She was wavering I think but I think she, she, my
sense is that she had the realization that she would have to
decide one way or the other because it would go beyond what
we were taught if she didn't make a decision.[26]

Donna returned to Alaska in the fall of 1959, not to Dillingham
but to teach music in Chugiak, a small homesteading community
twenty minutes north of Anchorage with its restaurants and, most
important, music stores.[27] To enhance her continued sense of freedom, she purchased a cream-colored Volkswagen Beetle, and before school began, she and three of her friends from Dillingham
headed south to the Kenai Peninsula to visit Seward, Homer, and
Ninilchik. Tressie Vander Hoek, her best friend, had met Donna
during her one-year residence in Dillingham while her husband,
Guy, worked on the new high school (just like Richard had done).[28]
Roberta Tew and Martha Jay, Church of Christ lay missionaries
that had befriended Donna in Dillingham, surprised Donna by flying to Anchorage to join her on this gal pal trip.
    While Donna wrote about this adventure in her letters home and
took photographs along the way, no letters described in great detail
the important conversations she had with her friends. Tressie's interviews, therefore, provided excellent clues into their trip, either
camping or staying in church basements (where she said they encountered a group of Dillingham children). She said that Donna

felt especially free since Richard was still in Dillingham working on the school and not at his shop in Anchorage.[29] Tressie remembered how much happier Donna seemed teaching in Chugiak than in Dillingham, crediting her newfound glee with not having to deal with Richard on a daily basis and therefore having more time to establish real friendships with her colleagues (as well as continue her friendship with Tressie, who had moved to Anchorage). Back in Dillingham, Donna had often trekked nearly a mile out to Tressie's house on Windmill Hill to hide from Richard, hang out with Tressie and her son, Richie, often complaining about his oppressive persistence. As the school year progressed, Donna became busier, Tressie explained, and she had less and less time to "goof off. . . . She seemed to be happier in Chugiak."[30]

Donna began to complain in her letters that by December 1959 she missed her family, something that Tressie corroborated. Christmas without her family was difficult, and although she had access to the airport in Anchorage, she could not afford to fly home in 1959. To make matters worse, her beloved kitten, Chena (given to her by Richard in September), was hit by a vehicle and severely injured. Now she was going to spend Christmas very much alone, in her little trailer across from Chugiak Elementary School. In hopes of alleviating her sadness, Richard volunteered to fly her out to Dillingham to visit her friends Bobby and Marty over the break while he fixed items tagged on the school by inspectors.[31]

Subsequent interviews with Tressie and Richard's family corroborated Donna's depression about being without her family again, as well as her decision to fly with Richard to Dillingham to visit her friends over Christmas break. They warned him about flying with a passenger without a pilot's license and about the weather. Donna met Richard at Anchorage's Merrill Field on December 30 around ten in the morning. Richard's family and one of his co-workers explained that Richard had not received clearance to fly due to weather conditions, low ceiling, and the potential for storms. Instead of calling off the trip, he suggested they wait for flight clearance at Peggy's Café, across the street from the airfield, calling home and to fellow plumber Donald Wagner numerous times. Donald tried to convince Richard to put off his trip until the next day, as each hour they waited gave them one less hour of daylight.

Interviews with Donald proved illuminating regarding Richard's last few hours. By 2 p.m., they awaited clearance at Peggy's Café. The weather out west was socked in by storms, making flying difficult. Still just a student pilot, Richard was not instrument rated, meaning he flew only by visual contact with the ground below—therefore, he needed daylight to navigate the difficult terrain, which included Clark Pass, Lake Iliamna, and numerous other mountain ranges. Around 2:30 p.m., Richard finally received clearance, but only two hours of sunlight remained—and the trip would take them nearly four hours, assuming they had no headwind. They loaded into the Cessna—the first time he had flown with her alone—and headed west. They never made it.

Interviews with Richard's family members as well as numerous bush pilots and air traffic control officials explained more about the flying conditions, regulations on student pilots, and the thought processes of Richard on that cold December day. Richard contacted Air Traffic Controller Lt. Earl Gay at the King Salmon control tower at 4:50 pm, some six minutes after the sun had set, and Gay knew Richard was in trouble. A blinding storm with very strong winds had overtaken the area and the transcript of the communication indicated that Gay quickly learned that Richard had no instrument training. Gay didn't know that a petrified Donna sat next to Richard in the plane—after all, it was illegal for a student pilot to fly with passengers. Gay attempted to determine Richard's location and head him in the proper direction. Unfortunately, two minutes after their last communication, Gay could not make radio contact anymore. He feared the worst. With the sun below the horizon, the search had to wait until the next morning. First beginning at Etolin Point (south of Dillingham), and working north, east, and west, every available pilot took to the air. By January 1, they realized they could not find the plane quickly, and Donna's minister (who headed the Civilian Air Patrol search) contacted her parents.

Donna's father, Reverend Leslie D. McGladrey, borrowed money and flew to Alaska to help with the search. He could not fly, but as he wrote, "Extra 'eyes' are welcome in search so we hope to ride along and help some pilots look." He continued, "We will be issued arctic clothing before we are allowed to take off. Everyone here still talks of a 'good chance of survival,' and tell tales of things

fully as bad as this that have turned out okay."[32] Writing many letters back, he described the frustration and futility of searching for a
white plane on the snow-covered tundra of Alaska. Interviews with
numerous others involved in the search effort, although many years
removed, also revealed the frustrations of searching for downed
planes in the middle of winter: being grounded due to poor visibil-
ity with conditions of blowing snow and trying to locate a plane
buried under drifts. Many of those I interviewed remembered this
particular plane wreck like it was yesterday.

Some members of Chugiak remembered Donna well, including
her former landlord, Margaret Swanson, the widow of Paul Swanson, the Chugiak school agent. Paul was in charge of finding housing for all teachers, including Donna. In fact, when Donna arrived,
the Swansons had no housing for her, so according to Margaret,
Donna actually lived at their house with them until a trailer was
available. Margaret had been the recipient of some of the items in
Donna's trailer after her death. "Oh, it was the best pea soup I ever
had," she said of the pea soup Donna had made and put in her
freezer before she died.[33]

Zona Dahlman, one of Donna's teacher colleagues at the Chugiak Methodist Church, smiled at a description that Donna had
sent home of her friend Zona: "4th grade, single, teacherish, nice,
pal together. Love skiing and square dancing."[34] Zona remembered
Donna well and remembered something else that was a bonus: her
kitten, Chena. Donna loved that kitten, but at one point thought
she would have to give Chena up. She developed a severe case of
hives and feared an occurrence of cat scratch fever, or at the very
minimum allergies. She could not bear giving up her cat, which she
loved so dearly. Donna described in many letters what a sweet kitten it was. Zona, however, told a much different story, "It was an
attack cat!"[35] Zona remembered that Donna would sit down on her
couch with Chena, who was asleep on the window ledge behind
her. Waking, Chena would stalk her, then the kitten would leap at
her neck with claws drawn. With the memory seemingly very fresh,
Zona described how sometimes Donna needed help disengaging
Chena from her neck. She often came to school with scratch marks
on her neck, arms, and legs. She remembered the yummy pea soup,
where Donna's trailer was located, the troubles that the teachers

had acquiring housing, the fun they had square dancing and hanging out together as friends—all of the things that Donna had talked about in letters home.

Les and Dorothy Fetrow, longtime members of the Chugiak Methodist Church, barely remembered Donna, but they remembered meeting her father when he arrived in January 1960 to join in the search for Richard's downed plane. Together with Leslie's letters, the Fetrows provided the background for Leslie's interaction with the community of Chugiak. They remembered "like it was yesterday": Leslie's talk at the church on Sunday morning, describing his search for Donna out in Bristol Bay, his heartfelt frustration and anguish at not finding her and having to return home to his job knowing that Donna had likely not survived and remained out on the frozen tundra. They remembered the small congregation, filled mostly with their family members, in tears. Les took Leslie fishing, to get his mind off of his sorrows, and remembered him with great fondness. Conversations with them were well timed; within a few years, they passed away or could not remember any longer.[36]

Also in Chugiak lived Hilda and Hermann Kroener, the former eighth-grade student of Donna's and her husband, who had worked with Richard. The Kroeners proved to be, next to Verna Lee Heyano, the most important informants on the entire project in Alaska. The name Hermann Kroener was familiar to the McGladrey family: Hermann had traveled with Donna and Richard to Stella Eva Newton's Susitna homestead in October 1958. Even more, he had taken the photograph of Donna and Richard in the motorboat that appeared in Donna's photo album—one of the only Alaska photographs that Verna had included in Donna's album (see figure 10.2). Hermann worked for the Newton brothers as a plumber and had gone to Bethel with Richard and Charles—the same trip that carried Donna. Perhaps most sobering, Hermann was with Charles when he rented a float plane, then hiked five miles over the Alaskan tundra to the crash site when Orin Seybert, president of PennAir, found the wreckage of the Newton's plane in mid-June 1960. He and Richard were the first people on the ground at the crash site before the Civil Aviation Authority was able to remove Richard's and Donna's remains. Over forty years later, and with Charles New-

Figure 10.2 Richard Newton and Donna McGladrey on the Susitna River. Photograph courtesy of Hilda and Hermann Kroener.

ton's and Orin Seybert's descriptions of the crash site location, Hermann was able to bring out some older FAA maps and measure to within a half mile the actual location of the downed plane and help me locate it on a map during a tremendously revealing interview.[37]

Hilda, much like Verna Lee, provided a plethora of information about growing up in Dillingham and classroom activities (and antics by the children). She described, as Donna had and Verna Lee explained further, the depressed economic situation in town and how that sometimes led to despair, and therefore alcoholism. More important, she was the first to share with me information about Donna in the classroom—and Hilda's perspective proved invaluable. After taking music with Donna and being inspired, Hilda realized that she wanted to be a music teacher just like Donna. Hilda was "in [Donna's] music class, and I loved every bit of it. She was so, seemed like she was just so vivacious, I just loved being in her class because she just, boy she, and she made us do the right thing!"[38] She continued, "and I used to wish I was as pretty as she was. Just peaches 'n cream complexion, and the blonde hair . . .

and seemed like there was never a strand out of place. And her figure was gorgeous and just, she was just a nice person."[39] She talked
about how Donna taught them how to sing on key and eventually
in harmony (which Donna described in her letters). Hilda described
how Donna taught them to sing in rounds, something the children
had never done before, as a way to help them understand harmony.
Hilda then broke out into song, singing one of the songs that
Donna had taught her more than forty years before.

Donna wrote about yelling at the students until she turned blue,
and on occasion using corporal punishment. Hilda explained that
Donna had to be harsh sometimes because the boys teased her in
class. She said, nevertheless, that Donna was a great teacher and she
wanted to be just like her. She explained that even though she
wanted to be a music teacher, she met Hermann Kroener when he
did some work on their house after Richard's death. They fell in
love with each other and a short time later were married. She
laughed, saying that she had wanted to be a music teacher not a
fisher, but ended up marrying a plumber who fished every summer.

Finally, Hilda remembered being devastated when she heard of
Donna's and Richard's deaths. "It shouldn't have happened," she
repeated. "They never should have flown that day." From former
students to local commercial and air cargo pilots like John Paul
Bouker, all agreed. "They had get-homitis," Bouker said. Hilda
reiterated, "there are old pilots and bold pilots, but no old bold
pilots."[40]

A few years later, in April 2007, Hilda and Hermann's son, Mar-
vin, found the wreckage, which had never been recorded on an accessible map, by using the information gleaned from newspaper
reports from 1958 and 1959 in the Anchorage, Bristol Bay, and
various other newspapers, as well as my previous interviews. It was
just as Charles had described it in his letter to my grandfather some
forty-eight years ago:

> The plane exploded and burned on impact. The left door was
> torn off and lay about five or six feet out and a little behind its
> opening. The left ski and main gear was lying about five feet
> behind it. The nose gear was under the front seat and the right
> main gear was under the baggage compartment. They were

known to be wearing two knit sweaters. Each had a parka, and three sleeping bags were in the plane, however, the only cloth found was a small polka dot piece of blouse and a very small piece of green shadow plaid wool shirt. The heat was so intense that 2 steel wrenches were fused together. The entire fuselage except the empennage or tail feathers was melted down to a few small blobs of metal. Death was between breaths, instantaneous and merciful. They suffered from the fire not at all.[41]

Donna's father failed to find her. Alaska hid the Newtons' white Cessna under snowbanks throughout the winter, and the tundra only revealed itself to a pilot who flew off the typical trajectory between Egegik on the Alaskan Peninsula to Dillingham's hospital due to a medical emergency. Although Donna did seem most favored by her parents, in the end, she moved the farthest from home. About her decision, her sisters drew the same conclusions:

DOROTHY: Well, we really felt that she wanted to do this and so we were kind of proud of her going away on an adventure like that, and we were happy for her that she was doing something she really wanted to do, but it was awfully far away because there wasn't email and . . . you just didn't pick up the phone and call because we were too frugal to make long-distance phone calls like that.

JOAN: I think I felt just a tiny bit uneasy at her going so far as I recall, not, not for any good reason.

DOROTHY: Well, mother liked to brag about her.

JOAN: Yeah, she did. . . . Dad was not much given to talking about those things that I recall. I mean, he, he always just grinned. He was proud of all his kids no matter what they did at least that's the impression I got. . . . She seemed to be happier in Chugiak. I don't think that the pressures were so, so heavy. And she still had her friendships. She must've been looking forward to that little trip going back to see Martha and Roberta, who ironically died in a plane crash ten years later.[42]

When this project began, questions to informants were simple but integral in formulating the project. As the project grew larger, I quickly understood the importance of oral history to understanding Donna's life in the context of community, both Dillingham and Bristol Bay as well as Chugiak. More important, thanks to the perspectives that these informants shared, the final project, *Between Breaths: A Teacher in the Alaskan Bush* (Albuquerque: University of New Mexico Press, 2006), is much more robust and contextual. Interviewees helped me understand what it was like growing up in Dillingham and Chugiak, living in remote places such as bush villages in Alaska, as well as understanding aeronautical history, stories of others who had lost relatives and friends, and local history, homesteading history, the fishing industry, southwest Alaska, Alaskan history in general, and so much more. These interviews, supplemented with research at local, state, regional, and national archives in Illinois, Alaska, and Washington, DC, gave a far broader context for Donna's life in the Alaskan bush.

In the end, the scope of this oral history project was far greater than I had ever expected. After compiling more than fifty hours of interviews with numerous informants, and only a portion of them transcribed, these tapes informed a significant portion of *Between Breaths*. Without her letters, interviews with her family, and being able to track down and interview friends, colleagues, and other acquaintance who understood what it was like to live in bush Alaska during the 1950s, the book never could have happened. To these informants, many of whom I have considered dear friends now, I will always be grateful.

Notes

1. Susan Armitage and Sherna Berger Gluck, "Reflections on Women's Oral History: An Exchange," *Frontiers: A Journal of Women Studies* 19, no. 3 (1998): 6.

2. Donna McGladrey to Verna and Leslie McGladrey, September 1958, Dillingham, Alaska. This letter and all subsequent letters and photographs (unless otherwise indicated) are in the author's private archive collection. During transcription, Verna eliminated phrases and words from Donna's original letters, inserting in their place, " [items omitted]," which was unacceptable to me as a researcher.

3. Joan Eik and Dorothy Mathews, interview by author, June 2000, Blaine, Minnesota. All recordings are in author's possession.

4. Dorothy Mathews, interview by author, June 2000, Blaine, Minnesota.

5. Joan Eik, interview by author, June 2000, Blaine, Minnesota.

6. Ibid.

7. Joan Eik and Dorothy Mathews interview.

8. Dorothy Mathews interview.

9. They purchased three photographs of Donna on the horse and put one in each of the girls' albums, a stark reminder of their parents' preference, they recalled.

10. Joan Eik and Dorothy Mathews interview.

11. Ibid.

12. Ibid.

13. Ibid.

14. Joan Eik interview.

15. Sandra Mathews, *Between Breaths: A Teacher in the Alaskan Bush* (Albuquerque: University of New Mexico Press, 2006), 89.

16. Mary Anne Mateson, interview by author, March 2000, Palmer, Alaska.

17. Richard, Royce, and Charles Newton had hired German immigrant Hermann Kroener to work with them. All three men have passed away, Charles first in the late 1980s, then Royce in 2000, then Hermann within a year or two of our last interviews.

18. I learned all of this while conducting interviews in Palmer, Alaska, with Royce's widow, Ruby Newton; Charles's widow, Mary Newton; and Richard's sister closest in age, Mary Anne Mateson, during my first research trip to Alaska in 2000.

19. Mathews, *Between Breaths*, 85.

20. David Carlson wrote in a journal daily about the goings-on in Dillingham for over fifty years. Several of the journal entries mention Donna McGladrey's performances in church and her student performances to raise money to purchase band instruments. Photocopies of his journal pages can be found in binders at the Dillingham Public Library in Dillingham, Alaska.

21. Donna McGladrey to Malvin and Joan Eik, November 4, 1958, Dillingham, Alaska. Letters in author's collection.

22. Mathews, *Between Breaths*, 73.

23. Ibid.

24. Hilda Kroener, interview by author, July 2001, Chugiak, Alaska.

25. The wind in Bristol Bay blew with great intensity, making wind power generation a logical source. In one particular day, the sustained winds were tremendous and the windmill began to spark, scream, and then tip. Because of its enormous size, people were afraid it would cause tremendous damage if it fell. According to Smith, he scrambled to the top of the windmill to stop the blades, but he could not move the lever. The wind tore the blades from the

windmill across the tundra, and the blades were never found by the residents. Lyle Smith, interview by author, July 2001, Dillingham, Alaska.

26. Joan Eik interview.

27. Dillingham had offered her another contract, but it would have required her to teach English as well as music (and likely physical education, as well). She opted for Chugiak instead.

28. By the fall of 1959, Tressie had returned to Anchorage with her husband and son, Richie (named for Richard Newton).

29. Unfortunately, Roberta Jay and Martha Tew died in an airplane wreck in the 1960s, so I was unable to interview them. They would have provided key information about Donna's life in Dillingham and her relationships with Richard and other men in the community.

30. Mathews, *Between Breaths*, 118.

31. According to Mary Newton, Matanuska Heating and Plumbing Company had finished their work on the high school, but inspectors had tagged a few items that needed fixing prior to the school's scheduled opening in early January. Therefore, there was some urgency to their arrival in Dillingham. Mary Newton, interview by author, July 2001, Palmer, Alaska.

32. Letter from Leslie David McGladrey to Verna McGladrey, January 4, 1960, Elemendorf Air Force Base, Alaska. Letter in author's private collection.

33. Margaret Swanson, interview by author, July 2000, Chugiak, Alaska.

34. Donna McGladrey to Verna and Leslie McGladrey, Chugiak, Alaska, October 27, 1958.

35. Zona Dahlman, interview by author, July 2001, Chugiak, Alaska.

36. Margaret was in a retirement home and has since passed away, and Les and Dorothy Fetrow have developed various ailments, which has impaired their memories of the past. Shirley Mauldin, interview by author, July 2001, Chugiak, Alaska.

37. Orin Seybert founded and is the owner of Peninsula Airlines, and has flown in Alaska for more than forty years. In June 1960, he was flying "on the deck" (low) from Egegik to Dillingham to deliver a patient to the hospital at Kanakanak, just outside of Dillingham. He had to hurry, so he took a shorter route over more open water and spotted a downed craft—which he promptly reported. The plane turned out to be Richard's Cessna. Orin Seybert, interview by author, July 2000, Anchorage, Alaska.

38. Hilda Kroener, interview by author, March 17, 2001, Chugiak, Alaska.

39. Ibid.

40. Hilda Kroener interview by author, July 2007, Dillingham, Alaska; John Paul Bouker, interview by author, July 2007, Ekuk, Alaska.

41. Charles A. Newton to Mr. McGladrey, Anchorage, Alaska, June 16, 1960.

42. Joan Eik and Dorothy Mathews interview. Roberta Tew and Martha Jay had both become pilots and were real pioneers in Alaska's aviation history. Roberta acquired a pilot's and a commercial license, her instrument rating, and

even became a flight instructor. She was the first woman to fly for Western Alaska Airlines, according to Michael Moran, the son of Myron Moran, who helped lead the search for the Newton crash so many years ago. Michael Moran, phone interview by author, 2007. Unfortunately, in the winter of 1968, the F-27 that carried Roberta and Martha, as well as thirty-nine others (many of whom lived in Dillingham), suffered a catastrophic event. According to interviews, the wing fell off, but according to newspaper reports, an explosion caused the tail section to break off. Just short of Lake Iliamna near San Pedro Bay, the pilots lost control of the aircraft and they all lost their lives. Mathews, *Between Breaths*, 182.

11

Searching for the Rest of the Story

Documenting the Dee School of Nursing

JOHN SILLITO, SARAH LANGSDON,

AND MARCI FARR

Historians John Sillito, Sarah Langsdon, and Marci Farr illustrate one area in which women's work "has always been gendered"[1] in documenting the experiences of women who trained as nurses at Ogden, Utah's Dee School of Nursing. This documentation was possible only through oral history. Oral history allowed the authors to move beyond the institutional records, which documented only the classes available to discussing the motives, experiences, and female networks of the students. The women were delighted to share their memories along with photographs and personal papers. The Weber State University Special Collections Department has become the repository for this wisdom.

IN OGDEN, UTAH, on July 12, 1905, storekeepers closed their shops, schoolchildren lined city streets, public officials turned away from their duties, and hundreds of prominent and ordinary citizens gathered at the Ogden Tabernacle to mark the funeral of Thomas D. Dee. The *Ogden Standard* called him the city's "foremost citizen," noting that "no other man in Ogden was identified with so many and diverse enterprises."[2] Indeed, over his lifetime,

Dee made a major impact on Ogden's business, religious, educational, political, and governmental life. His death came a few days earlier as a result of contracting capillary bronchitis after falling into the chilly Ogden River while searching for additional water sources for the city.[3]

For his widow, Annie Taylor Dee, the shock of his sudden death brought back sad memories of the loss of their oldest son, Thomas Reese Dee, a decade earlier. In an attempt to save young Thomas, surgery was performed on the family's dining room table because no suitable medical facility existed in Ogden. The combination of these losses led Annie Dee to resolve that she would spend her life and resources bringing better medical care to the city she loved. Her determination led to the creation of a hospital that still exists, though in a much different form, as well as a nursing school that operated from 1911 to 1955.[4] The latter aspect of that story forms the focus of this essay.

Recently, we conducted an oral history program at Weber State University that was intended to deepen our understanding of the nursing school, the nurses themselves, and the effect the school and its graduates had on northern Utah. To create perspective, we also offer a general overview of the history of the hospital and, more particularly, the nursing school associated with it. We outline the extant archival and printed sources that document the nursing school's growth, development, and decline. Finally, we describe the way the oral history project expanded the documentary heritage already existing in our Special Collections department. Despite the wealth of material housed at Weber State, it became apparent that we required more depth to understand the nurses and their training. How did they view this experience? What could we learn about the texture of their lives, which lay invisibly within the official records? Because the last class had graduated more than a half century ago, we believed an oral history program was essential to capture the memories of an increasingly diminishing group of women.[5]

In July 1909, a little over four years after her husband's death, Annie Dee began her efforts to create a hospital with a contract let under the auspices of the Thomas D. Dee Company. Prior to that, Annie and other family members, assisted by their friend, Dr. Robert Joyce, who was also the family physician, studied many of the best hospitals in the United States, Canada, and Europe. The Dees envisioned a facility that would not be a strictly "charitable hospital"; investors would not receive dividends, and all funds exceeding operating expenses would be used for maintenance and improvements.[6] Ogden architect L. S. Hodgson was selected to design the hospital, which was described by the *Deseret News* as one of the most modern medical facilities in the country, one where every aspect would "be complete and perfect in its detail."[7] The contract to build the hospital was awarded to C. J. Humphris of Ogden for $46,625.[8]

On February 3, 1910, the Thomas D. Dee Memorial Hospital Association was incorporated with Annie Dee as president. A few days later, she and her children conveyed to the association the legal title held by the Dee Company to a three-acre tract of land located on the city's east side at Harrison Boulevard between Twenty-Third and Twenty-Fourth Streets. The articles of incorporation stated that the association's purpose was "maintaining, operating, and conducting hospitals and other institutions for the care and treatment of sick, wounded, injured, or infirm persons; [and] of maintaining schools and other places for the education and training of nurses." The enterprise also gained the support of a number of prominent citizens, local businesses, several fraternal and social organizations, and the Relief Societies of both the Ogden and Weber stakes of the Church of Jesus Christ of Latter-day Saints (LDS). This breadth of support for the proposed hospital demonstrates the crucial degree of the area's medical needs and signifies Ogden's status as an expanding commercial and population center in northern Utah.

Although the facility was not technically complete until 1911, the dedication took place December 29, 1910. As city, county, medical, and business leaders looked on, Annie Dee "for and behalf of the Thomas D. Dee company, and the family of my beloved husband," formally tendered to the populace of Ogden and Weber County "the exclusive use and title to the grounds, together with the hospital and other buildings," with the goal of "relieving, curing, and restoring those suffering human beings that shall come under . . . care and treatment within these walls."[9] In addition to space for seventy-five patient beds, the new building included room for offices, with a furnace room and laundry constructed in the rear.

Two days after the dedication, fifteen patients were transferred from Ogden General Hospital accompanied by five graduate nurses: Maude Edwards, Beda Nelson Woodbury, Winifred Howard Jarvis, Alice Manning, and Mary Hornsby. Three student nurses were also transferred: Anna Hansen, Ethel Edwards, and Marie Rasmussen. Maude Edwards was named superintendent of nurses, and Dr. Robert Joyce became chief of a staff that included thirty-two physicians.[10]

Within the first few years, however, problems arose, and by 1914, insufficient funds threatened to shut the hospital doors.[11] In response, the Catholic Church offered to take over operations. Father Patrick M. Cushnahan, pastor of Ogden's St. Joseph's parish and a member of the hospital board, promised to retain the hospital's name, operate the facility in perpetuity, and keep it "open to all suffering humanity in a manner that Ogden City can be proud of."[12] Ultimately, however, in March 1915, local business leaders and the presidents of the Ogden and Weber stakes arranged for the hospital's transfer to the control of the LDS Church, while retaining the Dee Hospital name.[13] Since then, both the name and location have changed, twice moving the facility further south on Harrison Boulevard. Currently, as part of the Intermountain Health Care System, the McKay-Dee Hospital continues to expand the sophistication of its medical technology and service to the community.

As previously mentioned, nurses were part of the hospital's development from the beginning. Trained initially at the Ogden General Hospital, the five nurses and three student nurses who transferred in 1910 formed the first faculty and student body of the Thomas D. Dee Hospital School of Nursing, as specified in the articles of incorporation. The establishment of the nursing school was part of a national trend that was also reflected throughout Utah. Between 1894 and 1911, nursing schools were established in conjunction with St. Mark's, Holy Cross, and Groves-LDS hospitals, which were all in Salt Lake City, as well as Budge Hospital in Logan. Though each nursing school was tied to a hospital, some were also linked to religious denominations. From its inception, the Dee

Hospital was prepared to meet the need for a school of nursing in Ogden.[14]

The first students enrolled in a two-and-a-half-year program under the direction of Maude Edwards, who was also the hospital's director of nursing. After Edwards resigned, Annie J. Hall, a graduate of St. Mark's Hospital Training School for Nurses, took over in 1912 and is "generally given credit for raising the standards of the training school." She lengthened the training period to three years and opened an obstetrics division to encourage childbirth in the hospital rather than at home.[15]

The nursing program was strenuous. Nurses worked a twelve-hour shift in the hospital with a two-hour rest period if they were not too busy, and one-half day off each week. Classes were held in the evenings. Initially, the student nurses lived in the basement of the hospital, and at different periods in homes in the neighborhood. Discipline was strict, and the nurses were required to check in and out and observe a 10 p.m. curfew, though once a month the curfew was extended to midnight. Combining both theory and practice, the students were exposed to various aspects of medical care and assigned uncompensated private duty as part of their curriculum. Additionally, the nurses were expected to prepare meals and supervise wards in the evenings.[16]

The first graduation took place in June 1913, with eight nurses (five from Utah and three from out of state) receiving their pins and graduation certificates. The program was held in the Weber Academy auditorium, where Annie Dee presided over a hall decorated with the "training school colors, American Flags, potted plants . . . cut flowers . . . and an enlarged portrait of Thomas D. Dee." Elder David O. McKay, a member of the LDS Church's Council of Twelve Apostles who had strong ties to the local area, acknowledged the "debt of gratitude owed by the community for the hospital" and the "self-sacrifice and hard work . . . necessary to the successful nurse," as instilled by the nursing school. The Florence Nightingale Pledge was administered by Episcopal Reverend W. W. Fleetwood, pastor of Ogden's Church of the Good Shepherd, after which speakers from the medical community discussed the "vital role" of nurses. These ceremonies set the pattern for future graduations, and as the *Salt Lake Tribune* noted, the graduation became a significant "annual event."[17]

Reflecting the challenges facing the hospital itself, during its first five years the nurse training program lacked stability and was overseen by four different superintendents. In 1915, after the operation of the hospital had been transferred to the LDS Church, Stella Sainsbury, a graduate of the LDS Hospital School of Nursing, became superintendent of nurses. Over time, the program became stronger.[18] The opening of a student dormitory east of the hospital provided a major step toward stability (see figure 11.1), as described in one account:

> The home was beautifully furnished with a piano, phonograph, and a choice assortment of records. Miss Sainsbury had a private apartment with sitting-room, bedroom and bath. Other supervisors roomed alone and student nurses lived two in a room. Student rooms were lovely and cheerful with built-in double dressing tables with glass tops over flowered chintz. Each nurse also had her own clothes closet and drawer space. Twin beds were furnished for each room. Classes were now held in a large room in the basement, which was also used as a recreation room. This was a great improvement.[19]

Another major event for the nurses revolved around the country's entry into World War I in April 1917. Superintendent Sainsbury enlisted and was replaced by Stella Peterson, a fellow graduate of the nursing program at the LDS Hospital. There was a dramatic need for nurses to support the war effort, and a unit of five from the class of 1918 volunteered; after specialized training in New York City, they were sent overseas.

Equally challenging was the influenza epidemic of 1917–19, which dramatically affected both the hospital nursing staff and students. So extreme was the epidemic that the hospital closed some floors, limited both maternity and surgery cases, and dedicated all available space to influenza patients. A morgue was set up in the basement, and listed among the deaths were two student nurses. As the need for beds increased, the hospital built a frame annex on the north side of the original building. The additional beds relieved overcrowding in the hospital proper. This building remained in use as an isolation unit until 1920, when it was closed and subsequently torn down.[20]

Figure 11.1 Nurses home dedication. Annie T. Dee (right, fourth down) is joined by civic and family members including LDS Church President Joseph F. Smith (holding hat) in dedicating the nurses' home in 1917. (Courtesy Weber State University Stewart Library Special Collections.)

Between the two world wars, changes in the nursing school were minimal. The students' responsibilities expanded to include staffing the business office and information desk, operating the switch-board, and continuing to prepare and serve meals for the staff. A public health clinic was added, becoming the first in a Utah nursing school and a precursor of the Ogden City/Weber County Health District, established in 1936. Prior to that, in 1932, the nursing school had affiliated with Weber College, and a decade later it affiliated with the University of Utah, allowing third-year students to gain additional specialized instruction.

The entry of the United States into World War II in December 1941 posed challenges for nursing educators. To meet an acute shortage of nurses, the US Cadet Nurses Corps was organized in 1942, providing a stipend, as well as funding for tuition, uniforms, and books. The program was discontinued in 1949.[21]

Over time, it became apparent that nursing education in Utah would be better served by moving the programs from hospitals to institutions of higher learning. Again, this decision reflected national trends. In 1942, the University of Utah created a department of nursing education and offered its first bachelor's degree in 1948. Four years later, Weber College received approval from the Utah State Board of Education to initiate a program in practical nursing to support patient demand not only at Dee Hospital but also at St. Benedict's Hospital, which had been established in Ogden in 1947 by the Sisters of St. Benedict.[22]

In the mid-1950s, the Dee School of Nursing and Weber College participated with six other colleges and hospital affiliates in a national study program supervised by the Columbia University Teachers' College. The study underscored the need for more medical and scientific knowledge as part of the nursing curriculum. As a result, the Dee School of Nursing was phased out, Weber College took over the classes, and the hospital became the setting for clinical experience. During its forty-five years of operation, the Dee School of Nursing had graduated more than 700 nurses, who formed the backbone of the nursing profession in northern Utah (see figure 11.2).[23]

It is clear that those involved in creating and maintaining the Dee School of Nursing foresaw its historical importance and created several sources of documentation. Beginning in the 1920s, for example, a yearbook was published. First called the *Dee Crier*, later the *Dee Annual*, and finally the *D'Ami*, it included student and faculty photos and information about the school. An alumni asso-

Figure 11.2 After forty-five years of training nurses, the Dee School of Nursing graduated its last class in 1955. (Courtesy Weber State University Stewart Library Special Collections.)

ciation was created in 1915 and periodically produced updates of the lives and careers of the graduates. In 1995, the alumni organization achieved an extremely important milestone with the publication of *Autobiographical Sketches of Alumni Following Hospital Graduation, 1913–1955*. This chronology featured each graduating class and included biographical and family information, recollections of the training experience, accomplishments after graduation, and other information.[24]

Additionally, the Weber State University Special Collections department, whose mission is to document the history of Ogden city and Weber and Davis Counties has been actively acquiring records of the Dee family, the hospital, and the nursing school. Among the holdings are three major collections. First, because the hospital was so intertwined with the Dee family, especially in the early years, the 1988 acquisition of the Thomas D. Dee and Annie Taylor Dee Family History Collection provides a major source for historical study. Second, a large group of Thomas D. Dee Memorial Hospital records came to Weber State a year later, supplemented further by another accession in 2002. These two collections contain valuable correspondence, financial and legal documents, newspaper clippings, architectural records, and photographs. Finally, the Thomas D. Dee School of Nursing Collection, acquired in 1989, includes student files, internal publications, state reports, and other data on the workings of the school itself. From the files, we know when the women came to school, how they progressed during their training, and when they graduated. Still, as previously indicated, despite this vast amount of documentary evidence, there were gaps in our knowledge of both the Dee School of Nursing, the later careers of the nurses, and the impact its graduates had on the nursing profession in northern Utah and elsewhere. Moreover, in broad terms, we were interested in what had drawn these women to nursing, and how this career path had provided them with significant opportunities in a time when only limited avenues of professional activity were available to women. As Grace Hall Walling, niece of supervisor Annie Hall, commented about the early days of the Dee School of Nursing: "It seemed like the whole atmosphere was to train these women to be very successful and have a profession which was more than being married and having children and doing house chores."[25] Clearly the way to accomplish all of this was to rely on the technique of oral history. On July 7, 2008, an article appeared in the *Standard-Examiner* that briefly outlined the nursing school's history and announced our interest in interviewing graduates. An overwhelming response to the article allowed us to interview some forty graduates from as early as the class of 1936, right up through the last class in 1955. Armed with earlier documentary evidence—and intent on using that evidence to fill in the gaps—we sought to create the parameters of the project.[26]

As we proceeded, some pertinent questions became apparent. They began with basic biographical information but broadened to include the graduate's decision to become a nurse and attend the Dee School. What memories, we asked, recalled a typical day and lent resonance to the routines and traditions of nursing? How did the nurses recall key events, including World War II? These questions reminded us that some of the nurses' family connections gave insight to the school's history, predating their own attendance. Finally, it became apparent that the interviews produced data that added to the documentary evidence and cast light on an era, as well as a training program, and increased our understanding not only of individuals but of the community at large.

We began, of course, by asking why these women chose nursing as a profession. Frequently that decision involved personal experiences, either with nurses or with women as unofficial caregivers. For example, Ruth Stevenson Shupe (class of 1941) recalled, "When my mother died I decided I wanted to become a nurse so that I could help take care of the sick."[27] Similarly, Emma Lou Stander Goddard (1946) noted, "I knew in second grade I wanted to be a nurse when I saw my mother's . . . starched, white [uniform] with cap."[28]

Others had experiences with the Dee Hospital itself. One good example is Dorothy Mills Bird (1947) who not only recounted her youthful experiences visiting at the hospital as a motivator but also specified an economic factor. As she noted:

> What got me started thinking about being a nurse was when [my] mother was ill at the . . . Dee Memorial Hospital. I can remember going up to the fourth floor, a big medical floor, fifteen or so patients to a room, and we walked down the long hall; the curtains around her. I walked over across the hall into what may have been the kitchen. I looked down and saw nurses walking from the hospital up to the [nurses] home. They had on their blue capes, and I thought "Wouldn't that be wonderful to be a nurse." We didn't have much money and I did not know how I would ever be able to be a nurse until one day in gym [class] while we were getting dressed a few friends . . . were talking . . . and they said "Oh, have you heard about the new nursing program for army? You can join and the army will pay for your nursing." I got all excited and asked them where and everything about it. Out of that whole group of girls, . . . I was the only one who applied.[29]

A similar view came from Patricia Pilcher Layton (1954), who recalled that as a young girl, she thought nursing might prove to be an enjoyable and rewarding profession. When she mentioned that thought, her mother registered her in the program before she could have a change of heart. Her mother's motivation was not her daughter's interest as much as economic necessity. As Layton recalled, "My father died two months before I was born, and she had three other children to care for. She had a hard time. She realized the importance of a female having an occupation or a profession."[30] Regina Urban Turner (1947) was a high school graduate attending a business college in Spokane, Washington, when she decided a secretarial career might not be for her: "I was very good in shorthand and typing but terrible in bookkeeping. I was young and a bit discouraged and ready to do something else." About that time she encountered a high school friend, Louise Barr (Burbonnais) (1946) who had graduated from the Dee School the previous year. As Turner recalled, she "gave me some information on the cadet program. So I applied and was accepted at the Dee Hospital. My family could not afford to send me to college financially. And this was the big opportunity of my life and I just had to make a go of it."[31]

Economic necessity also motivated an earlier generation of nurses as well, who came of age during the Great Depression. Ruth Donaldson Brown (1943) observed that her experiences during the Depression made her realize that if she wanted to continue her education past high school, she would have to pay for it because "Mother and Dad did just not have the money. They were too busy raising all [their] kids." Realizing that nursing was the only post–high school training that interested her or that she could afford, Brown "worked all summer, saved every penny I had, to get the money to go into nurses' training. I wore the same brown, rumpled stained skirt all during nurses training. . . . All of us were so poor."[32] The experiences of Grace Palmer Rasmussen (1938), living in a remote rural area of northwest Utah, reinforce this point: "I decided on nursing due to encouragement from my mother as well as the fact that I did not have money for attending college. I . . . had to leave home at age 15 to finish high school. I lived with different families and worked for my room and board so I could finish the last two years of high school."[33]

In some instances, the prevailing reason for becoming a nurse was friendship, even female solidarity. For example, Audrey Kennedy Peart (1932) planned to go to a business college; however, a friend whose older sister had graduated from the Dee School talked her into going into nurse's training instead. As she later recalled:

> We could be roommates and live together while in training. She was two years older than I. One of the rules was you had to be eighteen years old and I wouldn't be until October. Our family doctor from Randolph where we lived did sign my application saying I was eighteen years old. Although my mother and father were disappointed in my decision, they supported me and helped me to get ready to enter the Dee Hospital Nurses training in September.[34]

For some women, nursing school offered a chance to relocate to a more "cosmopolitan" area. Delpha Greaves Allen (1948) commented, "I thought if I didn't leave Grace, [Idaho] in six months I was going to be stuck there forever. I was working in my dad's store and help was hard to find because the war was on. My two friends and I decided to put our applications in at the Dee Memorial Hospital in Ogden. We graduated in May and were accepted in the class in June."[35] Alta Roskelley (1936) offered another interesting perspective:

> I did not know what I was going to do with my life. My friends had all gone on to college and I did not want to be behind them. I was struggling with what I was going to do. One day a man walked in the office (my uncle's doctor's office) and he said, "You know, you ought to be a nurse," I said, "Oh, I can't stand the sight of blood, I could not do that." The more I thought about it the more I thought it was something I should try to do. My uncle did not want me to go to Logan, he wanted me to go to an accredited school. He knew people here in Ogden and suggested I come to the Dee Hospital.[36]

Still others saw nursing as a rare opportunity to find a niche in society. For example, Elsie Okamota Shiramizu (1950), whose family had come to Utah as part of the Japanese relocation during World War II, recalled that she discussed her future options with a counselor at Davis High School. At the time, Elsie thought she needed to drop out of school to help her family pick tomatoes. But her counselor urged her to make a different decision and encouraged her to stay in school and keep her grades up so that she could apply for one of the two nursing scholarships the Dee Hospital offered local high school graduates. That night, Elsie "told my mother about it, and we talked all night, the pros and cons. Mom said, 'Well, you know they can take away your job, but not your degree.'"[37]

Another area that came out in most interviews concerned the nursing graduates' frustrations with the school's strict rules and regulations and the effect they had on their private lives. Curfew, recalled Ruth Brown, was a particular source of irritation. It seemed incongruous with the other aspects of her training and responsibility. As she put it, "I could never understand why we could go on a floor and be a charge nurse for sixty-two patients, and then we had to be in at ten o'clock at night."[38] Another perspective comes from Jane Shurtliff Morrin (1941), who commented, "There were a lot of rules really. We had room inspections once a week; they checked to see if our beds were made properly and everything was picked up and neat. And then every night our lights had to be out at ten o'clock."[39]

During the interviews, it gradually became apparent that more than curfew dictated the nurses' private time. Ruth Shupe recalled that the student nurses "were expected to be up between 6:00 to 6:30 a.m., to be showered, attend chapel, have breakfast, and be to classes at 7:00 a.m., or to work at the hospital, the 7–3, 3–11, or 11–7 shift. It was very hard to stay awake at night. We could rest at times if it wasn't too busy. We also had classes to attend during the day."[40] Another strict rule emerged from the memory of Ruth Donaldson Brown: "I think the first two years we were paid $5 [a week]. If we broke something like a thermometer they would take that out of the $5. We were very careful not to break things!"[41]

The nurses found the program demanding on them physically and economically. It was also a major time commitment. As Regina Urban Turner recalled:

> We spent a lot of time studying. We had to do our washing;
> [the hospital] did our uniforms and things like that, but you
> always had to wear a slip and we had to do our personal wash-

ing. . . . We had chapel every morning before we went to work. We would meet at the chapel in the nursing home for about fifteen minutes and had song and a prayer for us to go to work with. We would line up [for inspection] and there were times when Mrs. Miner would pick up our uniform and make sure we had a slip on. Or you held out your hands, since your fingernails had to be clipped way down. We had to also wear hair nets and make sure our hose were clean and mended. [During the war] you couldn't even buy cotton hose . . . we would have to sew up the runs.[42]

Glenda Heaton Johnson (1950) mentioned the importance of a compatible roommate, because you "had to depend on her, first of all, for a lot of news and for a lot of help with finding out changes, meals; we very often went to the cafeteria, ate, and picked up another meal for our roommate, who had worked the night shift and was too tired to get up and go to lunch." Johnson remembered the time as one of cooperation among the students, "and actually as I look back it was kind of fun. We grew to know one another . . . there was a lot of camaraderie. We became like a big group of sisters."[43]

The nurses remembered their interactions with doctors, often fondly but occasionally with some resentment. Alta Roskelley recalled helping the doctors "on with their coats, walk[ing] behind them. . . . They would get on the elevator first, things like that. That was something that was very foreign to me. I thought they were kind of like little gods."[44] Melva Castleton Crookston (1952) was more direct, noting that "some of the doctors were kind of rude to you."[45] On the other hand, Regina Urban Turner admitted that the "doctors and nurses were very dedicated and certainly were the foundation of what has become a 'miracle age'" in terms of medicine.[46]

The interviewees also remembered their nursing supervisors. Eva Dean Last Rudalch (1945) recalled, "One of my most vivid memories of training, that made a great impression on me, was Mrs. Oetta Glasscock reminding us every morning, 'First and foremost you are a lady.' It has been chiseled in my mind. I never forgot it."[47] Finally, Glorya Stokes Telleson (1954) noted that in her last job as a nurse she encountered a former nursing instructor as a patient: "I visited her, tried to elicit memory of that lost time forty-four years ago. She feigned remembrance, but as she and I held hands and talked, I realized that the sparkle had dimmed forever. Now she was in my care, and the receipt of the skills and knowledge she had imparted to me long ago."[48]

Indeed, many nurses interviewed also carried vivid memories of patients. As Josephine Heslop Manning (1944) noted: "If you took care of a patient with pneumonia, you always remembered the symptoms, you always remembered the treatment, where if you read it in a book [it was different]. But you can . . . see a lot of different things if you are actually taking care of a patient. That's why I think living it for three years was the best way to get that kind of training; because we lived it though experience."[49] Similarly, Sine Scharling Post (1945) recalled the experience of one of her classmates:

> We found out that it didn't hurt a patient to get out of bed right after surgery, even if we didn't do it back then. Virginia Nelson [Green] was bathing a patient, a man from Mexico, who had his appendix removed the night before. As she was making his bed she braced her knee against the bed, and gave the draw sheet a swift pull so it would be nice and smooth. This flipped the man out of bed, which was about a foot from the wall. He fell out on the wall side, and scrambled out from under the bed, and stood before her in his little hospital gown, shook his finger at her, and said, "Seester, you craze!"[50]

Without a doubt, World War II marked a formative period in the nurses' lives, their training, and their careers. The memories of December 7, 1941, remained vivid for Jane Shurtliff Morrin: "The Japanese attacked Pearl Harbor; it was on a Sunday. And I had that day off. I went to work on Monday and of course it was pure chaos. We had several Japanese nurses that were staff members. There were patients there that absolutely refused to let those girls in their rooms, yet they were wonderful people."[51]

Another perspective came from Josephine Heslop Manning, who recalled, "I was in training only about six months when World War

II started and things changed so much. That was one of the terrible things that left a mark on you. . . . Things happened during those three years that I would always remember." Manning particularly remembered a train wreck that occurred on December 31, 1944, on the Lucin cut-off, when the Pacific Limited was on its way from Ogden to California. Among the fifty dead were thirty-five soldiers and sailors. As Manning recalled:

> They sent a bunch of nurses out, and then they were going to bring back all the patients back, but they couldn't get to the other side. The train that ran into the first one was on the Utah side and the others were already into Nevada, so they took them to San Francisco. But all the dead they brought back to our hospital. They would take them to mortuaries except the military. And those . . . men [came] to our hospital until Hill Field could come and get them. I will always remember that.[52]

Another significant event during World War II was the creation of the previously mentioned Cadet Nursing program. As Delpha Graves Allen commented: "They were short of nurses during the war so the government set up the Cadet Nurses Corps. If you joined, they paid for everything. The only thing you had to do after you graduated was stay active in nursing. That meant active in a hospital."[53] Faye Longhurst Ball (1946) confirms this view, recalling that in January 1943, "the first class of 1946 started (at the Dee School of Nursing), the three year diploma nursing program and became members of the United States Cadet Nurse's Corps. This program was started because [of] an acute nurses shortage and was designed to prepare young women in the shortest possible time to practice as graduate nurses in either civilian or military service."[54] Similar views were expressed by Phyllis Naegle Purdy (1941): "I joined the Navy Nurse Corps quite soon after I got out of training. I felt it was my patriotic duty. I really got an experience in the navy. I . . . learned a lot. I was naive, I grew up in Utah, and boy did I get my eyes opened. I got out in the world, and it was a good experience for me."[55] Lois Heap Murray (1947) commented on social aspects during the war years, particularly as they influenced nurses in training: "When I went to school, if a teacher got married, she could not work afterwards. She had to be home. It was only during World War II that we even got out, like Rosie the Riveter. We got out and had jobs, women were finally allowed to work because of the great need and demand for a workforce."[56]

Jean Graham Woodfield (1945) offered this summation: "The war changed everything; you had to go without things because everything was rationed. We were given coupon books and had to bring them and turn them in so we could get sugar or anything else that was rationed. . . . We had to mend our nylons because you knew you were not going to get another pair. Shoes were also rationed and you were very careful with them."[57] Other shortages existed, as well. As Regina Urban Turner recalled: "We did not have many doctors practicing in Ogden from 1944 to 1947 because of the military demand during World War II. We made do with the help of a few residents and interns."[58]

One surprising aspect of the oral history project was the information some nurses knew about events and individuals predating their own time in school. For example, Grace Hall Walling shared memories of her aunt, Annie Jessie Hall, one of the early nursing supervisors and in many ways a legend in the school's history. Usually interviewees referred to her as "Annie" but Walling remembered her as "Aunt Jessie." Filling gaps in the documentary record, Walling, who, as previously noted, saw the goal of the program as training women to be professionals, also observed:

> There was a lot going on in that time, and Aunt Jessie was very interested in furthering the profession of women in nursing and she was very nitpicky about cleanliness, especially with the nurses and the hospital. They actually were trained to be bedside nurses, and patients did not get out of bed with whatever their problem was so they were fed in bed, they were bathed in bed, and this was the job of the nurses.[59]

Walling also provided a glimpse about the experiences of her mother, Dorothea Allan Hall (1916), who lost her mother when she was nine years old. As Walling recalled, Dorothea's mother insisted that her husband send their two daughters back to live with family members in New York after her death, believing that there were

> wild people out here [in Ogden]. The schooling wasn't nearly as good. In the summertime, because my grandfather worked on the railroad he would have a pass, and he would bring the girls for short visits back to Utah. . . . So because my mother's [Dorothea] lifestyle with family in the East was not that wonderful, she got here and could see that the hospital would feed her and give her a place to live and then give her a profession. So it was an easy decision. That is why the nurses became her family.[60]

Finally, it became apparent that despite the many hardships, including economic stress, war-related traumas, and restrictions on time and personal life, most of the nurses interviewed remembered that era fondly. As Glenda Heaton Johnson recalled,

> The Dee Hospital had the greatest staff, they were wonderful. In fact, our night supervisor was somewhat of a rascal! We used to have good jokes and laughs; she would wait for us to get off duty, put us in her car, and take us down to the café. We would have a great big breakfast, tell jokes and laugh. Then she would take us back to the dorm and we would go to bed. There was this camaraderie with us.[61]

Lois Heap Murray remembered that most of the nurses were so poor they could not afford much of a social life. Still, they were able to have some off-duty fun: "One thing we did was we wore our uniforms and went down to the Berthana [ballroom] where we would roller skate. There were a lot of service men and they treated us a lot better. They would not try to get smart or anything. We always wore our uniforms for safety!"[62]

Despite the camaraderie, some tensions remained, and personal adjustments were necessary for the trainees who lived in close quarters as they managed the pressures of school and work. One example surrounds Elsie Okamota Shiramizu, who told us:

When I first started I did not have a roommate. I was a rare breed too because [of] being of Asian background, and the rest of them were all LDS. There were two of us that were not LDS. I was kind of a loner anyway because I did not know anything about Mormonism. . . . They ignored me initially because I was a rare breed, but eventually it got to a point where we became a family.[63]

As of this writing, the Dee School of Nursing has been closed for longer than it existed. Many of the graduates went on to become charge nurses, private duty nurses, and nursing instructors at Weber State. Though the numbers of graduates are diminishing over time, they still meet annually at a luncheon to sing the Dee School song and reminisce. The number of graduates still in practice is small, but for some forty years they acted as the mainstays of the nursing profession, particularly in northern Utah. The oral history project allowed us to capture and make available their stories before they were lost. As they spoke, we became acquainted with the women behind the charts and photographs printed in the official records and class yearbooks. Each recounted experiences with the doctors, patients, and one another. We learned of the challenging work they undertook, the demanding instructors, and the sacrifices they made. We learned that female network patterns—formal and informal—and solidarity was a central element in the decisions of most of the women to pursue nurse training. They were influenced by their friends, mothers, and older siblings and, in turn, many of them influenced another generation when they became nursing educators or when their children pursued a nursing career as well. They also told us of the fun, such as sliding down the icy hills on steel bedpans. They remembered the camaraderie they enjoyed at the time and over the years. As we conducted the interviews, we were also able to accomplish an ancillary goal by adding documentation to our holdings, including photographs, student publications, diaries, letters, and even uniforms. More important, the oral history project put faces and stories on these records and artifacts and made it possible for us, as well as future generations, to know these women and their contributions.

In the article "Human Values in Oral History," James Bennett observes that there is basic agreement that oral history, "as understood by most professional historians," consists of "information that comes from interviewing persons who were present at events at issue." More important, he states, despite some who deride oral history as being trivial or lacking significance as a primary source, "the truth is that oral histories relate to the most important question anyone can ask: How should I live my life?"[64] As a result of our project, we found that the nursing school graduates we interviewed answered that important question both professionally and personally. In the process, the project also allowed us to discover and collect the "rest of the story."[65]

Notes

1. Susan H. Armitage, "From the Inside Out: Rewriting Regional History," *Frontiers: A Journal of Women Studies* 22, no. 3 (2001): 44.

2. "Funeral of Thomas D. Dee," *Ogden Standard*, July 12, 1905; "At the Tabernacle," *Ogden Standard*, July 13, 1905.

3. Thomas D. Dee, Death Certificate, Utah Division of Vital Statistics, Death Certificates, 1904–56, Series #81448, Utah State Archives and Records Service. Additional details on Dee's death are found in Warren L. Wattis, "Tribute to the Dead," *Ogden Standard*, July 13, 1905.

4. See Eleanor B. Moler, *Building a Dynasty: The Story of the Thomas D. Dee Family* (n.p., 1987), 96.

5. It should be noted that during the forty years of its existence, the graduates were all female, with one exception. That exception was Ray VanderSteen, who graduated in 1953 along with forty other nurses. Born in Ogden, Utah, his wife, Donna, had just completed her nursing degree when he applied and was accepted to the program. According to his application, his work as an orderly at Dee Hospital and helping care for the sick stirred an interest and a desire to pursue his education in nursing. As he noted in his application, "I think the Dee is a very good training school," and he wanted "to become a registered nurse and obtain my degree." See Ray VanderSteen, application for admission, Thomas D. Dee School of Nursing Collection, Ms. 41, Weber State University (WSU), Special Collections, Bx 23, Fd 7 (hereafter cited as Dee Nursing Collection, WSU).

6. "Contract Let for Dee Memorial Hospital," *Deseret News*, July 17, 1909.

7. Ibid.

8. See original records in Thomas D. and Annie Taylor Dee Family Collection, Weber State University, Stewart Library Special Collections, Ms. 52, Bx

14, Fd 5 (hereafter cited as Dee Family Collection, WSU). According to the *Deseret News* account, the main building would consist of a four-story, red-brick structure, approximately 60 feet by 148 feet, able to accommodate 100 patients. The paper noted that the patients were divided into male and female rooms. They would be "roomy and . . . furnished with the latest style of furniture," and each floor would have its own kitchen, allowing patients to have their meals served in their wards. On Hodgson, see Teddy Fullmer, "Leslie Simmons Hodgson: Architect of Ogden," typescript, WSU.

9. "Dedication of Thomas D. Dee Memorial Hospital," *Ogden Morning Standard*, January 2, 1911.

10. Moler, *Building a Dynasty*, 51.

11. See Thomas D. Dee Memorial Hospital Collection, Weber State University, Stewart Library Special Collections, Ms. 51, Bx 1, Fds 3, 10–15 (hereafter cited as Dee Hospital Collection, WSU). See "Editorial," *Ogden Standard*, October 24, 1914. The paper noted that the closing of the hospital would create a "severe loss" for the community and called on Ogden's prominent citizens to take "quick action" to prevent the closing.

12. P. M. Cushnahan to Mrs. Thomas Dee and Family, November 8, 1914, Dee Hospital Collection, WSU, Bx 1, Fd 25. Cushnahan also pledged that the church would assume "the present indebtedness amounting somewhere between $21,000 and $25,000," that there would be "absolutely no distinction on account of race or creed," and that the hospital would be open to "all respectable surgical and medical practitioners."

13. Ibid. In addition to the offer from Rev. Cushnahan, the only other option came from the LDS community, which is the option the board selected by unanimous vote. In the wake of the decision, Cushnahan resigned as a member of the board. See letters from the board dated February 25, 1915, to Cushnahan and the Hospital Committee of the Weber Club, explaining the board's decision that accepting the offer of the LDS Church was "the best one possible under the circumstances."

14. Sandra Hawkes Noall, "A History of Nursing Education in Utah," PhD diss., University of Utah, 1969, 38. For information on the development of the Salt Lake hospitals, see Jessie Embry, "Diploma Nursing at Salt Lake City Religious Based Hospitals," *Utah Historical Quarterly* 76 (Summer 2008): 281–99. A broad overview of national trends can be found in Barbara Melosh, *"The Physicians Hand": Work, Culture and Conflict in American Nursing* (Philadelphia: Temple University Press, 1981), esp. 37–76.

15. Moler, *Building a Dynasty*, 52.

16. Ibid., 53.

17. See "Dee Hospital Graduates' Exercise," *Ogden Standard*, June 10, 1913; "Diplomas Given to Eight Nurses," *Ogden Morning-Examiner*, June 10, 1913; and "Nurses to Be Graduated," *Salt Lake Tribune*, June 9, 1913. The graduates were Ethel M. Edwards, Marie Rasmussen, Ruth Harbison, Leota A. Embling, Anna Hansen, Lucille Dunbar, Frances Burrett, and Jean H.

244   SILLITO, LANGSDON, AND FARR

Sharp. See "Graduates of the Thomas D. Dee Memorial Hospital School for Nurses," *Ogden Standard*, June 7, 1913, which contains pictures of the graduates. The Florence Nightingale Pledge reads: "I solemnly pledge myself before God and in the presence of this assembly, to pass my life in purity and to practice my profession faithfully. I will abstain from whatever is deleterious and mischievous, and will not take or knowingly administer any harmful drug. I will do all in my power to elevate the standards of my profession, and will hold in confidence all personal matters committed to my keeping and all family affairs coming to my knowledge in the practice of my calling. With loyalty I will endeavor to aid the physician in his work, and to devote myself to the welfare of those committed to my care."

18. Noall, "History of Nursing Education," 39.

19. Moler, *Building a Dynasty*, 54–55. See also Dee Family Collection WSU, Bx 14, Fd 9.

20. Moler, *Building a Dynasty*, 55.

21. For an overview, see *The US Cadet Nurses Corps, 1943–48*, Public Health Publication no. 38 (Washington, DC: Government Printing Office, 1950), and "US Cadet Nurses Corps," *Trained Nurse and Hospital Review* 111 (September 1943): 202–3.

22. See Richard W. Sadler, *Weber State College: A Centennial History* (Ogden, UT: Weber State College, 1988), 109. For an overview of developments at St. Benedict's see Bernice Maher Mooney and J. Terrence Fitzgerald, *Salt of the Earth: The History of the Catholic Church in Utah, 1776–2007*, 3rd ed. (Salt Lake City: University of Utah Press, 2008), 245–49.

23. Moler, *Building a Dynasty*, 70.

24. Helen Farr, ed., *Autobiographical Sketches of Alumni Following Hospital Graduation: Forty-two Years of Graduate Nurses, Eighty-two Years of Alumni History* (Ogden, UT: Thomas D. Dee Memorial Hospital, School of Nursing Alumni Association, 1995). From time to time, the alumni organization would also do updates of graduates, which occasionally included responses to questionnaires. Though not oral interviews per se, these books were especially useful as we prepared to interview some of the nurses because we were able to build and expand on what they had recorded more than a decade earlier. In a handful of cases we have used this information to make a point, often because the nurses are not available for interviewing.

25. Grace Hall Walling, interview by Marci Farr, July 28, 2008, Dee School of Nursing Oral History Project, Stewart Library Special Collections, Weber State University, Ogden, Utah, 1–2. All other oral histories cited are part of this project.

26. Charles F. Trentelman, "The Right Remedy: Family Matriarch Paved Way for Ogden Nurses," *Standard-Examiner*, July 7, 2008.

27. Ruth Stevenson Shupe, interview by Marci Farr, September 9, 2008, 2.

28. Emma Lou Stander Goddard, interview by Marci Farr, October 29, 2008, 1.

29. Dorothy Mills Bird, interview by Marci Farr, July 16, 2008, 1.

30. Patricia Pilcher Layton, interview by Marci Farr, August 4, 2008, 1.

31. Regina Urban Turner, interview by Marci Farr, September 11, 2008, 5–6.

32. Ruth Donaldson Brown, interview by Marci Farr, August 8, 2008, 3–4.

33. Grace Palmer Rasmussen, in *Thomas D. Dee Memorial Hospital School of Nursing Alumni Association Roster* (Ogden, UT: n.p., 1995), 67.

34. Audrey Kennedy Peart, interview by Marci Farr, September 30, 2008, 1.

35. Delpha Greaves Allen, interview by Marci Farr, July 22, 2008, 1.

36. Alta Roskelley, interview by Marci Farr, July 14, 2008, 1.

37. Elsie Okamota Shiramizu, interview by Marci Farr, July 22, 2008, 7–9.

38. Brown interview, 13.

39. Jane Shurtliff Morrin, interview by Marci Farr, October 3, 2008, 3.

40. Shupe interview, 2.

41. Brown interview, 13.

42. Turner interview, 7.

43. Glenda Heaton Johnson, interview by Marci Farr, September 9, 2008, 3.

44. Roskelley interview, 20.

45. Melva Castleton Cookston, interview by Marci Farr, August 1, 2008, 7.

46. Turner interview, 3.

47. Eva Dean Last Rudalch, in Farr, *Autobiographical Sketches*, 84.

48. Glorya Stokes Telleson, interview by Marci Farr, August 19, 2008, 19.

49. Josephine Heslop Manning, interview by Marci Farr, August 5, 2008, 18.

50. Sine Scharling Post, in Farr, *Autobiographical Sketches*, 72. Green graduated in the same class (1945).

51. Morrin interview, 7.

52. Manning interview, 25.

53. Allen interview, 3–5.

54. Faye Longhurst Ball, in Farr, *Autobiographical Sketches*, 76.

55. Phyllis Naegle Purdy, interview by Marci Farr, August 27, 2008, 2–3.

56. Lois Heap Murray, interview by Marci Farr, July 28, 2008, 11–12.

57. Jean Graham Woodfield, interview by Marci Farr, August 5, 2008, 3–4.

58. Turner interview, 1.

59. Walling interview, 1–2.

60. Ibid., 12.

61. Johnson interview, 19.

62. Murray interview, 8.

63. Shiramizu interview, 14–15.

64. James Bennett, "Human Values in Oral History," *Oral History Review* 11 (1983): 10–11.

65. Although it is beyond the scope of this essay, the existence of our oral history program, as well as the printed and manuscript records that are housed at Weber State University, provide a significant database for future studies of both the hospital, and more particularly the nursing school itself. Copies of the interviews, and the class annuals, can be accessed by emailing dc@weber.edu.

12

The Utah Eagle Forum

Legitimizing Political Activism as Women's Work

MELANIE NEWPORT

Historian Melanie Newport discovered that oral history was the only way for her to study the Eagle Forum, a conservative political organization that has helped shape the political culture of the West. Although many of these women believe that a woman's place is in the home, they also believe that women need to preserve traditional family values in the community and practice what some historians have called "municipal housekeeping." Eagle Forum records are not open to researchers, and talking to participants was Newport's only source of information. The oral history provided more than just stories. Newport was able to develop relationships with women who felt marginalized by the "liberal bias of higher education." The interviewees were pleased that Newport took their views seriously, and Newport acknowledges that conducting the oral history interviews opened her mind as well. Her willingness to listen opened doors for further research.

WHEN ALASKA GOVERNOR and vice presidential nominee Sarah Palin burst onto the national political stage during the 2008 presidential elections, observers gawked at the contradictions between her conservative religious politics, ideas about gender roles, and her own presence in the public sphere. Surprised at the presence of a mother of five in a major election, observers from left to right struggled to make sense of her values and her insistence that her identities as a mother and Christian were in fact not at odds with her place in national politics. One commentator angrily decried, "An individualism exemplified by Palin, the frontierswoman who somehow has managed to 'balance' five children and her political career with no need for support—is leading to a culture-wide crack-up."[1] Though it remains to be seen if Palin's moment constituted a "a culture-wide crack-up," her religiosity and motherhood were part of an established tradition of conservative women's political work in the West.

The political influence of conservative women in the West has been well documented. In the 1950s and 1960s, "housewife activists" held coffee klatches and volunteered for Republican political campaigns.[2] "Goldwater Girls" strove to elect Arizona senator Barry Goldwater president in 1964.[3] In California, conservative women flocked to events and rallies for Foundation for Economic Education and the Christian Anti-Communist Crusade. Women defined their participation in a variety of political activities— through the Republican Party, anticommunism, and education initiatives, for example—as a critical expression of their commitment to traditional family values. Because women were at home during the day, they performed political "housework," such as staffing precincts and stuffing envelopes. Educating each other on important issues, women built political networks to generate support for a wide range of socially conservative issues from the 1970s to the present.

Governor Palin also spoke to the central conundrum for the women who came to accept and advance the Republican Party's conservative agenda—the paradox of justifying women's work outside the home while using politics to protect the interests of "traditional families." Perhaps nowhere was this paradox as central to state political discourse than in Utah, the birthplace of the Tea Party and the heart of the Church of Jesus Christ of Latter-day Saints (LDS). Since the battle to prevent the passage of the Equal Rights Amendment (ERA) in the 1970s, the Utah chapter of the Eagle Forum has been a critical influence in shifting the state's politics to the right.[4] Appealing to a largely LDS constituency, the

Eagle Forum became a mouthpiece for conservative women and a lightning rod for controversy. Oral histories with feminists, LDS women, and Eagle Forum activists reveal not only the reasons and motivations for conservative women's activism but the strategies they have developed to justify and legitimize the political work they do outside the home.

The story of the political mobilization of conservative women in Utah begins not with a Latter-day Saint but a Catholic. Eagle Forum founder Phyllis Schlafly was a product of the "distinctive women's political culture" of the emerging New Right. An educated mother of six, Schlafly got her start volunteering with the Junior League and the Republican Party. Her political views gained local prominence when she ran for congressional office in 1952. Despite losing, Schlafly stayed involved with politics as an anticommunist writer and through her work with the Republican Party and as a chapter president of the National Federation of Republican Women. Donald Critchlow notes that Schlafly was exceptional in her "ability to translate conservative ideas to grassroots activists and motivate them to achieve political goals."[5] This power reached maturity when Schlafly, previously "apathetic" to the proposed ERA, learned of the moral and political implications of the amendment. The amendment's passage through Congress concerned Schlafly, who believed the proposed amendment would rob women of their privileges, including their rights to be homemakers, to use women's-only public restrooms, and to be restricted from live combat. She founded the STOP-ERA (Stop Taking Our Privileges Equal Rights Amendment) organization in 1972. In 1975, she launched the Eagle Forum to support a sustained battle for the defense of conservative values. As with STOP-ERA, Schlafly used her own political and religious contacts to rapidly establish chapters across the country.

In spite of the scale of this mobilization, Schlafly biographers and historians of grassroots conservatism have neglected the activities of the thousands of women involved with the Eagle Forum.[6] Once Schlafly chose a state chapter president to locally lead the primarily female organization, she stepped out of the picture. Through state chapters, members distributed a bevy of anti-ERA materials to their communities and lawmakers. The Eagle Forum combined the lobbying strategies of the Republican Party with the grassroots organizing of the National Federation of Republican Women to create an issue-oriented social movement to preserve "traditional values."[7]

The Eagle Forum had tremendous appeal in the conservative political culture of predominantly Mormon Utah. As with the rest of the country, Utahans had taken a serious interest in anticommunism. LDS Apostle Ezra Taft Benson was a known advocate of the John Birch Society; one historian notes that as a result, "An ultraconservative political subculture developed among a minority of Mormons" during the 1960s.[8] Conservative ideals became further connected with Mormonism as the church proclaimed its stance on a number of "moral issues"—alcohol sales, pornography, homosexuality, and the ERA. Utah historian Martha Bradley asserts that as soon as the LDS First Presidency equated preservation of the family with conquering the ERA, there was little room for opposition to the amendment within the church.[9] As leaders urged LDS Church members to take action, the Eagle Forum found a willing pool of women in Utah eager to defeat the ERA.

The presidents of the Utah Eagle Forum represent the major phases of conservative women's activism in Utah. During the ERA fight, Carol Garbett of Kearns, Utah, was de facto state leader of STOP-ERA during her tenure as Salt Lake County chapter president. Garbett was later selected as a state delegate to the Houston International Women's Year conference, which suggests that her involvement with the Eagle Forum lifted her to a visible profile not necessarily evident in other records.[10]

With the failure of the ERA, the Utah Eagle Forum took a more subtle position in state politics. In the early 1980s, Schlafly chose Dorothea Masur, a Catholic woman from Logan, to lead the Utah Eagle Forum. Masur, a state legislator from 1980 to 1982, kept the group at a low profile, choosing instead to focus on the group's legislative lobbying power. During the 1980s, about fifty members sustained the Eagle Forum's lobbying mission.[11]

Amid family health issues and charges of shoplifting, Masur was replaced by Schlafly with vice president Gayle Ruzicka in 1991.[12] Ruzicka, a Mormon active in Eagle Forum chapters in Idaho and Arizona, made significant changes to the Utah chapter's strategies.

Using existing Mormon networks to spread news about political issues and the establishment of local chapters, Ruzicka substantially increased participation and the political influence of the Eagle Forum within the state. The Eagle Forum is widely regarded as the bellwether for conservative women's sentiments in Utah. Ruzicka herself has become a formidable if not notorious figure in state politics. As a result, the Eagle Forum in Utah enjoys a prominence unequaled by most other chapters nationwide.

Oral history is integral to understanding the Utah Eagle Forum's past and present. As an organization, they have kept few records; Ruzicka admits to being unfamiliar with the group's activities before her arrival in Utah.[13] The National Eagle Forum Archives holds expansive documentary records, many of which are restricted to researchers. With few resources made available by the organization itself, researchers are limited to newspaper articles and a few documents saved by local feminists. Although newspaper articles outline the activities and agenda of the Eagle Forum, they say little about its character and organization. Indeed, the informal nature of Mormon women's social networks means that much of the day-to-day machinations of groups like the Eagle Forum are lost to historians.

Oral histories, then, take on tremendous significance. Interviews with Eagle Forum participants as well as feminist perceptions of the group reveal a significant change in the character of Mormon women's activism. Oral histories collected in two distinct historical moments—following the International Women's Year activities and before the presidential elections in 2008—document the transformation of conservative women in Utah. Feminist descriptions of hysterical housewives in oral histories of the 1970s gave way to oral histories in which conservative women themselves described their roles as political change makers. In both sets of oral histories, conservative women have a reach extending far beyond the home.

Although not all of the Eagle Forum women interviewed participated in the 1976 International Women's Year (IWY) activities in Mexico, Utah, and Texas, the oral histories chronicling those events provide important insight into how feminists perceived their opposition. Such perceptions have not only influenced popular perceptions and portrayals of conservative women by the media and historians but have also contributed to how the Eagle Forum women view their contributions to state politics oppositionally. This sense of identity—a collective sense of being confidently able to accomplish change in the face of great opposition—inspires and motivates the Eagle Forum to fight a sustained battle for their values and justifies Mormon women's work outside the home.

Several different oral history collections exist in Utah with regard to the ERA fight. Between 1975 and 1977, JoAnn Freed collected a number of oral histories with Utah women who participated the Mexico City IWY conference.[14] Many of the attendees of the Mexico City conference interviewed by Freed were organizers of the 1976 Utah IWY conference, and it is noteworthy that few of the narrators acknowledged the anti-ERA agenda propagated by the Eagle Forum and other organizations at the time. Such a silence stands in stark contrast to oral histories collected by students for the IWY project housed at Brigham Young University.[15] Interviewed in the early 1990s, pro-ERA narrators focused primarily on their experiences at the Utah IWY conference. The conference became one of the largest in the country after organizers encouraged leaders of the LDS women's organization, the Relief Society, to promote the participation of LDS women. Following the issue of an official directive urging ten women from every LDS congregation to attend, attendance exceeded expectations by thousands. Fifteen years later, feminist narrators passionately and vividly recalled the behavior of this unanticipated glut of women and in doing so made manifest their opinions of conservative women's political behaviors and roles. The interviews allude to the larger failure of feminist women to control the discourse of gendered politics in Utah.

Esther Landa, a well-known former president of the National Council of Jewish Women and Utah activist, spoke disdainfully of conservative participants at the Utah IWY conference. She characterized them as uniformly LDS and uninformed, thwarting the intentions of feminist leaders. With imagery that brings to mind pillaging barbarians, Landa stated that the IWY conference had been "destroyed by this horde coming in."[16] Landa's remarks pointed to a wider sense that conservative women had not earned the right to participate in the public sphere. This notion is further supported by

IWY representative Ramona Adams, who depicted conservative women's "naiveté" as "ignorance in action."[17]

Perhaps the most emphatic critique in the collection of oral histories came from Marilee Larta, who said, "I have never seen such rude, vicious women in my life that came. If they are the best of what was happening in the wards, they were the worst examples of womanhood that I had ever seen."[18] This angrily responsive language, even fifteen years later, implies not just harsh feelings over conflict at an event but deeply ingrained perceptions of conservative and particularly Mormon women's political participation. It was not just that the women attended the conference en masse, or that they arrived at the conference uninformed. Larta's comments imply that the women's activity in Mormon congregations and what she saw as their inability to be ladylike in a non-Mormon space disqualified conservative women from accepted participation in the conference. Representing the wrong kind of womanhood, the activists were condemned for behaving in ways that challenged civil discourse and the feminist mission of the conference. Interestingly, this policing of women's political participation undermined the IWY's overall mission to engage women in dialogue about the meanings and goals of modern womanhood.[19]

In contrast with the feminists, conservative women attending the conference remembered it more favorably. Perhaps the prime example was general Relief Society General President Barbara Smith, who issued the call for LDS women to participate in the IWY and in the ERA struggle. Smith was a vocal supporter of what occurred at Utah's state IWY conference. Of the women who attended, she said, "They were great to come. They were great to stay. They did the very best they knew how and I think they should be commended. And I really think the people who are talking against what they did at that time don't realize what a tremendous responsibility they assumed."[20]

Smith's remarks point to the reality that the IWY represented a first time entree into the public sphere for many of the conservative and Mormon women who participated. That Mormon women found greater support for this activity from church leadership than local feminists (some of whom were themselves LDS) set up a critical boundary in Utah political culture. Conservative housewives could not look to feminist organizations for opportunities to shape political discourse; they had to create opportunities that suited their chosen roles in the family and made space for them as legitimate political actors. The Eagle Forum's emphasis on the political capacity of housewives built the foundation for a sustainable conservative women's movement in Utah.

Oral histories with 1970s feminists highlight the ways feminist and conservative conflict at the time shaped local understandings of which political communities were hospitable to Mormon women seeking impact beyond family and congregation. Although oral histories give feminists the opportunity to control the narrative, they also tell us something vital about the milieu conservative in which women found themselves at the dawn of the Reagan era. Feminists interpreted the political behaviors of conservative women as evidence that they lacked the ability to think for themselves, were manipulative and too bold in pressing their agenda, and were only respected by other conservatives. Such interpretations drove conservative women to carefully construct political strategies and identities to challenge accusations about the hypocrisy of political work outside the home.

These oral histories point to the genesis of polarization between female political actors but, more important, raise the question of how conservative Mormon women responded to the IWY experience and the broader polarization of women's politics. Oral histories with members of the Eagle Forum show how, through the deployment of an effective lobbying mechanism and a particular code of behavior, one organization created a political milieu congenial to conservative women eager to do the work of democracy in Utah.

In this polarized political culture, I set out to conduct oral history interviews in the summer of 2008. Negative portrayals by the media had made women of the Eagle Forum wary of interviewers. While reviewing a release form, one woman asked if there was a way she could place a restriction on writers taking her words out of context. Though I could not make that guarantee, I did my best to reassure her that she would have the opportunity to review and edit the transcript. She was surprised. Though often quoted in the newspaper, this woman had never had the opportunity to review what she had said. Presenting the interview as a collaborative effort between narrator and interviewer helped build a sense of trust that relaxed the interview atmosphere. This concept of shared authority is not new. The guidelines of the Oral History Association are reasonably explicit in emphasizing the narrator's role in the oral history process well after the interview goes a long way in building positive relationships and perceptions of what oral historians are setting out to do.[21] When working with groups as tightly networked as the Eagle Forum, such relationships are especially important.

Another important component of the preinterview process was explaining not only my intentions for conducting the interviews in the first place but why I was interested in Eagle Forum. Though the narrators agreed that creating an archival resource where one did not presently exist was important, they were more engaged by my acknowledgment of the presence of a liberal bias in higher education and in the emergent field of conservative history. All of the narrators expressed surprise that historians were taking conservatism seriously because they did not expect it.

Although one scholar of conservatism noted that he avoided using oral histories because he "wanted [his] book to be history, not journalism," oral history provides historians with an opportunity to reach out to the people they study.[22] Just as telling the story of marginalized groups can alter popular misconceptions, oral history interviews can help bridge chasms created by a tradition of conflict between these groups and historians. The relationships we build through interviewing, not just the content of the interviews, have a significant bearing on opportunities for future scholarship.

This matter weighed on my mind greatly as I scheduled and conducted interviews. For me, one of the challenges of conducting interviews with members of an organization so renowned for its stringent, black-and-white views on things was concern was that my behavior, in some subtle way, might jeopardize my position with these women. I deliberately selected modest outfits so as not to offend—or solicit even the most subtle amount of attention from—these women, who are all practicing Mormons and moral conservatives. Not that I would otherwise dress unprofessionally, but my appearance mattered more to me than than usual. I debated the presence of a campaign magnet on my car, ultimately removing it because I wanted to feel neutral. Though these may seem like simple and even silly concerns, they were indicative of my perceptions coming into the interviews—that the women of the Eagle Forum were discerning and possibly judgmental. For some reason, I was terrified that the nature of the interviews would be changed if my own identity as a liberal feminist was manifest. Though I did not try to test this hypothesis, it was a bias that brought a measure of caution to my interviews. I had internalized so many misconceptions about the women I was to speak with. Oral history interviews are perhaps one of the few opportunities historians have to confront their biases face to face. This reflective exercise made me acutely aware of the challenges members of Eagle Forum faced as they entered the public sphere to do political work.

Though all of the narrators interviewed attributed their involvement with the Eagle Forum to an inborn sense of morality that came with a Mormon upbringing, each told a different story about how she became involved. These stories reflected the changing approach of the Eagle Forum over the years. As a young mother, Gayle Ruzicka found that the Eagle Forum provided her with a way to obtain information and fight against the ERA from home through letter-writing campaigns. "The LDS Church . . . suggested to all of us that were members that we do something and get involved. And that's what led me to Eagle Forum. But I was a young mother with lots of children and was very limited in what I could do, but I did what I could do." Ruzicka's sense of political possibility was shaped by quieter motivations and strategies than previously suggested by feminist narrators of the ERA struggle. Her understanding of what women could do as wives and mothers appealed to Karen Clark, a young housewife from South Jordan. At a 1989 presentation at the Sandy Library, she first heard Ruzicka's perspectives on education, abortion, and homosexuality. Clark was invited to the Eagle Forum's monthly board meeting and was appointed a chapter president. Leadership in the Eagle Forum provided her with a means of political action without compromising her commitments to home and family. She recounted, "I met here as a chapter in my home so I could be with my family and not have to leave them. And when I went to the Capitol, I took my little ones with me."[23] For Ruzicka and Clark, the home orientation of the Eagle Forum provided an opening for political participation.

Yet for others, it was the work the Eagle Forum did outside the home that made it so appealing. Dalane England, a small business owner and seasoned "concerned citizen" who had lobbied independently at the Capitol for years, had a number of conversations about the Eagle Forum before she really knew what they did. She had asked people, "What do they do that's so whacko? What do they do that's so over the top? No one ever answered that question. . . . I kind of had this thinking that they were kind of a little bit out-there organization." This changed gradually as England attended an Eagle Forum conference in 2001, but she was never fully aware of what the group did until her daughter, a Teen Eagle legislative intern, encouraged her to meet with Eagle Forum at the state Capitol. Countering a common perception in Salt Lake City that the Eagle Forum has a domineering presence there, England remembered, "I had never realized who they were and that they were there." With this group of women England found a new means of efficacy. In the Eagle Forum, all of the narrators found people who shared their views and a means for becoming effective activists that fit with their faith and preexisting political views.

Oral histories help reveal how women feel about their political involvement, and in doing so tell us much about Mormon political culture. It has commonly been assumed that LDS women have not historically been politically independent thinkers—and certainly comments from women at the state IWY conference about the presence of manipulative men with walkie talkies might support that train of thought. The diversity of views expressed by different narrators suggests that although these women diligently follow counsel from primarily male Mormon leaders to be politically active, they do so after much personal study and consideration of the issues. Though Karen Clark remembered her first encounter with the Eagle Forum as including both Gayle Ruzicka and her husband, Ruzicka herself said nothing about her husband's political views or involvement beyond the very general statement that politics are discussed in her home. That Ruzicka, along with the other narrators, sees her activities with the Eagle Forum as independent of her husband but supportive of her role as wife and mother indicates that these "housewife activists" are the ones setting the political tone in their homes, or at the very least, that they have the time to devote to politics.

Supporting this idea are several innovations introduced by Ruzicka early in her involvement with the Utah Eagle Forum. Oral histories provide insight into a well-known yet simple and efficient system for disseminating information quickly to participants throughout the state: the phone tree. In its current incarnation, information shared through the phone tree starts with the issues vice president, who reviews policy information and passes it on to the president. The president reviews the information and decides which policies to pursue and emphasize. For matters of legislative importance, the secretary takes the message drafted by the president and faxes it to chapter presidents. Chapter presidents then initiate the "five-call-five-call-five," where five women will call five women who then call five more women. Simple strategies applied consistently to a bevy of conservative issues have proven strikingly effective over time.

What oral histories reveal about this process and the organization itself is that for a group known for such stringent policy positions, the Utah Eagle Forum is run with a surprising amount of flexibility. As Gayle Ruzicka explained:

> The reason that I didn't do a membership was that I wanted people if they could participate on the things that they agreed. You know, in this world of politics, sometimes you'll agree on something and sometimes you'll disagree. We set the telephone tree up in way that if we started calls out to people and we hit somebody that says, "You know what, I don't feel that way" or "I don't agree with you on this one" we would have somebody else we could move to next and just say "Okay, I understand" and move on. And so I wanted everybody to feel free to be on the telephone tree without saying "I'm a member of Eagle Forum."[24]

Such flexibility—a general agreement on most but not all things—surely contributes to the successes of the Eagle Forum. Adaptations like the phone tree use existing Mormon community and family networks to provide women with the opportunity to quickly obtain information and act on it immediately.

Next to the phone tree, the Utah Eagle Forum is known for its presence at legislative meetings and at the Capitol both during the forty-five-day legislative session and during interim meetings throughout the year. Dalane England noted that the lobbying effort was part of the attraction of the group, despite have previously perceived the Eagle Forum as "out there."[25] Of her initial experience lobbying with the Eagle Forum, she said: "So I just went up there and started working with them and it was wonderful, because it's not so lonely. You have this, really an organization who they're experienced, they're informed, they know the issues, they know the bills, they're not alone, they work with each other . . . so it would just so well organized, that I could be a part of this."[26] Though the appeal seemed less than universal—most of the women interviewed lamented the time they spend away from their homes during the legislative session—the women emphasized their commitment to being there. Though some press reports have implied that the Eagle Forum's presence is overbearing, participants view their time lobbying as the greatest expression of their commitment to what they refer to as their most important issue—"the family."

In terms of language, the phrase "the family" comes up most frequently when participants in the Utah Eagle Forum talk about what motivates their participation. Frequently, discussion about the family is intertwined with language typically employed in Mormon teachings, for example, describing the mission to protect the family as a "calling." All of the women interviewed expressed a commitment to perpetuating prolife legislation and concerns about the "gay agenda." Also under the broad umbrella of protecting the family are parents' rights. Couched in libertarian language, the women of the Eagle Forum fight vigorously for the right for parents to have control over the education their children receive—from legislation involving school notifications of activities to fighting for vouchers and home schooling rights. Though these issues are a part of the national Eagle Forum agenda, oral histories reveal which issues are most important to participants in Utah and why such issues are emphasized.

The code of behavior developed over the course of the Eagle
Forum's history suggests an interaction with media portrayals and
ideals of womanhood. When talking about the Eagle Forum and
the Teen Eagles intern group, Gayle Ruzicka emphasized that participants at the Capitol are always well groomed and wearing skirts
and dresses. She noted that when informed of impolite behavior by
participants, she strives to quickly correct it. Dalane England expressed how this behavior fit in with her own values, saying, "I
loved the perspective they come from, because it was never hateful,
never belligerent; it was never 'go in and create some ruckus.' It
was always 'be respectful to everyone, even those you disagree with'
which I think is a basic principle."[27] Cultivating this culture of po-
liteness and ladylike behavior in the organization is a vital step in
presenting the Utah Eagle Forum as a nonthreatening yet politically powerful coalition of women.

The Eagle Forum pioneered a watchdog role for conservative
women in Utah—a role that complimented their own sense of purpose as women, wives, and mothers. They stood vigilant to thwart
new dangers and enlarge the legislative boundaries of conservatism.
They labored to safeguard the seats of their supporters. These tasks
required the continuing commitment of women aware of what was
going on in state politics. Said Ruzicka: "If there's something that's
near and dear to you, you should pick up your phone and call your
legislator. But everybody can't find out what's going on. We're at
the legislature, we know what's going on, we're watchdogs for that
and we put the information out."[28] With this straightforward mind-
set, the Utah Eagle Forum harnessed the power of a conservative
base to become a powerful factor in the making of public policy.
Gayle Ruzicka is now regarded as a formidable figure in state politics, and the Utah Eagle Forum enjoys a prominence unequaled by
Eagle Forum chapters elsewhere.[29]

Oral histories with feminists and members of the Utah Eagle
Forum provide historians with many new insights into the activities
and motivations of conservative grassroots activists. Conservative
women responded to early feminist claims of hypocrisy with the
establishment of institutions like Eagle Forum. The passionate con-
victions of the women interviewed conveys why the Eagle Forum
would be a good fit in Utah's political and religious climate and

also about the creative methods employed by grassroots activists to accomplish their goals within that setting. Using strategies to fit existing social networks and gender roles and emphasizing common values in the vernacular of Mormonism, the Eagle Forum has gone from a small lobbying group to a powerful advocate for family values and individual rights in Utah. Oral histories help us see the ways women have empowered themselves through the Eagle Forum. Of their place in Utah politics, Gayle Ruzicka said of the Eagle Forum, "We are conservative so you know, people like to label us as right-wing extremists. We are not; we're a very conservative organization. There's lots of people out there far more extreme, if people like to say than we would ever be considered. We are probably politically very mainstream for Utah."[30] That a mainstream conservative women's organization can be one of the most powerful political influences in the state speaks to the importance of appealing to the political capacity of wives and mothers. As historians of the West undertake the history of conservatism, it is vital that the voices of the grassroots activists shaping policy and legislation are not lost. Oral history can make that possible.

Notes

1. Jessica Grose, "Why Sarah Palin Incites Near-Violent Rage in Normally Reasonable Women," *Jezebel*, September 5, 2008, accessed February 27, 2012, http://jezebel.com/5045934/why-sarah-palin-incites-near+violent-rage-in-normally-reasonable-women; Jodi Kantor and Rachel L. Swarns, "A New Twist in the Debate on Mothers," *New York Times*, September 1, 2008, A1; Belinda Luscombe, "Why Some Women Hate Sarah Palin," *Time*, October 2, 2008, accessed February 27, 2012, http://www.time.com/time/politics/article/0,8599,1846832,00.html#ixzz21wmSMZdk; Judith Warner, "The Mirrored Ceiling," *Opinionator*, September 4, 2008, accessed February 28, 2012, http://opinionator.blogs.nytimes.com/2008/09/04/the-mirrored-ceiling/.

2. Lisa McGirr, *Suburban Warriors: The Origins of the New American Right* (Princeton: Princeton University Press, 2002); Catherine Rymph, *Republican Women: Feminism and Conservatism from Suffrage to the Rise of the New Right* (Chapel Hill: University of North Carolina Press, 2006); Michelle Nickerson, *Mothers of Conservatism: Women and the Postwar Right* (Princeton, NJ: Princeton University Press, 2012).

3. Michelle Nickerson, "Moral Mothers and Goldwater Girls," in *The Conservative Sixties*, ed. D. Farber and J. Roche (New York: Peter Lang, 2003), 60; Michelle Nickerson, "'The Power of a Morally Indignant Woman': Republican Women and the Making of California Conservatism," *Journal of the West* 42 (Summer 2003): 36–37.

4. Melanie Newport, "Grassroots Power: The Utah Eagle Forum, 1972–2009," master's thesis, University of Utah, 2009.

5. Donald T. Critchlow, *Phyllis Schlafly and Grassroots Conservatism: A Woman's Crusade* (Princeton: Princeton University Press, 2005), 6.

Phyllis Schlafly: The Sweetheart of the Silent Majority (Chicago: Regnery Gateway, 1981); Critchlow, *Phyllis Schlafly and Grassroots Conservatism*; Rymph, *Republican Women*; David Farber, *The Rise and Fall of Modern American Conservatism* (Princeton: Princeton University Press, 2010).

7. Rymph, *Republican Women*.

8. Jay Logan Rogers, "Utah's Right Turn: Republican Ascendancy and the 1976 US Senate Race," master's thesis, University of Utah, 2008, 6.

9. Martha Sonntag Bradley, *Pedestals and Podiums: Utah Women, Religious Authority and Equal Rights* (Salt Lake City, UT: Signature Books, 2005), 99–101. See also Neil J. Young, "'The ERA Is a Moral Issue': The Mormon Church, LDS Women, and the Defeat of the Equal Rights Amendment," *American Quarterly* 59 (2007): 623–44.

10. Carol Garbett, interview by author, December 15, 2008, Salt Lake City, Utah.

11. Dorothea Masur, interview by author, August 12, 2008, Ogden, Utah.

12. "Ex-Ogden Legislator Faces Charge in HAFB Shoplifting," *Salt Lake Tribune*, September 28, 1990, B15; Gayle Ruzicka, interview by author, June 5, 2008, Highland, Utah.

13. Ruzicka interview.

14. JoAnn Freed Collection, Utah State Historical Society, Salt Lake City, Utah.

15. Martha Sonntag Bradley Research Collection, Brigham Young University, Provo, Utah.

16. Esther Landa, interview, August 6, 1991, Martha Sonntag Bradley Research Collection, Box 17, Brigham Young University.

17. Ramona Adams, interview, September 19, 1991, Martha Sonntag Bradley Research Collection, Box 13, Brigham Young University.

18. Marilee Larta, interview, August 9, 1991, Martha Sonntag Bradley Research Collection, Box 17, Brigham Young University.

19. Martha Sonntag Bradley, "The Mormon Relief Society and the International Women's Year," *Journal of Mormon History* 21 (1995): 110.

20. Barbara Smith, interview [transcript], October 14, 1992, Martha Sonntag Bradley Research Collection, Box 2, Brigham Young University.

21. Oral History Association, "Principles and Standards of the Oral History Association," *Evaluation Guidelines*, http://alpha.dickinson.edu/oha/pub_eg.html;

Michael Frisch, A Shared Authority (Albany: State University of New York Press, 1990).

22. Critchlow, Phyllis Schlafly and Grassroots Conservatism, 10.
23. Karen Clark, interview by author, July 7, 2008, South Jordan, Utah.
24. Ruzicka interview.
25. Dalane England, interview by author, July 9, 2008, Bountiful, Utah.
26. Ibid.
27. Ibid.
28. Ruzicka interview.
29. Phyllis Schlafly, interview by author, July 23, 2008, St. Louis, Missouri.
30. Ruzicka interview.

Part III

Essential Sources

13

Creating Community

Telling the Story of the Mormons in Fort Collins, Colorado

LINDA M. MEYER

*Historian Linda M. Meyer examines one religious community, a con-
gregation of the Church of Jesus Christ of Latter-day Saints (LDS)
in Fort Collins, Colorado. Unlike many towns and cities in the
Intermountain West, Fort Collins was not settled by Mormons, and
members of the LDS Church were relative newcomers to the area.
Although the LDS Church Library provides rich primary sources
about Mormon congregations in other locations, it offers very little
information related to Fort Collins. Oral history provided one of the
few ways to find out about the Mormons who settled on Colorado's
Front Range. Through her interviews, Meyer found that the experience of being part of a religious minority created a greater sense of
community among church members. This was further influenced by
the volunteer work necessary to build the local chapel. The interviews
also corrected some misinformation from a few printed sources. Most
significant, the interviews provided stories that enhance understanding of the community. The Mormon community has continued to
grow in Fort Collins and surrounding areas to the point that Church
President Thomas S. Monson announced in April 2011 that a temple
will be built in that city.*

DURING THE PAST half a century, many rural towns in America disappeared as an increasing number of their younger generations

moved to the cities. Some people may interpret this loss of small towns to mean that the nation's sense of community is breaking down. In his book *Community and Social Change in America*, Thomas Bender proposes new definitions of *community* that do not rely on a specific location but instead focus on mutual interest and emotional ties.[1] According to Bender and others, experiences of community exist even within the impersonal setting of a large urban area. A community was once defined as a group of people who lived in close geographic proximity and participated in interdependent relationships, sharing significant portions of their lives. The concepts of interdependent relationships and sharing remain an essential part of the new definitions, which involve deep feelings of connectedness to others within the group. As Philip Gulley expresses it, "Community isn't so much a locale as it is a state of mind. You find it whenever folks ask how you're doing because they care, and not because they're getting paid to inquire."[2]

Oral histories proved to be a rich source of information as I set out to study the ways members of the Church of Jesus Christ of Latter-day Saints (LDS) in Fort Collins, Colorado, interacted to create an identifiable cultural community during the twentieth century.[3] In the late 1990s, I conducted nineteen oral history interviews with individuals involved in the early years of the Fort Collins LDS Church.[4] These oral histories provided context and valuable insights concerning the creation of the LDS community in this northern Colorado city.

Brigham Young's followers colonized many areas throughout the western United States, but northern Colorado was not among them. Thus, the community experiences of the first Latter-day Saints in Fort Collins differed greatly from those of their counterparts in Mormon colonies located outside of Utah, such as Rexburg, Idaho, or Mesa, Arizona. The Latter-day Saint immigrants who founded Rexburg, Mesa, and other early LDS towns brought well-established church traditions to their new settlements and enjoyed the advantages of being part of the dominant culture, whereas the early Fort Collins Mormons struggled to define themselves as members of a tiny minority. The stories of the LDS "old timers" supply interesting details regarding their community-building activities in the mid-twentieth century. Those who participated in the

Fort Collins congregation during the 1940s told of church meetings and socials in the local Odd Fellows' Hall, small gatherings of Mormon women for activities of the Relief Society (the LDS women's organization), and the beginnings of a sense of religious identity in this mostly non-Mormon college town.

In addition to fleshing out the lean framework provided by written records, in some cases the oral histories provided the only source of information concerning past events. An interview with one individual often led to contact with a person who had not been on my original list of potential narrators. Some provided information concerning the locations of additional historical documents and other primary source materials or offered new names to research in sources I had previously accessed. In all cases, the participants offered insights into their social and religious activities and interactions, told through colorful narratives illustrating the Mormon experience in Fort Collins.

My initial conception of the role of oral histories from the old timers was that the stories would add interesting flavor and provide background for the names and dates I discovered in historic documents of the area. I soon found that the stories represented the very heart of the study of Mormon community-building in northern Colorado. For an earlier project, I had researched the chain of title to the land on which the first LDS chapel was built in Fort Collins. From the microfilmed warranty deeds in the office of the Larimer County clerk and recorder, I determined that this formerly vacant lot at the intersection of Peterson and Locust Streets had been purchased by the LDS Church in late 1948 and was sold to the Salvation Army in 1963. Pondering these dates, I wondered about the role this piece of real estate had played as a center of the Mormon community in those fifteen years. Additional questions came to mind: What other Fort Collins locations had provided a sanctuary for LDS worship services before 1948? Who were the first Mormons in Fort Collins, and when did they start gathering with others of their faith for fellowship and spiritual edification?

To begin the process of filling in the story, I started conducting oral history interviews with some of the more senior members of the Fort Collins congregation. During these interviews, participants were asked questions regarding their lives in the town and involvement with LDS Church activities in the area. Since many of the early Fort Collins church records prior to 1942 were lost in a fire, there were large gaps in the information available from local documents. The memories shared through oral histories provided details that might otherwise have been lost. Also, many times a narrator offered other sources of information. Tyler Woolley frequently admitted that he couldn't remember dates or other details, but then he would pull out a hand-written record, such as a list documenting the names of Fort Collins bishops between 1951 and the 1980s. Another narrator, Forest Stonemets, served as a bishop of the Fort Collins congregation during the 1960s. He had created a scrapbook, featuring dedication programs, news clippings, and photographs of the construction of the second LDS meeting house in the town. Although many of these sources might contain errors, their existence contributed greatly to the growing body of evidence that could be investigated in piecing together the cultural history of the Fort Collins Latter-day Saints. These additional sources came to light as a direct result of the question-and-answer sessions of oral history interviews.

Although none of the participants in this project had kept a diary or personal journal, many led me to primary documentary sources regarding church member activities during a given period of time. These sources, while providing additional information, often raised new questions. Lamar Esplin brought out a photocopy of a Fort Collins church record that he had obtained many years earlier on a trip to Salt Lake City. Dated 1940, the document listed the names of sixty-eight members of the Fort Collins branch. Esplin was puzzled by the number listed, as he showed me a copy of the 1954 dedication program for the first building constructed by Fort Collins Mormons, the Peterson Street chapel. A short history of the Fort Collins LDS congregation printed on the back of the program mentioned that the group had grown from "a dependent branch with 49 members in 1940 to a fully organized ward with 241 members in 1954."[5] (A Mormon ward is a congregation analogous to a Catholic parish.) Since the official church record listed sixty-eight members in 1940, either the number or the date on the dedication program (or both) must be in error. This error was perpetuated, as the information was copied into the 1964 program for the dedication of a new church building on Lynnwood Drive, and it also appeared in an article in the local newspaper at the time of the new building's dedication.

Clues relating to the actual size of the congregation in 1940 were offered in the Esplin interview. Lamar and Phyllis Esplin arrived in Fort Collins in 1942, only two years after the organization of the Fort Collins branch, and they remembered the number of members meeting at that time as being very small. Typically, only about half of the individuals listed on the membership records are active participants in church meetings, so a total of thirty to thirty-five active members would fit with the Esplins' descriptions of their early meetings at the Odd Fellows' Hall.

The interview with the Esplins brought to my attention inconsistencies in the written record and provided information helpful in my attempt to write an accurate history of the Mormon community in Fort Collins. At a later date, I traveled to the LDS Family History Center in Salt Lake City. After searching through numerous microfilm documents, I determined that the Fort Collins Branch of the Western States Mission of the Church of Jesus Christ of Latter-day Saints was organized on December 13, 1931, with a total of forty-nine members.[6] I also found a possible reason for the error in the history provided in the program for the Peterson Street chapel dedication. The Denver Stake of the LDS Church was organized in 1940, and at that time, the Fort Collins branch became a part of that stake organization, rather than a unit of the Western States Mission. A document discussing the organization of the Fort Collins branch as a dependent unit of the Denver Stake may have been used by an earlier historian to set the creation date of the Fort Collins branch at 1940. My interview with the Esplins played a pivotal role in raising the question of inaccuracy of some of the historical records and in pointing my research in the right direction to solve the problem.

In addition to providing additional sources of written documentation, my narrators offered the names of other people still living in the Fort Collins area to interview. Phyllis Esplin mentioned that Lily Hout, daughter-in-law of William Luther (Bill) Hout, an early president of the Fort Collins branch of the church, was still in town

and could be a good source of information concerning church activities in the 1930s. Blanche Chadwick Martens directed me to
Rosella Bauer Harris, who had grown up in Fort Collins and joined
the church in 1929 with other members of her family.

Offering Insights Concerning Social
Interactions and Identity

Unlike the names, dates, and locations gleaned from written documents, the oral history interviews provided glimpses into the feelings of community identity that emerged among Fort Collins Mormons as their numbers increased. Common themes appearing in
the narratives of those who arrived earliest in the city included religious isolation, self-sacrifice, unity of purpose, and a sense of the
small size of the LDS community before the 1950s. For narrators
who had moved from Utah during the 1940s, the tiny Fort Collins
congregation of ten to fifteen families contrasted sharply with the
large, well-established, and fully staffed church organizations common in the state of their origin.

These themes were evident in an interview with a retired animal
science professor and former bishop of the Fort Collins student
congregation of the church. Newlyweds Lamar and Phyllis Esplin
moved to Fort Collins in 1942, when Lamar began working for the
agricultural college that became Colorado State University. They
had grown up together in Logan, Utah, and both attended Utah
State University before Lamar went on to pursue graduate work in
animal science at Texas A&M and the University of Illinois. Lamar
spoke of the days during World War II, when nine or ten Mormon
families would hold their Sunday meetings at the Odd Fellows'
Hall downtown. The men, who gathered for a separate priesthood
meeting early in the morning before Sunday school classes began,
took on the responsibility for emptying ashtrays, sweeping the
floor, and setting up chairs for the Sunday services. Phyllis added
that in those early days, the women would attend weekday Relief
Society meetings at the home of one of the women. The group was
so small that the entire Relief Society could fit into one car to drive
to where the meeting was held.[7]

The stories told by converts to the church differed in perspective from those of lifelong members. Several of the oral history narrators contrasted the opportunities for community building available in Fort Collins with their isolated experiences of life as converts in more rural areas. Blanche Ellgen Chadwick Martens grew up on a ranch near Craig, Colorado. Her mother, Elizabeth Culverwell Ellgen, became a Latter-day Saint three years before she met Herman Ellgen III (Martens's father), who didn't join the church. Instructed in church beliefs by her mother at home, Martens had few opportunities for attending church with other members. The Mormon missionaries would sometimes walk eleven miles from Craig to the family ranch to visit with them and with the Chadwicks, another LDS ranch family, for a week before returning to town. After her first marriage to Robert Chadwick, Martens moved to a ranch near Fort Collins and finally became part of a Mormon congregation. Her interview emphasized the theme of self-sacrifice as she described the dedication of her son, Dale Chadwick, in riding his bicycle seven miles into town every morning to attend a before-school seminary class for teenagers.[8]

Another narrator, Esther Bailey Park, experienced similar isolation from the church on the Bailey family farm near Indianola, Nebraska. Park's mother was baptized by two traveling missionaries in 1909. There were no branches of the church near their farm; thus, for more than twenty years the family's only contact with the LDS Church came through the visits of passing missionaries. Park and her sister were baptized after their sixteenth birthdays, and their father accepted baptism shortly before his death in 1930. Unable to keep the farm going in the midst of the Depression and hearing of an opportunity for employment harvesting cherries, seventeen-year-old Esther and her mother joined her older sister in Fort Collins in summer 1937 (see figure 13.1). They knew of no other Mormons in Fort Collins for several years, but one day in 1943 the owner of the restaurant where Park worked made the comment that "those Mormons are meeting at the hall down the street," and they had the opportunity to experience being part of an LDS community for the first time.[9]

Although she spent her childhood in town, an early Fort Collins convert experienced feelings of religious isolation similar to those

Figure 13.1 The family of Blanche Ellgen Chadwick Martens after moving from their ranch to a Fort Collins home, 1962. Left to right: Elizabeth Ellgen, R. Gale Chadwick, Kent Chadwick, Blanche Chadwick, Robert Chadwick, and Kay Chadwick. (Dale Chadwick was serving a church mission to Finland at that time.) Photo courtesy of R. Gale Chadwick.

of her rural friends. At the time of her interview, Rosella Bauer Harris was one of three people listed on the 1940 LDS branch record who still lived in Fort Collins.[10] She was five years old in 1926 when her family was introduced to the church by two Mormon missionaries serving in Fort Collins. The family received weekly doctrinal instruction from the missionaries and their successors for several years. During that time, Rosella knew of no church members in town, although she heard that the missionaries were teaching other families. The Bauer family drove to nearby Loveland on occasion after 1927 to attend church meetings in the home of George Myron Baker, a Mormon who worked as a department store salesman. On December 15, 1929, Rosella, her parents, her older brother, and two cousins who lived with them officially became members of the LDS Church when they were baptized by immersion in the old Fort Collins YMCA swimming pool.

When the Fort Collins Branch of the Church of Jesus Christ of Latter-day Saints was organized two years later, eight of the forty-nine people listed on the membership records were members of the Bauer family. Rosella recalled that at the beginning, branch members attended Sunday meetings in each other's homes. As the branch slowly grew over the next decade, they started meeting in a rented room in the Odd Fellows' Hall at 117 East Mountain Avenue. Mrs. Bauer sponsored children's meetings in her home during the 1930s; these usually served her own children and a few neighborhood youngsters, who learned such handicrafts as the construction of birdcages from straws and yarn.

Before the end of the decade, tragedy struck the Bauer household. Rosella was sixteen when her father died of a heart attack in 1937. Her mother died of cancer within six months, and a year later Rosella married Ernest Harris. After farming in Fort Collins for three years, Rosella and Ernest Harris moved to Cheyenne, Wyoming. More than twenty years later, Rosella Harris returned to find a well-established LDS ward in Fort Collins.[11]

The oral history interviews of Mormons who came to Fort Collins after World War II moved from the common themes of isolation and minority status to those of community expansion and growth. The topics of unity and self-sacrifice continued to surface, especially in stories of the LDS efforts to build houses of worship in the city. But the LDS social life was certainly not "all work and no play." As church membership increased in Fort Collins during the late 1940s, the Mormons became better acquainted with each other through dances, picnics, and parties, in addition to their regular Sunday meetings. An interview with Sterling Olsen, who moved to Fort Collins in 1948 to work in soil research for the US Department of Agriculture, recalled a "Gold and Green Ball" (an annual formal dance that had become an LDS tradition) held in the Odd Fellows' Hall in the late 1940s. Some of the LDS college students managed to obtain decorations that had been used on a sorority float for the College Days parade that spring, and they had the old hall looking very festive. The church members could not decide which of the seven teenage girls in attendance should be queen of the ball, so they crowned them all.[12]

Another narrator, Tyler Woolley, related that in addition to renting the Odd Fellows' Hall for Sunday meetings and other activities, the Fort Collins Mormons sometimes held dances and other social activities in the basement of the historic Old Main building on the nearby college campus. Woolley and his wife, Lucile, joined others moving from Utah to Fort Collins in 1948 when he found work at the college as a professor of biology, specializing in entomology. During his first few years in Fort Collins, he and other LDS men met at the Odd Fellows' Hall early on Sunday mornings to prepare the hall for their worship services.[13]

In addition to providing human interest stories, the oral history interviews filled many gaps in the written sources concerning meeting places of the Fort Collins Latter-day Saints prior to the construction of the Peterson Street chapel. I now knew that by 1942, when the Esplins relocated to the area, the Mormons were holding Sunday services in the Odd Fellows' Hall, and that they continued

Figure 13.2 A meeting of the children's organization of the Church of Jesus Christ of Latter-day Saints in Fort Collins, April 15, 1951. This photograph was taken a few months before the congregation moved from the rented meeting place at the Odd Fellows' Hall to their newly constructed chapel on Peterson Street. Photo courtesy of R. Gale Chadwick.

gathering there until their first meeting house was completed in 1951 (see figure 13.2), although at times they used other facilities for their social activities. In his interview, Esplin provided another bit of information when he recalled that the Odd Fellows moved from a location on East Mountain Avenue to one on West Mountain Avenue in the early 1940s, and the Latter-day Saints moved along with them. By 1947, the number of Mormons in Fort Collins had increased sufficiently for the branch to plan fundraising activities to build their first house of worship. After the lot on Peterson Street was purchased by the church, contractor A. W. Burt began construction on the building in 1949.[14]

Fort Collins branch members assisted with the construction in the evenings and on Saturdays; Sterling Olsen recalled working on framing, roofing, and bricklaying. Olsen also drove to Salt Lake City to request permission from the central church leadership to build a partial basement for a furnace room and storage area.[15] Excited at the prospect of owning their own meeting house, the members enthusiastically volunteered their time in building and fundraising activities. Although their work was overseen by a professional contractor, most of the Mormons were not skilled in the building trade, and one narrator, Donal Johnson, called the Peterson Street chapel "an architectural disaster." Johnson, a former dean of the College of Agriculture at the local university, recalled that "in order to have activities, you had to move all the pews, and the floor was so uneven, that you had to move the benches back into the exact places" so that they would not wobble.[16]

In September 1951, the Fort Collins Latter-day Saints began holding meetings in their new chapel. Church policy dictated that new church buildings were not dedicated until all construction debts had been paid, so the Fort Collins members didn't hold the dedication ceremony until March 28, 1954. Narrators shared amusing memories of Sunday meetings and social activities held in the Peterson meetinghouse. The members enjoyed dances and theatrical productions, and since the building had no stage or curtain, the actors entered and left the pulpit area through the front windows.[17]

In addition to donating funds and labor for the Peterson Street chapel, the Mormons also supported the construction of a larger meeting house, a stake center, in Denver. The Denver District of the

Western States Mission of the LDS Church, formed on October 30, 1938, encompassed branches in Denver, Englewood, Barnum, Pueblo, Fort Collins, Cheyenne, and Laramie. On June 30, 1940, the Denver District became the Denver Stake.[18] As a part of the Denver Stake, the Fort Collins branch members assisted in fundraising for and labor on the new stake center. Sterling Olsen remembered driving to Denver on Saturdays to help with the construction; as one of his assigned tasks, he cleaned the excess mortar from the brick walls after the masons assembled them.

Members of the Denver Stake completed construction on their new stake center in spring 1950. Fundraising and construction labor for two new buildings in the years between 1947 and 1951 kept the Fort Collins Latter-day Saints very busy, and the oral histories offered many stories of close friendships that developed as the members worked, played, and worshiped together.

In the decade following World War II, the GI Bill and resulting expansion of the agricultural college in Fort Collins led to many job opportunities that attracted educated Mormons to the city. The steadily growing membership of the congregation quickly outgrew the Peterson Street chapel, and within ten years the Latter-day Saints were searching for a new meeting house site. The original plans for the first building made no allowance for classroom space; members assumed that they would add it as the need arose. Blanche Martens recalled teaching a Sunday school class of young children in the church hallway. She laughed as she described the children's faces peeking out from behind the heavy coats hanging on hooks in the hall.[19] Sharyn Smith, who moved to Fort Collins from Loveland in 1957, taught a class of eleven-year-old girls in the kitchen; since there were no chairs, the girls sat on the counter and stove. Her husband, Owen Smith, remembered that even the furnace room in the basement was used as a classroom.[20]

Realizing that simply adding classrooms to the small chapel on Peterson Street would not solve the crowding problems, church leaders began discussing the construction of a larger building. A parcel of land in a new subdivision on Lynnwood Drive was purchased in November 1960, and fundraising activities began again; one program to gain contributions for the building fund brought LDS middleweight boxing champion Gene Fullmer to town to address a dinner audience in April 1961.[21] Members held ground-breaking ceremonies for the new meeting house on June 26, 1961, and completed the first phase of construction, including the chapel and classrooms, one year later.

In addition to raising money, the Fort Collins Mormons donated their labor on this building as they had on the earlier chapel and the Denver stake center. Sterling Olsen recalled the early morning and evening work details staffed by volunteers. One rainy day, only four men appeared: Sterling Olsen, Lamar Esplin, Forest Stonemets, and Irving Dunn. Plans called for the roof of the new chapel to be supported by four pairs of massive beams, which were lying in the alfalfa field, waiting to be fastened to the concrete footings that had been poured earlier. After a mechanical device lifted each pair of beams upright to their thirty-foot height, one man would have to climb a rope attached to the top of the beams to fasten them together at the peak. After a short discussion (in which one man asserted that he was too old to climb up there and another professed a fear of heights) Olsen found himself elected to the job. Four times he shinnied up the rope, fastened the beams (and tried not to look down), and shinnied back down again, while the others held the beams in place and shouted encouragement. Olsen added that all four men later served as bishops of Fort Collins wards.[22]

Church growth in the city continued at a steady pace, within the decade creating a need for a larger building, a stake center, to be located at the corner of Swallow and Stover Streets. By the 1970s, church policy regarding congregants working on their buildings had changed, and professional construction workers carried out all the work on a new structure. No doubt this improved the quality of the construction and conformed to new insurance regulations, but as narrator Burns Sabey commented, the local members lost a "wonderful bonding experience" found in building their own meeting house.[23]

Nevertheless, in 1970, with undimmed enthusiasm, Fort Collins Mormons took on the challenge of raising funds for construction. In a major project involving the whole stake, church members delivered all the routes of the new northern Colorado weekly newspaper, the *Triangle Review*. Once each week for several years, dozens of family cars converged in the parking lot of the Lynnwood chapel to load bundles of newspapers. The enterprise required good planning and dedicated teamwork, and carriers suffered a few mishaps. Lorna Lindsay, delivering her quota of papers one wintry evening, slipped on the ice and hit her head. She stated, "I literally saw stars, and not just the ones in the sky."[24] Fortunately, she sustained no permanent injuries. The new building took shape at a steady pace, and on February 6, 1977, members of the Fort Collins Second Ward, led by Bishop Owen Smith, held the first meetings in the new stake center.[25]

Many of my narrators told stories of events and activities of the Fort Collins LDS congregation (especially during the devoted effort to build three meeting houses in Fort Collins and the stake center in Denver) that created strong feelings of friendship and fostered the development of a Mormon community. In addition to these comments, the oral histories provided insights concerning the ages and interests of the Fort Collins members. For example, Tyler Woolley described MIA activities in the late 1940s in Fort Collins. The MIA, or Mutual Improvement Association, was created for young people of the church over the age of twelve. There were very few Mormon teenagers in Fort Collins during the 1940s and 1950s, so the MIA participants were the students who had come for a college education.

A final common theme of the oral history interviews deals with the resourcefulness and initiative of the Fort Collins Latter-day Saints. Tyler Woolley told a story explaining why the Lynnwood Drive building has a garden-level partial basement, since basements were discouraged by church authorities in Salt Lake City. The lot selected for this building was on high ground, with a six-foot drop in slope down to the future parking lot. Woolley, at that time serving as bishop of the congregation, did some calculations and figured out how much backfill would be needed to put the building on level ground, rather than digging out a basement. He also determined that all the basement windows would be above ground level. Taking these calculations to Salt Lake City, he conferred with the officials at church headquarters and managed to win approval for the basement plan. This was fortunate, because the construction crew had already commenced digging the basement.[26]

Forest Stonemets, a convert to the church, had a way of taking matters into his own hands when asked to provide service. While others sat in councils and planned future activities, Stonemets rolled up his sleeves and got it done. During his interview, he commented, "I've got a lot of different ideas, because I wasn't born and raised in this organization."[27] Apparently, the church leaders in the area appreciated his can-do attitude, because he was asked to serve as bishop of the Fort Collins congregation and received a sustaining vote by the members on the first day they held services in the new Lynnwood Street chapel. Prior to its construction, the members dug a well on the property to determine the depth of the water table and ensure that the basement would not be flooded. Since there was already a well, Stonemets decided that he didn't want to hand-water the new lawn surrounding the building. Rather than waiting to submit a request to church headquarters through the usual channels, he hired a company to install a pump and irrigation system and paid for the work with a check from his personal bank account. When called to task for not having the project authorized, Stonemets replied that it was all taken care of, there was no need to be concerned about it; he then invited the members to make a donation toward the irrigation system if they felt so inclined. He reported that the donations covered his expenses in installing the system.[28]

In another story, Stonemets recalled being asked to find a way to increase the attendance of Fort Collins members at the temple built in south Denver in 1986. His solution was to charter a bus, scheduled to leave the Fort Collins church building at 4 pm on a Friday afternoon, to transport the members to Denver for the evening temple session. In addition to providing transportation for elderly members who were reluctant to drive, the bus fostered fellowship during the three-hour round trip. Expenses for the bus were also covered by individual donations, and the service proved to be so popular that frequently every seat was filled. The events recalled by narrators Woolley and Stonemets showed the initiative common among Fort Collins Mormons as they built their meeting houses and looked for creative solutions to the challenges they encountered.

The recorded memories of the Fort Collins Latter-day Saints turned an interesting research topic into a fascinating opportunity to understand the lives and interactions of a dedicated, faithful, hardworking yet fun-loving group of people who created a cohesive community in this western college town. While preparing to write on the topic of Mormon community building in Fort Collins, I spent several years researching names, dates, locations, and other data. I wanted to ensure that my facts were accurate, that I reported the historical events correctly, and that the framework I constructed for this history stood on a solid foundation. I appreciated the additional documentation provided by many of my narrators as I recorded these oral histories, and I found even more value in the stories they told. Truly, these stories made the names and dates come alive for me, as I hope they will for any others who take the time to listen to them.

Notes

1. Thomas Bender, *Community and Social Change in America* (New Brunswick, NJ: Rutgers University Press, 1978), 6–8.

2. Philip Gulley, *Front Porch Tales* (Sisters, OR: Multnomah Books, 1997), 22.

3. Portions of this chapter are excerpted from the author's master's thesis. For additional historical information about the LDS Church, the city of Fort Collins, and the people interviewed, see Linda C. McGehee, "The Development of the Fort Collins Mormon Community during the Twentieth Century," master's thesis, Colorado State University, 2000.

4. Original oral history tapes and notes remain in the author's possession.

5. From a history included in the program for the chapel dedication, March 28, 1954.

6. "December, 1931 Quarterly Report of the Western States Mission of the Church of Jesus Christ of Latter-day Saints," *Denver, Colorado District, Western States Mission of the Church of Jesus Christ of Latter-day Saints, Membership Records 1908–1942*, Microfilm #0001836 in the LDS Family History Center, Salt Lake City, Utah.

7. Phyllis and Lamar Esplin, interview by author, April 16, 1996, Fort Collins, Colorado, tape recording.

8. Blanche Chadwick Martens, interview by author, April 19, 1996, Fort Collins, Colorado, tape recording.

9. Esther Bailey Park, telephone interview by author, March 24, 1996, Fort Collins, Colorado.

10. The other two were Rosella's brother, Jack Clinton Bauer, and cousin Rose Bauer Pingree. Rosella Bauer Harris, interview by author, April 19, 1997, Fort Collins, Colorado, tape recording.

11. Ibid.

12. Sterling R. Olsen, interview by author, March 27, 1997, Fort Collins, Colorado tape recording.

13. Tyler A. Woolley, interview by author, April 23, 1996, Fort Collins, Colorado, tape recording.

14. "Latter Day Saints Organized First Independent Ward, 1951," *Fort Collins Coloradoan*, May 29, 1964, 7.

15. Olsen interview.

16. Donal and Ruth Johnson, interview by author, February 25, 1998, Fort Collins, Colorado, tape recording.

17. Ibid.

18. Wilfred W. Barber, ed., "Crestmoor Ward and Denver Stake," dedicatory booklet for the building at 740 Hudson Street, Denver, Colorado, October 15, 1950.

19. Martens interview.

20. Owen and Sharyn Smith, interview by author, April 21, 1997, Fort Collins, Colorado, tape recording.

21. *Fort Collins Ward Historical Report*, June 30, 1961, in possession of R. Gale and Judy Chadwick, Fort Collins, Colorado.

22. Olsen interview.

23. Burns R. and Elaine Sabey, interview by author, October 8, 1997, Fort Collins, Colorado, tape recording.

24. Willard and Lorna Lindsay, interview by author, November 3, 1997, Fort Collins, Colorado, tape recording.

25. Smith interview.

26. Woolley interview.

27. Forest Stonemets, interview by author, April 22, 1997, Windsor, Colorado, tape recording.

28. Ibid.

14

Every Mine, Every Cow Camp, Every Ranch

Oral History as Fieldwork

LEISL CARR CHILDERS

Historian Leisl Carr Childers looks at how oral history collected in the field, the places where people live and work, complicates knowledge about the effects of radioactive fallout from nuclear testing in the Great Basin and pushes inquiry in a new direction. Her research addressed the Nevada Test Site, where nuclear testing took place, and the isolated ranchers who live and work in the area. Her interview with one of the ranchers documented how radiation affected the lives and work of the people who lived in proximity to the Test Site. Her interview with a federal radiation monitor documented the unexpected friendships created between ranchers and representatives of the testing program responsible for keeping the population in the region safe. The interviews were the only way to understand both the importance of the area's geography and the friendly relationships between monitors and ranchers.

ORAL HISTORY OFFERS a valuable methodology for delving into a place, the personalities that inhabit it, and the work done there. From historians sitting in offices and archives among documents and photographs, it can be difficult to place human personalities in the space in which they live and work. According to oral historian Paul Thompson, "oral history is built around people," makes the historical narrative accessible, and seeks to collect the stories and experiences of the ordinary person. This methodology offers opportunities for conversation with people and physical contact with their homes and workplaces. This moves historians out of the institutionalized world of academia into an inquiry process driven by field research that often deepens and complicates the stories historians normally tell. By engaging in this type of active research through fieldwork, new evidence is introduced into the historical record that would otherwise be overlooked using traditional approaches to history.[1]

This essay addresses my discovery of a place and a set of important relationships that surfaced in oral histories collected in the so-called empty spaces of the Great Basin. Between 2003 and 2008, the Nevada Test Site Oral History Project at the University of Nevada, Las Vegas, collected interviews from people working on or affiliated with the nuclear testing program and those that had been affected by the testing during the cold war. Interviewees included scientists, administrators, secretaries, engineers, miners, electricians, welders, carpenters, military personnel, antinuclear activists, Native Americans, ranchers, and several residents of southwestern Utah called downwinders because of their unfortunate location relative to the clouds of radioactive fallout.

During the process of compiling the oral histories and related material for the archive, I encountered a federal report that piqued my curiosity. Generated in 1950 by the scientific team evaluating the cost of a continental nuclear test site, the document speculated as to the human impact of creating a testing facility. The scientists had preferred a site in the south central Great Basin because of the area's small population density, arid climate, and consistent prevailing winds that blew to the north and east, away from centers of population such as Los Angeles and Las Vegas that were less than 400 miles away, and because the location was more than 400 miles away from downwind centers of population such as Salt Lake City. The small towns within 400 miles of the dry lakebeds of Frenchman and Yucca Flat, where tests would take place, had much smaller populations and could therefore be easily monitored, although scientists considered these areas too large to evacuate. The scientific team regarded the communities within this 400-mile radius potentially in the path of significant radioactive fallout and determined that the "size of the risk" of a continental test site was that a small population, about 400 persons or 1 person per square mile across 400 miles, would receive some exposure. They estimated that in this sector adjacent to the test site, these persons had a low probability of receiving what was then considered to be a maximum (but recoverable) radiation dose.[2]

The report raised important questions that required exploration beyond the existing record, which contained few names and fewer descriptions of what had actually occurred during the testing program. Who were these people that lived within the zone between ground zero and Salt Lake City? Where did they live exactly, and how did they make a living? How were they affected by nuclear testing? Was their experience with the testing program the same as the downwinders in Utah? Several completed oral histories contained references to ranches or towns north and east of the test site. Others contained the names of a handful of individuals who traveled in the region monitoring radiation levels, interacting with local residents. Through the oral history project director's initial contacts, I got to know and conducted several interviews with ranchers such as Gracian Uhalde. I also interviewed several of the people employed as radiation monitors, such as Donald James, who worked in areas adjacent to the Test Site and became acquainted with the vast expanse of the Great Basin.

Through asking questions that pertained to their backgrounds, homes, and respective occupations, and by asking these questions in the places they lived and worked, I discovered that these two very different groups of people had built surprising relationships across an intriguing landscape. Uhalde and James developed a friendship that transcended distance, lifestyle, and ranchers' general dissatisfaction with the federal government, ameliorating the problem of radioactive fallout that occurred downwind of the Test Site. These interviews illuminated the importance of place and interpersonal relationships in historical study, in this case between ranchers, who lived in proximity to the nuclear testing program, and radiation monitors, who had been charged with keeping these ranchers safe, providing a missing perspective on environmental and cold war history in the American West.

Out of these interviews I identified two important categories of study that were difficult to uncover in traditional archival material, especially in redacted government documents between supervisors, their employees, and outsiders such as ranchers, and which oral history gets at in particularly effective ways. The first is the importance of place, particularly the proximity of people and activities in a particular place. The location of an event and its spatial footprint can be as important as the event itself, especially in rural spaces and outdoor laboratories where unanticipated atmospheric and geographic conditions, unforeseen animal movement, and other factors can alter expected outcomes. The second is the importance of interpersonal relationships and the ways in which they determine the efficacy of official federal policies. The decisions individuals make in translating official policies in the field can alter and adapt them to the needs of specific communities and individuals. Interpersonal relationships allow flexibility "on the ground" where none appears on paper.

The Importance of Place

The setting for these interviews was a space most Americans travel through but rarely consider. The Great Basin lies between the Wasatch Front in Utah and the Sierra Nevadas in California and is defined by its hydrologic boundaries—it is the only region in North America that drains internally. Once the site of two vast Pleistocene lakes, it is a veritable sea of mountains running north and south, alluvial fans, and basins punctuated by dry playas. Geographer John McPhee describes it as basin and playa, fault line and mountain range, another basin and playa, fault and range, and another, stretching from horizon to horizon. These are not gently undulating ridges and valleys formed by compression waves on the surface of the North American plate but pieces of dynamic fractured earth tilted at odd angles to each other from the stretching and pulling apart of the planet's crust. The ranges are constantly rising, sometimes violently and abruptly by geologic standards, while at the same time they are being eroded away by the elements.[3] Historians can glean much information from the work of geographers, geologists, archaeologists, and other scientists about the region, but without actually standing beneath the tall peaks and traveling across the playas in between, it is difficult to truly grasp its size. The deceptive nature of space and distance in the Great Basin, the relative location of ranches to the Nevada Test Site, and the connection between the environment and ranching ways of life within the region provide important levels of understanding that are best accessed through personal experience.

Writers from multiple academic disciplines have described the landscape of the Great Basin. In addition to John McPhee, geographer Richard Francaviglia, journalist Rebecca Solnit, and poet William Fox have grappled with finding appropriate language to describe the disorientation that occurs in the region's isolated space. Fox's work on cognition and landscape provides an insightful description about what happens to orientation and sight in the basin and range region. He writes that the Great Basin is the "frontier of cognitive dissonance," a "state of confusion defined as trying to hold two contradictory ideas or perceptions in mind at the same time." The normal means of understanding space and distance fail to work in this place. The dry, clear air makes physical features appear closer than they are in reality; the colors of the ranges do not shift from browns to blues as they recede. There are no trees on the valley floors to break up the open space, and very little verge is visible on the ranges. Most plant life comes in shades of gray, silver, and tan. Fox believes "The cognitive dissonance is caused by our visual expectations being wildly out of synch with these perceptual realities."[4]

Photographer Peter Goin describes the Great Basin as a "land of contradictions that often defy description. . . . Distances are deceiving as human scale becomes obscured and unpredictable." Arid and brutal, the Great Basin was the last region of the continental United States to be explored by the government, and when it was, weary surveyors described it in terms that evoked desolation and not paradise. Travelers who passed through the Great Basin began and ended their reports with the same disparaging descriptions of desolation. Noted humorist Mark Twain was not joking, however, when he described his travels across the region. "Imagine a vast, waveless ocean stricken dead and turned to ashes; imagine this solemn waste tufted with ash-dusted sage-brushes;

imagine the lifeless silence and solitude that belong to such a place; imagine a coach, creeping like a bug through the midst of this shoreless level," he wrote. Historian Elizabeth Raymond eloquently describes the historical perceptions of the region based on hardship of settlement. She explains, the "residents of the Great Basin . . . developed in self-defense a regional identity that grew from their pride in the basic accomplishment of simply having endured in such an unlikely place." Raymond sees little that would "redeem this landscape from its enduring symbolic role as America's resolutely unblooming wasteland."[5]

Because the Nevada Test Site (NTS) is located in the south central Great Basin, the majority of the region fell under the clouds of radioactive fallout. Most of the communities surrounding the NTS are small ranching towns nestled fifty to one hundred miles north and east of the nuclear testing area, just off Nevada state highways huddled near small springs tucked into the sides of mountain ranges. A network of dirt roads links these communities across land administered by the Bureau of Land Management in valleys that flow into one another, separated by tall peaks of limestone and granite. These toothy ranges were pushed skyward from someplace deep beneath the Earth's surface by forces greater than atomic bombs. In Coal Valley, Garden and Railroad Valley, Kawich Valley, Penoyer Valley, and Pahranagat Valley, tiny ranches barely stand out in a landscape barren of not much else but sagebrush. The arid climate of the Great Basin makes these communities very small and very tentative relative to the hostility and vastness of the region. They exist without easy access to basic services and supplies in an atmosphere that daily threatens to reabsorb their ranches and render irrigation work ineffective.

Most ranches in central Nevada were settled during the late nineteenth century by Mormon, Basque, or Italian immigrants and encompass only moderate tracts of acreage buffered by larger expanses of public land. The aridity of the Great Basin makes it necessary for livestock to range over wide, unfenced rangeland to survive. Small pockets of ranching communities dot the sides of mountain ranges where there was more adequate water and vegetation. The long Pahranagat Valley to the east shelters Alamo, Ash Springs, and Hiko; Garden and Railroad Valley to the north host Adaven, Currant, and Nyala. Most of these communities consist of clusters of homes with little or no services, often well off main roads such as Highway 93 or 25. Despite the growth of Las Vegas in the late twentieth century, Ely still provides most of the necessary amenities. Many ranching families have been there for several generations, passing their ranches from father to son. These families intermarried, producing a long list of relatives scattered from Ely and Tonopah to Las Vegas. Collectively they run cattle and sheep in the same way their fathers and grandfathers did, moving the animals on horseback from winter pasture to summer pasture.

Gracian Uhalde, a third-generation French Basque rancher in central Nevada, was born and raised on a ranch at Cherry Creek in Garden Valley, Nevada. He was the first rancher I sought to interview. The Uhalde ranch, situated one hundred miles southwest of Ely and fifty miles north of the test site, is difficult to locate, tucked back into a small canyon off a series of rarely maintained dirt roads (see figure 14.1). With no signs, GPS, or cell phone signal, and an incomprehensible Bureau of Land Management map, I followed Uhalde's verbal directions to his ranch for the interview. I drove north out of Las Vegas on Highway 93, turned left a couple hundred yards past a highway marker in the middle of a cutoff road between Alamo and Ely, went across Coal Valley through Water Gap to Garden Valley, and past a cattle gate along the side of a creek. I stumbled onto his ranch believing I had taken a wrong turn when I headed up the canyon. On top of this initial difficulty, I discovered that he was not even there from the two Peruvian ranch hands whose broken English managed to communicate that Uhalde was in Ely that week. I left my card on his kitchen door and drove home, hoping Uhalde had mistakenly forgotten our appointment and would call me again. But the second time I traveled to the ranch, only a single dog was home. It took three trips to get the interview with him. When I finally caught up with the elusive rancher, he cooked me breakfast for my trouble. The process of getting this interview, as well as the actual interview itself, spoke volumes about Uhalde's life: he never sits still for very long and often jumps from subject to subject quickly in conversation. The satellite telephone was a constant interruption as he talked to me, finished his chores, and cooked eggs, potatoes, and homemade bacon for our shared breakfast.

Figure 14.1 The Uhalde ranch.

Uhalde spent his childhood with the basin and range right out his front door. He gauges his distances according to familiar but relatively ordinary and nearly indistinguishable structural features that demark different playas, mountains, and canyons. Until I saw Coal and Garden Valleys and passed through Water Gap, his geographic vocabulary made no sense to me. There were moments during the first trip to his ranch when I was certain I was completely lost. I believe he was actually surprised that I found his home without any additional assistance, and as a result, viewed me more as an equal, familiar with the navigation of vast and relatively isolated spaces. It stands to reason Uhalde never thought I would make it to the ranch, and when I did, I earned a little respect for my effort. He told me that more than once he has bumped into stranded travelers on the dirt roads that crisscross his valley.

Because of its isolated location, the Uhalde ranch house has a pantry the size of a spare room to store food. Without the luxury of a neighborhood grocery store, ranching families make one trip to town for supplies every couple of months. Uhalde's pantry was full of canned vegetables, dried beans and rice, bags of potatoes, flour, and cornmeal. He cures his own bacon and other meats in a shed across the back yard adjacent to the laundry line. About a hundred feet to the side of the house, a large diesel fuel tank rests on struts. Twice a year, a tanker makes its way down from Ely to refill it. I had difficulty imagining a truck driver navigating the dirt roads that are covered in talc-like sand and rock and are not easy to negotiate even with a four-wheel-drive vehicle. The roads are not passable for most of the winter because no county or state vehicles plough them, and it can be bitterly cold. In the summer, the temperatures tend to be above ninety degrees on the valley floors. The wind is always blowing no matter the season. The planning and patience it takes for Uhalde to maintain a life at the ranch impressed itself deeply on my imagination.

After Uhalde and I talked (and because he hates to sit for too long), he took me for a ride in his beat-up truck past the old home-stead and up to the lookout hill where he had watched atmospheric nuclear tests as a child. He parked his truck facing south, pointed at the horizon, and told me that they could see the mushroom cloud right over the tops of the mountains immediately across the flat val-ley (see figure 14.2). When they saw which way the fallout cloud was heading, they knew whether they could stay out and work or whether they had to hurry inside and shut all the windows and doors. I was shocked that testing had taken place within sight of the ranch, with only a single mountain range in between. The pop-ular pictures taken by photographer Don English in Las Vegas of mushroom clouds to the north of town display a distance that seemed nearly twice what Uhalde had pointed across. In the crystal clear air of the ridge, the test site looked much closer.

The interview with Gracian Uhalde was as rich in experience as it was in history. Without gaining personal and physical contact with the place in which he lived and worked, it would have been extraor-dinarily difficult to begin to understand his experiences. The disori-entation produced by the deceptive nature of space and distance in the region, the relatively close proximity of his ranch to the NTS, and seeing in person the connection between the environment and ranching ways of life provided a better understanding of Uhalde's story. In addition, the place where this interview occurred created

Figure 14.2 The view of the Test Site from the Uhalde ranch.

insight as to the identity of those 400 persons the government report discussed, where they lived, what their life was like in the Great Basin, and why it was so easy for the atomic scientists to believe that this was basically an uninhabited place.

The Importance of Relationships

The Great Basin, particularly Nevada, is best known politically for its libertarian stance and the late-twentieth-century popular protest of big government called the Sagebrush Rebellion. A 1979 quote from Nevada state senator Norm Gaser—"We're tired of being pistol-whipped by the bureaucrats and dry-gulched by Federal regulations"—indicates that the federal government has not traditionally been well liked in the region.[6] The perception that federal officials represent hardship and difficulty pervaded most ranchers' attitudes throughout the second half of the twentieth century and was partly generated by the secrecy and obfuscation that cloaked the nuclear testing program during the 1950s and 1960s. Most residents of the Great Basin, particularly the group known as the downwinders in Utah, were outraged at what they perceived to be the federal government's negligence of their safety. Against this backdrop, the relationship between Gracian Uhalde and radiation monitor Donald James developed and the primary reason their friendship became so important.

From 1951 to 1992, the Atomic Energy Commission (AEC), and its later incarnation, the Department of Energy (DOE), conducted the US nuclear testing program. Though the largest tests were detonated on several Pacific islands, the bulk of testing occurred in the sparsely populated area at the east end of the Mojave Desert and southern portion of the Great Basin. Situated in southern Nevada, approximately seventy miles north of Las Vegas, what became known as the Nevada Test Site hosted roughly half of all of the nation's atmospheric tests and nearly all of its underground tests. This stark and beautiful landscape essentially functioned as a scientific proving ground and an outdoor laboratory. Unlike indoor testing facilities, the effects of nuclear tests here were not confined to the boundaries of the Test Site.[7]

In 1953, the AEC and the public realized exactly how fluid the boundaries of the Test Site could become. On May 19, the AEC's test code named Harry detonated before dawn on Yucca Flat, producing a cloud of radioactive material that dispersed over the region's major highways and small towns east of the Test Site boundary. Radiation monitors and government officials stopped several hundred vehicles on Highways 91 and 93 and warned motorists to roll up their windows and keep their air intakes sealed. Men in white coats with Geiger counters told drivers that there was "no danger" but to stay inside their vehicle until they were out of the path of the radioactive cloud. Officials sent many of these vehicles to St. George or Las Vegas for decontamination in free car washes funded by the AEC. In addition, the agency's meteorologists observed just after dawn that the radioactive cloud was headed into some thunderheads over St. George and issued a warning to residents to stay indoors from nine in the morning until noon to avoid any potential fallout. An AEC spokesperson issued a statement to the media insisting that despite the appearance of danger as indicated by these precautionary measures, levels of "radiation had not reached a hazardous level" in any of these areas.[8]

In the early years of continental testing, 1951–70, the AEC contracted with the US Public Health Service (PHS) to monitor offsite radiation—occurring beyond the boundaries of the NTS—and inform the small rural communities surrounding the area, such as St. George in Utah and Caliente, Hiko, and Ely in Nevada, of the proper precautions needed to avoid protracted and dangerous exposure to radioactive fallout. Although not mandated by the federal government, this early radiation-monitoring program was part of the AEC's efforts to ensure the safety of the public and secure the relatively new and somewhat controversial continental testing site in the Great Basin. In related oral histories on the efforts to prevent onsite radiation exposure, Dr. Stuart Black, the AEC's leading health physicist, remarked that exposure of the general offsite population was not considered a problem in the early days—there were no standards until about 1955 for them, unlike onsite workers, who had occupational exposure limits. Atomic scientists and radiation experts involved with the testing program generally assumed that because test series were only about three months long, and fallout levels off site were significantly smaller than they were on site, there was no need to alarm the general population. Key to understanding the effects of fallout, according to Black, was the threshold exposure theory, which maintained that the human body could recover from a certain level of exposure.[9]

The radiation monitors the PHS sent into offsite communities were really just present in case something went terribly wrong, which was not something anyone involved in the testing program anticipated because of how many precautions were taken before tests were detonated, and to reassure the locals that nuclear tests posed no danger to them. In essence, the monitors were the public liaisons between the nuclear testing program and the offsite communities. But these monitors, caught between serving the public and guarding national secrets, sat at the center of a very difficult communication process. Their successful negotiation of the landscape between disclosing reassuring information to surrounding communities and protecting national security interests was entirely predicated on establishing personal relationships with the members of the communities they served.

In 1957, the *Los Angeles Times* interviewed ranchers and farmers around the NTS who claimed that nuclear testing was a threat to their families and livestock. They did not believe the AEC's claims that testing had not caused serious illness or injury to the health of livestock or residents. They reported with little effect that a rancher's son, Martin Bordoli, had died of leukemia; Father Ryan, a priest from Caliente, had become ill after driving through the test site's northern sector; and local highway employee Bert Wilson had suffered since 1955 from burns that would not heal.[10]

In the interview with Gracian Uhalde, he discussed his and his father's growing anger over the damage to their herds caused by radioactive fallout and his parents' increasing disillusionment with the government because of the nuclear testing. Uhalde's father purchased a Geiger counter in the late 1950s to measure the radioactive fallout, not trusting the government's monitors, who told him there was nothing to worry about despite burns on dogs, cattle, and sheep after test detonations and contact with fallout clouds. The measurements his father took on the Geiger counter indicated that their hay was heavily irradiated after many tests. Uhalde vividly remembered when the cloud from the 104 KT Sedan test in 1962 passed over his home when he was ten years old. The fallout rained like snow, and his mother would not let him play outside for three or four days afterward, fearing the burns it would produce. Referring to the decades of nuclear testing, he said, "My thought on the whole damn thing is, right down here at the Nevada Test Site, they created Frankenstein."[11]

Helen Fallini, at Twin Springs ranch only thirty-five miles north of the test site and a neighbor of Uhalde, recalled the early testing days. She said, "It wasn't supposed to hurt us in any way, shape, or form and yet we got that fallout so heavily that it was unbelievable." She watched her friend Minnie Sharp lose her hair and her neighbor Madison Locke develop significant radiation burns. Dogs and cattle on her ranch went blind and suffered radiation burns. She said the AEC treated her family and others in the fallout area like guinea pigs. After Martin Bordoli's death, his parents, Jack and Martha Bordoli (Martha was Helen Fallini's sister), sent a petition to the government asking for the suspension of nuclear testing. In response, AEC Chairman Lewis Strauss sent them a letter that insinuated stories of injuries and death due to radiation exposure were merely subversive, communist-inspired plots. Strauss insensitively suggested that the Bordolis keep their "sense of proportion" regarding the matter of radioactive fallout because the dangers that might occur from it involved only small sacrifices when compared to the greater evil of the use of nuclear weapons in war.[12]

In 1958, the US and Soviet Union agreed to a nuclear testing moratorium, which lasted until 1961. From 1951 until that moratorium, the PHS, the federal agency charged with public safety during the nuclear testing program, used reservists or temporary employees as radiation monitors." They came to Nevada during testing periods but were not permanent residents. Beginning in 1961, the AEC initiated a year-round testing program and, in cooperation with the PHS, set up a permanent monitoring program.[13] The government hired radiation monitors on a full-time basis and, unlike previous employees, these people moved to the region and became Nevada residents. By 1964, the PHS conducted routine sampling and monitoring within a 300-mile radius around the NTS and extended coverage as needed to track radioactive fallout. Ground monitoring consisted of mobile teams of two radiation monitors deployed to offsite areas prior to a test detonation. They tracked fallout with the assistance of the test control point and a two-way radio. Armed with four varieties of radioactive tracking devices, monitors chased radioactive particles across the Great Basin. They collected vegetation and milk samples and passed out film badges (for measuring cumulative radiation doses) to members of ranching communities routinely and when an event produced radioactive fallout.[14]

Frequent contacts with ranching communities "provided the opportunity to explain the role of the Public Health Service with respect to the programs of the Atomic Energy Commission," and "as a result of favorable public relations, a number of off-site residents took part in the environmental sampling program."[15] A *Chicago Tribune* article on radiation monitors in Hiko—about the 1966 Pin Stripe detonation, which vented a significant amount of radiation—remarked that monitoring "crews are assigned fixed routes and most of them are personally acquainted with every man, woman, and child in their area, as well as every cowpath." Monitors maintained "personal contact with everyone in the off-site areas who might be affected by a nuclear mischance."[16] The consistent presence of monitors reassured community members more than any other previous effort because they managed to convey sympathy and understanding to community members.

By examining interviews with several monitors, I began to understand exactly what it was they did to win the confidence of ranchers. Two in particular have been fondly remembered in ranching communities. The first is Kenneth Giles, who grew up on a Nebraska farm and came to Las Vegas in 1964 as a radiation monitor and continues in that position with the Desert Research Institute in Las Vegas. Radiation monitors, according to Giles, needed to be experts in science as well as knowledgeable about the communities they served. They needed to be people whom community members could believe. Radiation monitors like Giles were trained to just be upfront with ranchers. He commented, "None of these people had degrees, but they all were experts in their particular field." It did not hurt to be helpful: Giles used to bring groceries to the Uhaldes and still visits Helen Uhalde regularly in Ely. Once, she took Giles aside and showed him where the spare keys for the ranch were; she said if Giles needed anything while out in the field, he could help himself to anything in the kitchen, and if he starved to death, it would be his own fault.[17]

Donald James was probably the most fondly remembered monitor among ranching communities. He developed relationships with the Uhaldes and other ranching families north of the NTS. He found that many of the ranchers were bitter about the way the AEC had treated them in the past. He remembered Joe Fallini of the Twin Springs ranch showing him pictures of burned livestock and saying that he agreed testing had to be done but that the government did it with a "to heck with everybody" attitude. The testing officials told Fallini that the burns on his cattle were ringworm. But, James said in the interview, Fallini and others in the ranching communities adjacent to the NTS had suffered visible effects of radiation exposure. In avoiding the obvious connection between radioactive fallout and damage to ranching communities, James believed the AEC created a nearly insurmountable atmosphere of distrust.[18]

Uhalde remarked that most of the radiation monitors, especially during the early period of atmospheric testing, were "barely able to get around" in the vast spaces between ranches. "They came and took our milk cows because they wanted to test the iodine and the strontium-90 [that] gets in the milk first thing and all that whole baloney," he said. Uhalde remembered his father "being just livid" because he did not think the officials knew any more than the ranchers did "about what the hell they were doing," and because they were "being so secretive and so stupid about it that it could only mean something bad." Uhalde had no specific memories of the first officials who came around the ranch, just a feeling of disdain. It was not until Don James showed up that his family had any positive interaction with the government officials regarding nuclear testing. He said, "Don James was basically the first person that infiltrated—or maybe he came over to our side or something—but everybody liked Don James because I think he didn't have all the answers and he didn't really care. He was just here basically to have a good time and to do whatever he could do. He was a real human being, you know."[19]

Don James grew up in Erie, Colorado, on a farm and worked at the Rocky Flats nuclear facility producing detonators until 1961, when he moved to Las Vegas to learn radiation safety at the Test Site. As a radiation monitor, his job entailed everything from checking radiation levels in an assigned location the morning of a test to chasing a clouds cross-country to the Mexican or Canadian border—in 1964, he followed the Pike cloud all the way to Mexico. Monitors also took readings from permanent monitoring stations and got to know the locals. James understood that many of the ranchers were bitter about the way the government had treated them in the past. He said people were exposed offsite and there were visible effects of fallout in ranching communities north of the NTS, and all the government did by "lying" was create distrust. He believed the later monitors, including himself, were liked because they told the "truth" or personalized important information and related to the ranchers.[20]

After the permanent PHS monitors arrived—and the monitors from the Environmental Protection Agency and the Desert Research Institute in the 1970s and 1980s—they were liked because they knew the area and its residents and personalized sensitive and technical information. "We knew every mine . . . every cow camp, every ranch. We knew everybody," James recalled. He and a dozen other monitors gave talks, showed films, and demonstrated monitoring equipment so that the community members would understand how instruments took measurements and what they meant. "We'd tell them everything, we never held back on anything. You know, of course, the DOE [Department of Energy] says you don't say this, don't say that, or anything. When we were asked, we'd tell them . . . that's what they liked . . . they didn't appreciate [the previous] people . . . because they wouldn't say anything, and then when they did answer the people, they'd lie to them, and that just doesn't work."[21]

They also sympathized with the ranchers. On the days he picked up milk samples, James bought gallon containers of milk from grocery stores in Las Vegas where he lived and exchanged that milk for ranch samples so that the local children would not have to drink contaminated milk. During testing activity, he stayed outside with ranchers too busy to make it inside despite potential exposure to fallout. James attended ranchers' funerals and weddings and generally immersed himself in their communities.[22] His easy-going nature and acceptance among hard-working Nevada ranchers did more to ease the atmosphere of distrust than any previous official effort. Uhalde and other ranchers may not have liked the nuclear testing program, but they respected the job that James and his cohort of radiation monitors had to do, and they accepted radioactive fallout as a negative side effect of a difficult program.

Conclusion

Speaking with Don James and Gracian Uhalde impressed on me the impact of nuclear testing on ranchers who lived near the northern boundary of the NTS. In addition, the process I went through to actually conduct the interviews was an important aspect of my research experience. This was especially true in Uhalde's case. There is nothing so disorienting as traveling through the Great Basin on dusty back roads with no civilization in sight. I found more ranches tucked back into the mountain ranges than I expected, which belies the concept of emptiness. These interviews led me to ask questions regarding the assumptions made about the location in which testing was conducted and the federal government's definition of safety in comparison with the actual size and scope of the risk associated with a continental nuclear test site. They also provided detailed descriptions about how nuclear testing was actually experienced by adjacent ranching communities.

Oral history offers a valuable methodology for understanding the place where ranchers and radiation monitors did their work and getting at the relationships they created in that space. Through the interviews and accompanying field research I completed for the Nevada Test Site Oral History Project, I uncovered the importance of place and interpersonal relationships between Nevada ranchers and the federal government. The memories of individuals who engaged regularly with and were affected by both their environment and the testing program provide rich descriptive evidence. In particular, ranchers and radiation monitors who lived and worked in the same desolate isolation of the central Great Basin developed working relationships; these provide an important missing perspective on the nuclear testing program. They came to understand the geography and climate of the Great Basin in similar ways. Both groups negotiated the isolation of the basin and range, relying on each other for assistance and cooperation. In addition, I discovered that some radiation monitors found informal ways in which to communicate sensitive or even classified information to ranchers to help ease their fears over nuclear testing. In this way, oral history provides a special opportunity to provide essential depth to this project and new evidence regarding the human stories behind America's nuclear testing program in the Great Basin.

Notes

1. Paul Thompson writes that oral history, in some fields of study, allows evidence to be introduced from a new direction and can open up "important new areas of inquiry." Paul Thompson, *The Voice of the Past: Oral History* (Oxford: Oxford University Press, 1988), 8–9, 23–24.

2. For a larger explanation of the meaning of this document and the role it played in establishing the Nevada Test Site, see Leisl Carr Childers, "The Size of the Risk: An Environmental History of the Nuclear Great Basin," PhD dissertation, University of Nevada, Las Vegas, May 2011; "Discussion of Radiological Hazards Associated with a Continental Test Site for Atomic Bombs," Los Alamos Scientific Laboratory, September 1, 1950, Nevada Nuclear Testing Archive, Las Vegas.

3. John McPhee, Basin and Range (New York: Farrar, Straus and Giroux, 1981), 44–54; Anthony R. Orme, ed., *Physical Geography of North America* (New York: Oxford University Press, 2000), 385.

4. William Fox, *The Void, the Grid, and the Sign: Traversing the Great Basin* (Reno: University of Nevada Press, 2005), 10–13.

5. Peter Goin, "Magical Realism: The West as Spiritual Playground," in *Western Places, American Myths: How We Think about the West*, ed. Gary Hausladen (Reno: University of Nevada Press, 2003), 254; Mark Twain, *Roughing It* (Hartford, CT: American Publishing, 1872), 126–28, 136; Elizabeth Raymond, "When the Desert Won't Bloom: Environmental Limitation in the Great Basin," in *Many Wests: Place, Culture, and Regional Identity*, ed. David Wrobel and Michael Steiner (Lawrence: University Press of Kansas, 1997), 83.

6. Melinda Beck, "Sagebrush Revolt," *Newsweek*, September 17, 1979, 38–39.

7. The Nevada Test Site hosted 100 of 210 atmospheric tests and 828 of 844 underground tests. US Department of Energy, *United States Nuclear Tests July 1945 through September 1992* (Las Vegas: Nevada Operations Office, December 2000), xii–xiii.

8. AEC Press Releases, May 19, 1953, Nevada Nuclear Testing Archive, Las Vegas, Nevada; Richard G. Elliott to Distribution, May 19, 1953, Nevada Nuclear Testing Archive, Las Vegas, Nevada; John C. Clark to Kenneth E. Fields, TWX, May 20, 1953, Nevada Nuclear Testing Archive, Las Vegas, Nevada; "Robot Plane Survives 9th Atomic Blast," *Provo Daily Herald*, May 19, 1953; "Nevada Atom Test Affects Utah Area," *New York Times*, May 20, 1953; "A-Blast Cloud Brings Closing of Utah Town," *Chicago Daily Tribune*, May 20, 1953; "Utah Clear of Harmful Cloud," *Ogden Standard Examiner*, May 20, 1953; "Atom Fallout Blocks Two Nevada Highways," *Nevada State Journal*, May 20, 1953; "AEC Checks Utah Atomic Area, Denies Harm Done," *Ogden Standard Examiner*, May 21, 1953; "Nevada, Utah People Given Added Assurance They Will Not Be Injured by Fallout," *Nevada State Journal*, May 21, 1953; "St. George Gets Publicity from Radioactive Pall after Detonation," *Dixie Sun*, May 21, 1953; Chester McQueary, "Meeting Dirty Harry in 1953," Common Dreams.org, May 25, 2003; Department of Energy, *United States Nuclear Tests*, 2–5; Terrence R. Fehner and F. G. Gosling, *Origins of the Nevada Test Site* (Washington, DC: Department of Energy, 2000), 86–87; "Terrence R. Fehner and F.G. Gosling, *Atmospheric Nuclear*

Weapons Testing, 1951–1963 (Washington, DC: Department of Energy, September 2006), 105–106." Richard L. Miller, *Under the Cloud: The Decades of Nuclear Testing* (New York: Free Press, 1986), 173–77; Barton C. Hacker, *Elements of Controversy: The Atomic Energy Commission and Radiation Safety in Nuclear Weapons Testing, 1947–1974* (Berkeley: University of California Press, 1994), 103–5; Philip L. Fradkin, *Fallout: An American Nuclear Tragedy* (Boulder, CO: Johnson Books, 1989), 1–4.

9. Stuart Black moved to Las Vegas in 1964 and began work on the bioenvironmental research projects for the AEC such as the PHS/Environmental Protection Agency's dairy farm, conducted on the Test Site between 1964 and 1981, and the radioiodine study. Stuart Black, interview by Suzanne Becker, January 18, 2005, Nevada Test Site Oral History Project, Special Collections, University of Nevada, Las Vegas, online at http://digital.library.unlv.edu/ntsohp/.

10. "Bomb Tests Seek to Stress Safety," *New York Times*, May 12, 1957; "AEC Sets New Precautions for Nevada Tests," *Los Angeles Times*, May 14, 1957; Gladwin Hill, "Atomic-Test Area Calm on Fallout," *New York Times*, June 9, 1957; "A Searching Inquiry into Nuclear Perils," *Life Magazine*, June 10, 1957, 4–29; "Nevadans Charge Fallout Danger," *Los Angeles Times*, June 27, 1957.

11. Gracian N. Uhalde, interview by author, December 1, 2006, Nevada Test Site Oral History Project, Special Collections, University of Nevada, Las Vegas, Nevada, online at http://digital.library.unlv.edu/ntsohp/.

12. Helen Fallini, interview by Robert McCracken, October 25–26, 1987, Nye County Town History Project, Special Collections, University of Nevada, Las Vegas, Nevada; US House of Representatives, "Low-Level Effects of Radiation on Health, Hearings," April 23, May 24, and August 1, 1979, 14–39, 292–307; Robert McCracken, *A History of Railroad Valley, Nevada* (Tonopah: Central Nevada Historical Society, 1996), 283–86.

13. Beginning in 1963, the AEC conducted all testing underground. This helped ease the dissatisfaction of ranching communities adjacent to the NTS, but radioactive fallout continued to be an issue, resulting from several significant venting of tests throughout the rest of the 1960s and into the 1970s. Susan DeSilvia, *Extended Community: An Oral History of the Community Environmental Monitoring Program (CEMP), 1981–2003* (Las Vegas, NV: Desert Research Institute, 2004), 42–43.

14. Southwestern Radiological Health Laboratory, US Public Health Service, "Off-Site Surveillance Activities of the Southwestern Radiological Health Laboratory: from January through June 1964," Department of Health, Education, and Welfare, January 24, 1966, 1–6.

15. Ibid., 5.

16. Jerry Le Blanc, "The Radiation Watchers: With Scintillators and Thyroid Counters, Scientists in Nevada Protect Us from the Atomic Age," *Chicago Tribune*, February 4, 1968.

17. Kenneth Giles, interview by Suzanne Becker, February 10, 2005, Nevada Test Site Oral History Project, Special Collections, University of Nevada, Las Vegas, Nevada, online at http://digital.library.unlv.edu/ntsohp/; DeSilvia, *Extended Community*, 128–40.

18. Don James, interview by author, July 12, 2006, Nevada Test Site Oral History Project, Special Collections, University of Nevada, Las Vegas, Nevada, online at http://digital.library.unlv.edu/ntsohp/.

19. Uhalde interview.

20. James interview.

21. Ibid.

22. Ibid.

15

Oral History among the Orchards

A Look at the James George Stratton Family

KRISTI YOUNG

Folklorist Kristi Young uses oral history to show how the rural tradition continues in what is becoming a very urban west. While the Wasatch Front in Utah has grown into one continuous city, she has found a family that holds onto the rural lifestyle and their orchards in Orem and other areas in Utah County. The James George Stratton family has formed a community within the family and extending to their neighbors which is connected by work in the orchards. Their stories show the hazards of relying on family lore for history and show how that lore continues to influence the family and their neighbors. Although Brigham Young did not send the families to plant orchards, the fact that they believe they have a calling from a prophet to grow fruit gives them the fortitude to continue the assignment even as the world around them changes. Young's essay shows how folklorists use oral history to glean facts and cultural details and also probe perception.

AN INFLUENTIAL FARMING family in Orem, Utah, the Strattons have been involved with orchards since, according to family tradition, James Stratton was sent to Utah Valley by Brigham Young to grow fruit. Farming seems to be in the Stratton blood. Vern Stratton, a great-grandson of James, loves to farm. He claims that there were no other options for a farm boy before the end of World War II; fortunately, he enjoys his work and is still farming in his late eighties. It is a life in which a person learns to work and work hard but can still have a great deal of freedom. A college graduate, Vern might well have gone in another direction. But like his father, James George Stratton, who attended college at the University of Utah and the Utah Agricultural College for three and a half years and may also have been able to make other choices, Vern chose farming.[1]

This chapter examines the relationship the Strattons have with the land, their crops, and how their story is indicative of what other orchard families in Utah County experience by focusing on oral history. The majority of the material is taken from oral histories conducted for the Utah Heritage Project at Brigham Young University and housed in the Wilson Folklore Archive in L. Tom Perry Special Collections. Traditional historical sources provide some facts as well; however, oral history adds certain nuances to the written record that might be missing. Nevertheless, oral history is not foolproof. Memory tends to dim with time, and as a result traditional tales may blur historical fact, resulting in more knowledge about the person speaking than about the event that took place. Despite the wealth of information in oral history, written documents are still necessary and may even be discovered while pursuing oral histories. While the oral histories in this study come primarily from the Strattons, the stories of others from Utah Valley help make the history clearer.

The oral histories in this chapter paint a cultural history of Utah County with a particular emphasis on Orem. It is important to note that for the participants in this study, "Mormon country" means orchard country. There is a strong sense of place inherent in all of the stories. The participants are aware of their legacy and are active in passing along both collective and personal memory. The World War II era brought up many memories and stories that those interviewed were willing to share. For various generations that were part of this project, the acquisition of a work ethic was central. As the years have passed, the connection to the land has remained strong. However, the ways in which the land is used has changed in some cases.

Historians have long been interested in the West and its cultural climate as demonstrated by the enduring popularity of Wallace Stegner's *Mormon Country*.[2] As recently as the 1940s, much of the West was rural and concerns were not that different from the challenges the pioneers faced. This allowed some interviews with people who could shed light on the ways of the pioneers. The classic *Mormon Country* was published in 1942, and it looked at rural life in Utah and its challenges and benefits. Since that time, oral history has added to the historical picture. Over the years some of the rural areas have changed into urban areas with a sprinkling of agricultural enclaves. With urbanization has come a different set of problems than those outlined by Stegner. Some new problems deal with insecticides, maintaining farm land in urban neighborhoods, and finding second jobs that are compatible with agriculture. However, the Strattons of Utah County still straddle urbanization and the rural lifestyle and as a result represent a point where these lifestyles intersect.

Mormon Country/Orchard Country

For more than 100 years, Utah was primarily rural, with small pockets of city dwellers. Stegner's book described a predominantly rural church with the majority of members of the Church of Jesus Christ of Latter-day Saints (LDS) residing in Utah. Stegner created vignettes—both fictional and factual—to help his readers know what life in Mormon country was all about. At one time, life in Utah County, similar to the communities portrayed by Stegner, centered on the LDS Church and the orchards. Today in Utah there are more urban residents than rural ones and more non-LDS people moving into the state daily. Utah County remains over 88 percent LDS, so the church is still a large factor even if there are vastly fewer families relying on agriculture for their livelihood.[3] For a few families, like the Strattons, life still revolves the LDS Church and the orchards. It was the church that brought the Strattons to Utah from their native England, and activity in that church provides a structure for their lives currently. The church also explains why and how Utah was settled.

The question is, does the settling of Utah conform to conventional historical theory? Historian Frederick Jackson Turner claimed that Americans thrived on free land to the west of civilization. Later, historian Walter Prescott Webb went a step further than Turner, "claiming that geography itself (that is place) was an important determiner of culture."[4] Folklorist William A. Wilson writes, "As settlers poured into this free land west of the frontier, they were *changed* into the ruggedly independent, self-reliant, freedom-loving characters we have liked to call American."[5] Just how did mild-mannered city folk change into the ideal settlers of the American West? Was it wanderlust, geography, or perhaps religion? Looking at one group that settled an area of the American West, Wilson reaches the conclusion that "the emphasis should probably be more on the impact of the Mormons on the West than of the West on the Mormons."[6]

Although Webb's observation that geography or place is important, the culture in which the Strattons and other orchard growers move is influenced more by Mormonism than by geography according to Wilson. Although the settling of the West took place over 150 years ago, the descendants of these settlers still reflect some of the values and capabilities of their ancestors. These tie the generations together and create a pocket of the American West in Utah Valley where values of the old West are reflected.

The interviews done for the Utah Heritage Project definitely give a modern view of the American West tinged with the traditional suppositions of Turner and Webb. Wilson's observations creep in because Utah Valley is still Mormon country. The interviews indicate that there is a pride in ancestors, a love of land, a devotion to religion, and above all a heritage that is valued and honored.

Kimball Stratton talks about his great-grandfather, James George Stratton:

> He was sent down here by Brigham Young to grow fruit on the Orem bench for—to homestead the area. And they started out down in, on about Center Street in Orem, down by what is now the new Target store. And our old, the old stone house was just recently declared a historic place, and I believe they

moved it. I'm not sure what happened to that, but my great-grandfather was a pioneer in the area. Started farming, and then my grandfather was George, James George Stratton, and he and his brothers farmed the, what is now Orem area, and they, my grandfather was quite a big farmer in his day. They farmed the area where all of the Orem High is, all the parks and the City Center, they had thousands of acres of farms there, which was a feat. They farmed it all with horses, which is something I cannot imagine being done. It was thousands of acres. And they farmed it all with horses.[7]

Kimball's story is a good one, but some historical records do not match his account. Keven Stratton notes that James George was first sent to settle Fort Provo, and this is confirmed by family records.[8] The same family records indicate that John Henry was born in 1861 in Provo City.[9] There is some doubt about whether the family's sojourn in the Muddy Mission near Overton, Nevada, a journey undertaken at Brigham Young's request, took place before or after John Henry's birth, making it difficult to know when they returned to Provo. The family land (which was less than the "thousands of acres" that Kimball Stratton mentioned) was lost during the Depression, but the Strattons still had land in the northeast section of Orem and continued to farm there.

Brigham Young sent people to different locations, but there is no record indicating that settlers of what was then known as the Provo Bench were directed to grow fruit. There is actually no record that Brigham Young was behind the settling of the Provo area. On March 9, 1849, Frederick Williams announced that he was taking some of Brigham Young's cows and a group of settlers and going to Utah Valley.[10] Slightly surprised by this declaration, Young and governing bodies of the LDS Church decided to take a positive outlook on the settlement, even though it was done earlier than what they desired. The families who were part of the initial group going to the Provo area volunteered rather than being selected by Young, as so many groups were. Also, the settling of the Provo Bench (which is now called Orem) took place several years after the founding of Provo proper. So why is Kimball Stratton's story very important?

Folklorist Bruce Jackson writes of stories,

> Telling stories—is the primary way we tell what we know, express who we are. Or who we think we are. Or who we would like to think we are. Or who we would like our listeners to think we are.
>
> Which is to say: storytelling is active, organic, responsive, reactive; it is here and now.[11]

But stories do not reflect the reality of history. Finding out where the farm was and how much area it covered gives a more accurate historical view. It is also interesting to consider why these details were part of Kimball Stratton's account. Does his version reveal anything about what is important to James George's descendants?

Stratton's quote, although not 100 percent accurate, does indicate the awe he feels for what his ancestors did. However, as Jackson instructs us, story changes and Stratton's view of his ancestors is more important for what it tells us about his values and viewpoint rather than their lives. One of the benefits of oral history and how it contributes to our historical and present view of the West is knowing how those with roots in the West view themselves and their forebears. Ironically, to maintain the tradition of farming, some had to change their location within Utah County and even change their crops.

Kimball and his brothers eventually left the family's north Orem farms and went south to Santaquin in the southernmost end of Utah Valley, where they planted fruit trees and experimented with a variety of crops. Though currently farming in Santaquin, some of the brothers live in north Orem. They now grow bedding flowers in greenhouses in Santaquin. Flowers were not a crop in the early days of Utah Valley, but growing them has allowed Kimball and his brothers to remain close to the land they love. The ability to adapt is an important quality for the Strattons—the younger generations have not been able to make a living from the orchard in Orem—and is necessary for farmers in the West. For example, both Keven Stratton and Scott Smith, another Utah Valley fruit farmer, have adapted a watering system that was developed in Israel for arid areas and use it on their fruit trees. This is a further change from the irrigation practices of the last generation.

Keven Stratton works his small gentleman's farm with his wife and eight children. Although they grow enough to sell at a farmer's market, it is not enough to make a living. Like many farmers in Utah County, Keven also has a day job. He owns a golf course and is an attorney. But his commitment to the land—its use and the resulting crop—is great, as illustrated by this story:

> It was my wedding day, May 31st and we needed to get our tomatoes in. We had done about three-fourths the day before and then a huge rainstorm came in and we had to quit. You like to get your tomatoes in by the 20th so we were already eleven days late. We had to get them in because we were going to be gone on our honeymoon for a week. We didn't need to be to the temple until eleven. I got up early so there was plenty of time. I wanted to get the crew started. I was on the tractor and it was difficult because of all the mud from the rainstorm. The tractor got stuck. We were trying to get it out and Jerry Washburn drove by and saw me. We are like brothers. And so he told me to get out of there and get ready for my wedding. He was teasing me, kind of like an older brother would a younger brother. He was on his way to work; it was early in the morning. So everyone was helping. I went in to get ready and my dad came out and finished it.[12]

The land, the church, and family shaped the lives and the story of the Strattons and others in the valley. Even on a very important day, Keven was unwilling to neglect his land.

Vern Stratton does not farm with his siblings like James George Stratton did, but he and his surviving siblings meet at least once a month for Family Home Evening, a program of the LDS Church. Generally, it is held just for immediate, not extended, family. Although not working together, they are keeping the bonds of family—which are so essential for a family farm—together. For the Stratton family, the land is part of who they are. Folklorist Henry Glassie posits that "simultaneously changing and unchangeable, history is place. Place joins those who make and mark the land with those who remake it, accepting its tasks. It joins saint to rebel, warrior to farmer, God to man. In place, the person is part of history."[13]

James Stratton left his native England and came to Utah because of the church; this devotion to church is present in his descendants. Not only do they hold Family Home Evenings, but Keven and Zach committed two years of their life to serving full-time LDS missions. Keven is currently serving in a stake presidency, which requires more than twenty hours a week. The decisions that they make are consistent with the beliefs that they hold because of their membership in the church.

Sense of Place

One benefit of oral history is that it is possible to get a good sense of what it was like to live in the community. When it comes to the fruit stands in Orem, people are very aware of other stand owners and workers. Linda Richardson Ash and Kathryn Richardson Lunt are sisters who run a fruit stand in Orem. During their interview, they asked if we had interviewed Vern Stratton. They told us we should do so because he was rich and still kept doing it. According to them, he had a degree in horticulture and loved the orchards. Even though he was seventy-eight, he kept doing it because he loved it.

Then they began talking about Carlos Chavez, a man who works for Vern Stratton, and about his good qualities: "He's the neatest guy, isn't he? Yeah, he's a cool guy. Very honest, very—you know, he's just an example of somebody that came from Mexico and worked with Vern, and has just worked his way up. And he's as honest as the day is long, and when he brings you stuff, and it's not good, he'll make it good. He's just a neat guy."[14] Honesty turns out to be a quality that is valued in the area as a whole, and not just by the Richardson sisters. Many fruit stand owners only do repeat business with those that are honest. This applies to those they purchase from and whom they sell to.

Anne Stratton Perry manages her father's fruit stand. She agrees with the Richardson sisters and only deals with farmers who stand behind their product. She also related a story about a customer who tried to buy 200 bushels by saying he had a deal with J.T. Her father's initials are J.D., and he always goes by "Jack." She knew that the customer was lying and refused to sell the fruit to him.[15]

The Richardson sisters also describe how they frequently receive envelopes filled with money and notes saying that the individual had stolen from their store when they were young. They also say that they screen future employees by trying to hire only those whose families they know. Although that isn't foolproof, it makes them more comfortable about the honesty of their employees.[16]

Qualities like the importance of everyday honesty within a community are outlined in practical terms in oral history. It is through the practices and beliefs illustrated in their tales that the interviewees allow us to understand how their communities work and the practical reasons behind their choices. The impact of stories is much greater than the bland statement that their residents "value honesty."

Legacy and Memory

Dawn Jones refers to her parents' orchard as their "heritage or inheritance."[17] Kimball Stratton proudly declares that it was his "great-grandfather [who] planted the first peach tree in the state of Utah."[18] Keven Stratton displays stickers in his office proclaiming "Strattons," which were placed on the packing boxes years ago. The Strattons are recognized as a family with a great orchard heritage in Orem, Utah. Our study represents two sons of James George Stratton and some of their progeny—Herb (see figure 15.1), his son Keven, grandson Zach Stratton, Herb's brother Vern, and his son Kimball. The stories of these five people show the benefits of orchard life as well as representing the communal experience. Another way to express this idea is "the nature of collective heritage and the feelings it arouses reflect its personal heritage."[19]

There was no manual that taught a person how to do farm work. It was taught orally in a way familiar to folklorists: "We were just the help, you know. So that training would come down to other individuals and then that training would go from them to

Figure 15.1 Herb Stratton in his country store.

others and from them to others and then pretty soon it would get to us."[20]

Zach Stratton talks about how he is farming to put himself through school, just like his father and his grandfather, Herb. When he has farming questions, he turns to his dad and especially to his grandfather: "Pretty much everything I've learned from my dad and my grandpa. They—they're my grandpa and his brothers were the biggest farmers in Orem, probably even Utah County, for years and years, so they have a lot of expertise in it, and it's just been always easier to go to them 'cause they just always know what they're talking about."[21]

Herb also farmed his way through school, where he certified to teach math and English. He realized that he would need a job in addition to farming. But he continued to farm every year on his own and/or rented land. Probably the only years he didn't farm were when he was in Oregon working on his doctorate and when he was in the army during World War II. Herb refused to accept the agricultural deferment for which he was eligible and allowed himself to be drafted.

World War II

Workers were scarce before and during the war, and Herb remembers the convicts that came to work the land before he was drafted:

> There were prisoners working on the farms here, but those prisoners came from under contract with the, with the director of the prison. I remember he, I even remember his name, his name was Harris, his last name. And I used to—living there on the sixty-acre ranch, I used to kind of hobknob with him, but I liked them, you know, the prisoners. They were well behaved. They were, they were just young men, and I was younger, and I was in this ten, ten to eighteen stage. And they'd come and help us prune, and help us harvest and do all kinds of things. But they were under contract between my father, who ran the, the produce, and the state prison. At the point of the mountain. And that was kind of an interesting period of time.[22]

He goes on to tell how the prisoners seemed rather mysterious and exciting for a young boy. Overall he enjoyed his contact with them. In many ways it was a safe way of experiencing, to some extent, another way of living. These men looked, talked, and even worked like he did. Herb was in the army when the second wave of prisoners came to Utah Valley and did not realize that the German prisoners of war ever worked the orchards.

In his introduction to *Living with Stories: Telling, Re-Telling, and Remembering*, William Schneider writes, "Telling our stories is how we construct meaning from memory, but the process is selective and many factors influence how we tell stories and why we choose to retell certain stories."[23] When talking about the orchards, some of our interviewees provided information about the World War II prisoner of war (POW) camp located on James George Stratton's land. During 1942–43, young men were swept out of the valley and into the military, thus reducing the pool of agricultural workers. One solution was to bring in Japanese internees and Italian and German POWs to work in the orchards. Huts were constructed near 950 North and 800 East in Orem. First Japanese American internees were brought in to help with the orchards. Then Italian POWs were brought in to do some building on the fence surrounding the camp. Finally German POWs were brought in.[24]

Rey Allred recalls the following about the German POWs:

> There was a guard for I think every ten prisoners and we talked him one day into shooting a pheasant, 'cause there was a big rooster pheasant across the orchard. We said "I bet you can't hit that!" I think I was, if, it was '44. I was probably, see, I was probably, see, I was eleven years old, but I can remember sitting and talking, that was really exciting, 'cause here is a real soldier with a real gun and Germans that we hated! Your know, here they were! And they looked pretty, they looked like we did.[25]

Scott Smith also addressed the issue of prejudice against the POWs.

> Grandpa had, he had everything from prisoners of war who wrote him until the day he died that were German prisoners, and he'd served in the First World War, been wounded three times. Every reason to hate Germans. When these guys came and they were in the prison camps over here at Gatmire and down by Geneva Steel, Gatmire farm, I think it was on 1600 North. He treated those people kindly, and gave them gifts. I think he bought a couple of them coats, and did extra nice things for them, and they wrote—I've got letters from some of those POWs that wrote him until the day he died. He got Christmas cards from them. He got wedding invitations, and he thought the German people were the finest people in the world.[26]

Smith's account reveals one of the weaknesses of oral history— faulty memory. The farm on 1600 North was the Gilman farm, not the Gatmire farm, and the POWs were not housed there. They were on the Stratton farm on 800 North. But Smith, unlike

Rey Allred, who remembered correctly, was born more than a decade after the POWs left. He is remembering what he was told, and the point of the story is not where the POWs lived. Rather, Smith was focusing on the more important point of what a kind man his grandfather was. Stories like these demonstrate the heritage the individual has inherited as well as traits that are important to him.

Allred's and Smith's stories are interesting because they all deal to some extent with prejudice. For Allred it was part of his life. Smith, however, focuses on being nonprejudicial, which reflects his own values. The prisoners were paid small amounts of money for their labor. It is possible that this was how his grandfather's "presents" were purchased, but in handing down the story, this has changed into something else. Giving is more consistent with the grandfather Smith valued, and it is also possible that he is right and the items were purely gifts. Oral history allows its participants to mold the story.

This molding may also mean creating stories that another generation may take at face value. Before I interviewed his father, Herb, Keven Stratton told me to make sure that his father told me the story about how he (Herb) was born on the kitchen table. I specifically asked Herb to tell me about being born on the kitchen table.

HS: Well you know, I tease my mom, mom about that, but that wasn't, she says, "No, that's not—"

KY: Well that's good to know, family folklore. That's [*both laugh*] . . .

HS: That was really family folklore.

KY: Okay, all right.

HS: I teased her about that, she said "No," she said, "The doctor was taking care of me in, in our, in the bed-, bedroom.

KY: Well that's good. That's better than the kitchen table.

HS: She didn't like me that, to tease her about that. And I guess my son has heard—heard that. And I had to beg her forgiveness one time for sayin' that.

When I mentioned this version of the tale to Keven, he was surprised. He asked me about it twice during the course of the conver-

sation, and then we talked about how he has probably told this
story to his children thinking it was the truth.[27]

It is also important to realize that oral history may reveal more
about the teller of the story than actual events. This may lead to an
idealized or a horrific view of the West, depending on who tells the
story. There is no doubt that the German prisoners who heard the
pheasant shot would have very different tales to tell than the ones
told by Allred.

Work Ethic

Vern Stratton, father to Kimball and brother to Herb, makes his
living as a farmer. For him, one of the great joys of farming is the
work ethic it instilled:

> Well, I love the farm, of course, I'm a farmer myself. When I
> grew up, you didn't have a choice. You just worked on the
> farm. I was—during the Depression and right after the De-
> pression up until war time that there was—you just went out
> and worked, that's all. You didn't say you didn't want to, or
> you'd like to do something else. You just went out and helped
> and did the work. So, automatically you learned how to work,
> even if you didn't like it, you learned how to do it. And as I
> grew up and grew into a young man, I decided it wasn't that
> bad of a job, you know? Because you could earn a good living
> and there's a lot of freedom in the things you did. It wasn't
> repetitious, you know, the same thing every day. So, you're
> out in the fresh air with nature. It's a different life and it's a
> good life. It's a hard life because you have to work hard, lots
> of long hours sometimes. It used to be when we did every-
> thing by hand, very strenuous work, but it was still good. I
> know my kids, our eight children, they grew up. They were
> the best help I had 'cause they learned to work.[28]

His brother Herb remembers learning to work as a child around
the ages of five to seven:

It was our responsibility to help grow those strawberries. We had to irrigate them and weed them, calibrate them, and pick, harvest them, pick them, pick the berries, and then we had to help sell the berries. So we did it, it was a, from the ground to the consumer kind of operation, we did it all. It was interesting, and I can still remember helping put the plants in, in the ground, watering them and starting them to grow, and then as they grew they sent out runners, and then we had to plant, reach down and plant the little runners into the soil, make a solid bed with strawberries, to pick. And my older brother, who at that time was a teenager, used to get me out of bed at night sometimes to go out there and water, those strawberries. I'd have to hold the lantern for him. So, he'd get me out of bed and away we'd go.[29]

Herb taught his son Keven to work at a young age as well. "I remember as a boy I would be, I would sell fruit there at the fruit stand. . . . Eighth North was just a little two-lane road without any sidewalk or gutter or anything on it, and I'd get paid ten cents an hour to sell fruit."[30] While selling fruit is his earliest memory of working on the farm, Keven was gradually given more responsibility. He was able to put himself through his undergraduate years of college as well as law school primarily on money he earned farming. He reminisces about working with the farm:

It was my whole—it created my work ethic, you know. Yes, there is nothing like trees or vegetables needing water and knowing that if you don't do all you can to help the water get to where it needs to be and to the end of the row, that it dies, I mean, that there's some immediate consequences there, so that helped me to see that when things are, need to be done, they need to be done. When, if they're not done in a timely way, you can't put off tomorrow what needs to be done today. You need to get it done. But then there are some things that can, can be put on hold for a little while, but my whole work ethic is based on watching my family work hard, and seeing the harvest, or the fruits of their labors, yes. My father used to say that, the Lord said that "By the sweat of the, Adam was instructed by the sweat of your brow." And that's been a real foundation now that I, that you asked that question.[31]

Keven taught the same work ethic to his son Zach:

We'd go up to different markets in Salt Lake City and my dad would—there was one at Liberty Park in downtown Salt Lake City and I was eight years old, my [brother] K. J. was ten, and my dad left us change, you know, like twenty-five ones, and you know, ten, twenty $5 bills, and he just told us to sell. And, I'm being eight years old, people would come up, and I'd just do my very best, and, to sell them the fruit, but, yeah, he left us there all day, and so, ever since I was a little kid I've been doing it, and I've really enjoyed it.[32]

Zach is currently attending Brigham Young University, majoring in construction management with a minor in landscape management. He does not think that he would be happy doing a desk job. He is interested in working the land, although in a different way than his forefathers did.

Uses for the Land

Zach's grandfather Herb, who has worked the land since the early 1930s, has a view of the land that allows for different uses. He retired from his day job in education in 1979 and has devoted himself since then to farming as well as other uses of the land. He recalls:

Part of my farming was to expand my sales into the, what I call Stratton's Country Store, on the corner of 8th East and 8th North. That building no longer stands, stays there, but when I was, when I was twelve years old my father George said, "I've got these seedling peaches here that I can't ship. Can't ship, why don't you and your brother take them and pick them and sell them and you can keep the money." So we did. That's what we did. We took those peaches, we picked them and, and packed them in boxes and lugged boxes, there'd be a half bushel in a, in a box, and pack them and sell them for fifty cents, fifty cents a lug on the corner of 8th East and 8th North. That's where Stratton's Country Store started selling our peaches in 1937. I was twelve and my younger brother was ten, but that's what happened. That was the beginning of a whole new business, retail business right there.[33]

When Stratton's Country Store was demolished to make room for an expanded 800 North, Keven Stratton salvaged the sign, refurbished it, and placed it behind a table on a Stratton lot bordering 800 East (see figure 15.2), where his younger children carry on the tradition of selling fruit.

In addition to being a retailer, Herb found other ways to use his land. In the mid-1960s, when he was in his forties, he and a group of friends decided that Orem needed a golf course. The group approached the mayor and city council and received permission to study the feasibility of building a course. A year later the group of men were politely thanked and told "no." The city felt that a recreation center and new, larger city buildings were needed at the time and that a golf course could easily wait.

Herb recalls:

Well I was upset with that decision; I could not see why we couldn't have a golf course here in the city of Orem. So I went to our [family fruit] corporation . . . and I said, "Well the city doesn't want to build a golf course; why don't we build a golf course? Let's take this 60 acres and we'll add my 25 and then buy 25 and that will give us a, that'll give us 110 acres, we can build a golf course. And the family just said, they all voted as a group, they said "no." I couldn't get a, a unanimous, or I couldn't get a majority vote. They said, "If you, we don't want to do it, but if you want to do it, then you go ahead and do it. But don't include us." Isn't that funny, how families are? But we're all sitting around together, and so I said, "Okay, and who, who wants to talk about it?" Well I had two, two of my brothers said they would, that they would talk about it. And so the family authorized me to tell the city that we'd build the golf course, but it would just be the three of us, not

Figure 15.2 Sign for Stratton Country Store.

the whole family. But they authorized me, as president of the corporation to write a letter to the city, which I did, I wrote a letter to them and they said, "Well, we're delighted. Go ahead. Go ahead and do it."[34]

Work on the golf course began in 1965 and by 1967 it was ready for business. Herb continues:

> I viewed it as a way of converting my knowledge and my tech—the technology that we had, from agriculture, fruit production, into golf course construction, management, and offering it to the public. I felt like the, selling a greens fee ticket was about like selling a bushel of apples or a bushel of peaches, same thing, it's just a different product. You do the same, you go through the same process, through, you have a goal to reach and you have these different things. Well our goal with the golf though was, we had, we had such a strong commitment to the city with the—with that, with the group that we started with, but none of them wanted to join with us, so we, the Stratton brothers did. The three brothers joined together and built the first nine holes.

In 1979 when he retired from education, Herb bought out his brothers from the golf course. Later, he involved Keven, who currently runs the course in addition to farming and practicing law. Nine additional holes were added in 2003.

Conclusion

An aerial photograph from the 1940s shows the area around 800 North and 800 East in Orem as lush orchards. Today, a similar photograph would reveal primarily houses with fruit trees scattered here and there. In the 1970s, real estate development began in earnest and currently lots that once held a single home are being redesigned into streets of four or more homes. Much of the former Stratton farm land is now filled with houses. Even as the land is being repurposed, remnants of the old ways continue.

In 1942, Wallace Stegner wrote, "Mormon Country remains comparatively untouched by the tourist traffic; the society which is actually more interesting than the country in which it was planted keeps to itself, as aloof and self-sufficient as Brigham could ever have hoped it to be."[35]

Although the landscape and society has changed dramatically since Stegner wrote his book, there exists a portion that hesitantly gives up the reliance on the old ways. Doggedly, it hangs on to the self-sufficiency or, as the Mormon church calls it, "self-reliance" of the earlier pioneers. Fruit may not be present in orchards, but the majority of homes built on what was the Stratton property boasts a fruit tree or two. The fruit is canned or preserved by the family living on the property. Vegetable gardens are often present as well. A family generally works together on taking care of and harvesting and preserving their crop. Mormon families are not as isolated as their ancestors were since communication devices make the world ever smaller and the world has encroached on them. Tourists are big business in Utah now, and an influx of non-LDS people is creating a cultural landscape that is becoming more similar to surrounding states. But for some families, like the Strattons, the values and some of the activities that grounded their ancestors in the land and in the LDS Church are still very visible. Each generation continues to revolve around the church and its teachings as well as the land. Oral histories make it possible for us to see this trend. Through oral histories conducted with different generations today, we can even begin to see how family stories are changing with the generations. As a result, oral histories not only relay fact and cultural detail, they also signal to the listener or the reader what the interviewee thinks about his heritage.

The issues this chapter revolves around were also important to early settlers of the Provo Bench. Their lives centered around the orchards, and they were aware of the land and the restrictions they imposed on their lives as well as the possibilities it gave them and their children. They were also concerned about the work ethic of their families and others who came to work the land—similar to the various prisoners who became workers in the 1930s and '40s. Now the orchards are wedged between city blocks and Latino workers do the heavy work with descendants of original farmers providing the supervision. Innovative uses for some of the land has been adopted. It is a different place, despite the fact that values remain intact. There is a legacy now and a memory of the land and those who possessed it through the generations. These memories are passed down through stories. These stories become a touchstone explored through oral history.

Notes

1. Vern Stratton, interview by Andrew Jorgensen, March 25, 2005, Hereinafter cited as *Fruits of Their Labors: Orchards in Utah Valley*, 10, William A. Wilson folklore Archive, L. Tom Perry Special Collections, Harold B. Lee Library, Brigham Young University.

2. Wallace Stegner, *Mormon Country* (Lincoln: University of Nebraska Press, 1981).

3. See Peggy Fletcher Stack and Jessica Ravitz, "Redefining the Mormon Empire," *Salt Lake Tribune*, March 30, 2008.

Wilson, "The Concept of the West and Other Hindrances to the Study of Mormon Folklore," in *Worldview and the American West: The Life of the Place Itself*, ed. Polly Stewart, Steve Siporin, C. W. Sullivan III, and Suzi Jones (Logan: Utah State University Press, 2000), 187.

5. Ibid., 185; emphasis added.

6. Ibid., 189.

7. Kimball Stratton, interview by Andrew Jorgenson, 2004, *Fruits of Their Labors: Orchards in Utah Valley*.

8. Keven Stratton, conversation with author, October 28, 2008.

9. Ibid.

10. D. Robert Carter, *Founding Fort Utah* (Provo, UT: Provo City Corporation, 2003), 72.

11. Bruce Jackson, *The Story Is True: The Art and Meaning of Telling Stories* (Philadelphia: Temple University Press, 2007), 9.

12. Keven Stratton, interview by author, March 9, 2005, *Fruits of Their Labors: Orchards in Utah Valley*, 7.

13. Henry Glassie, *Passing the Time in Ballymenone: Culture and History of an Ulster Community* (Philadelphia: University of Pennsylvania Press, 1968), 120.

14. Linda Richardson Lunt and Kathryn Richardson Ash, interview by Sarah Siebach, July 23, 2004, *Fruits of Their Labors: Orchards in Utah Valley*.

15. Anne Stratton Perry, interview by Sarah Siebach, July 19, 2004, *Fruit of Their Labors: Orchards in Utah Valley*.

16. Lunt and Ash interview.

17. Dawn Jones, interview by Ilana Harlow, July 23, 2004, *Fruits of Their Labors: Orchards in Utah Valley.*

18. Kimball Stratton interview.

19. David Lowenthal, *The Heritage Crusade and the Spoils of History* (Cambridge: Cambridge University Press, 1998), 57.

20. Lani Hatch, interview by Al Schorsch, July 22, 2004, *Fruits of Their Labors: Orchards in Utah Valley.*

21. Zach Stratton, interview by author, November 5, 2008, *By the Sweat of Their Brow: Changing Agrarian Culture in Utah County.*

22. Herb Stratton, interview by author, November 11, 2008, *By the Sweat of Their Brow: Changing Agrarian Culture in Utah County.*

23. William Schneider, *Living with Stories: Telling, Re-Telling, and Remembering* (Logan: Utah State University Press, 2008), 2.

24. City of Orem, Utah, "City of Orem," July 9, 2008, http://www.orem .org/index.hph?option=com_content&ask=view&id=373&emid=347

25. Rey Allred, interview by Catherine McIntyre, July 21, 2004, *Fruits of Their Labors: Orchards in Utah Valley.*

26. Scott Smith, interview by Derek Jensen, July 21, 2004, *Fruits of Their Labors: Orchards in Utah Valley.*

27. Keven Stratton, conversation with author, November 14, 2008.

28. Vern Stratton interview.

29. Herb Stratton interview.

30. Keven Stratton interview.

31. Ibid.

32. Zach Stratton interview.

33. Herb Stratton interview.

34. Ibid.

35. Stegner, *Mormon Country,* 346–47.

Afterword

When History Talks Back

CLYDE A. MILNER II

HOW DO WE understand the past? Academically trained historians have their ways of researching and presenting a form of understanding. But nearly everyone early on in their lives has some personal connection to and understanding of the past. Families are important for this comprehension, as are local communities. For many people, their real "history" is not in books but in the memories they carry. The work of oral historians certifies that insight when an interview reveals the ways that individuals remember their pasts. This view of the past may seem highly personal, but as the studies in this book reveal, personal retrospection can produce vital information about collective perceptions of community and work.

Oral history can reveal much more. The fifteen diverse, insightful essays presented here demonstrate the importance of collecting oral histories in the American West. Although aspects of community and work appear in every chapter, other critical themes about oral history and the West are embedded in this work. The variety of locations and populations provide perceptions of families' and women's lives, ethnic and racial challenges, as well as economic and political struggles. We see a larger, more complex West through the lens of these studies. We also see the way that memory and stories shape our connection to the past. To each author's credit, the collaborative realities of the oral history interview are not ignored. The interviewer, even in subtle ways, can influence and shape the results of the interview. What's more, a series of interviews can enhance and modify the sense of community shared by a group of people.

As Jessie Embry explains in her examination of the Redd Center Oral History Program (chapter 1), efforts to undertake oral history interviews and the resulting oral history collections have become vital tools in scholarly research on the American West. This upward trend commenced by the start of the 1970s, if not earlier. Indeed, as Laurie Mercier recognizes (chapter 3), the volume of interviews gathered across the West is so substantial that this resource should be used more effectively by scholars. The holdings in various local, state, and university archives can be used for large-scale social and cultural history projects, much as Mercier proposes to do by revisiting her own work from the 1980s in Montana. The writings in this volume show that a new era may be dawning for applying the results of oral history in the West.

Where will this new era take us? I think it will greatly amplify our understanding of western history, especially from the mid-twentieth century to the present. The technology for undertaking interviews has progressed dramatically from the rudimentary efforts with wax cylinders and wire recorders to the impressive audiovisual clarity of digital formats today. As the technologies have improved, the volume of available interviews has expanded dramatically. How these oral history collections may be accessed for research may soon leap ahead with new search tools. In a manner similar to what happens with full-text keyword searches of historic newspapers, imagine the equivalent search through hundreds of hours of digitally archived audio files to find statements about certain ideas, events, places, individuals, and groups. If we can find important words that were printed in any digitized collection of papers, why not the equivalent for the spoken word in oral history collections?

Even if such technological marvels for searching audio files will soon exist, these advances will not necessarily address the full context of what oral history provides. The act of interviewing engages the present and the past. What happens is not simply a way to gather more information. A larger dynamic for individual lives and personal stories becomes evident. Yes, information does exist in the content of most interviews, but the interview itself, as the chapters in this book remind us, is more than fact finding. The questions, answers, digressions, amplifications, and silences that interviews may contain reveal the collaborative nature of oral history. Of course, the person being interviewed is the primary subject, but the interviewer also affects the event. José M. Alamillo reminds us in his chapter that "oral history is not just a research method but a political project. The process of engaging people with memories of their lives requires patience, self-reflexive alertness, careful listening, and political risk" (chapter 5). In an earlier version of her essay, Melanie Newport recognized when meeting with members of the Utah Eagle Forum that the "relationships built through interviewing, not just the content of the interviews, have a significant bearing on opportunities for future scholarship" (chapter 12). She also confessed that "oral history interviews are perhaps one of the few opportunities historians have to confront their biases face to face."

Oral historians know perhaps more directly than other historians that they become part of a process that both preserves and creates history. Barbara Allen Bogart concluded that her work in two locations—Fort Rock, Oregon, and Evanston, Wyoming—"made a contribution to a community's understanding of its own history. But I am also keenly aware that the version of history I created through oral history likely has become part of a feedback loop into the community's own view of its own past" (chapter 2). In a recently published study of a community destroyed by urban renewal in Frankfort, Kentucky—the colorfully named "Crawfish Bottom"—oral historian Douglas A. Boyd analyzed a set of twenty-five interviews carried out in 1991 after the neighborhood had already disappeared. Boyd asserts that the interviewees who had heard the consistently negative accounts of their neighborhood from outside sources now found "a psychological-emotional space in which they could finally celebrate their sense of place." In fact, Boyd believes that these interviews created a narrative of the community in public memory that did not exist in the same manner in the past. He informs his readers that "public memory is infused with multitudes of individual memories and is therefore inherently complex, malleable, and polyvalent." He bluntly states, "The concept of a community as a homogeneous human group bound together in time, space, and identity is not helpful and is, in fact, false." The multitrack of memory and narrative leads Boyd to the recognition of what he calls "the process of the folklorization of history in the ever-unfolding formation of public memory."[1]

Bogart and Boyd have recognized a similar process in what oral histories can create—a form of public memory. In my own writings, set in the American West, I often considered the problematic dynamics of both personal and shared memory. Harriet Sanders helped me see memory in this way. I did not conduct an interview with Sanders because she died in 1909. What I found at the Montana Historical Society in Helena was her 1863 diary, written during her overland trip to Montana, and her memoir of that same trip written thirty-four years later in 1897.[2]

By arriving in 1863, Harriet Sanders and her family could claim to be Montana pioneers. In fact, they came to the gold camps well before the 1864 creation of Montana Territory. She and her immediate family played prominent roles in the new society. Her husband, Wilbur Fisk Sanders, gained early fame as a vigilante and prosecutor of the road agents who robbed the miners. He later served as territorial delegate to Congress and eventually as US senator. A founder of the Montana Historical Society, he held the office of president of that organization from 1865 to 1890.

In 1897, the year she wrote her memoir, Harriet Sanders had been elected the first president of the Montana Women's Suffrage Association. Despite more than thirty years in Montana, Harriet did not write a full-scale autobiography. She focused on only sixteen years of her life in what she called "Reminiscences of My Trip across the Plains and My Early Life in Montana, 1863–1879." More than half of this memoir described the three earliest years, 1863–65, when she and her family traveled overland to the gold fields and settled in the mining camps of Bannack and Virginia City.

These were the years and events that could certify Harriet and her family as true pioneers. Many others had written (and no doubt spoken) about the same episodes. In the second paragraph of her memoir, she modestly wrote, "Our experiences across the plains were, I presume, similar in many respects to those of others." With these words as important signposts, Harriet's memoir indicates that at least by the 1890s a pattern of shared memory about the overland experience (as well as about the early days in the gold camps) had emerged among many Montanans.

These two documents show how one woman transformed her daily journal into an example of the shared memory of Montana pioneers. The same process can happen with an oral interview when a person's memory constructs the narrative. Internal evidence clearly demonstrates that Sanders used her original diary when she wrote the first part of her memoir. At one point, she asked that readers "Refer to my remarks in the Journal." Yet, despite having her diary at hand, she created a memoir that differed significantly from her original account and from the daily accounts of two other women in the same party. One of these women wrote a series of letters to her sisters in Ohio, and the other kept her own diary during the trip.[3]

What changed from her diary to her memoir is how Harriet Sanders presented indigenous Native peoples, that is, American Indians. She made them far more prominent in the memoir. In 1897, Sanders claimed that the party saw Indians "every day" or, on the next page, "daily" between Fort Kearny and Fort Laramie (June 29 through July 22 in the diary). The account in the diary reports only four days over this period when Native peoples are either met or sighted. She concludes in her memoir that their overland party during the entire journey "had been continually in danger of attacts [*sic*] from the Indians." The letters and diary written by the other women on the trip confirm what Harriet's diary also showed—that this emigrant party had no difficulties with the Indians.

Was Harriet Sanders in 1897 lying about her trip in 1863? I doubt that either she or her fellow pioneers at that later date would have seen her memoir in such a harsh light. In fact, I doubt that any of them would have asked that question. A good oral historian would not have asked that question so directly either but may have crafted a way to learn more and place the memoir in a larger context. By making the Indians a greater danger in her memoir, Sanders did what many other pioneers had done. In his massive study of the overlanders on the California and Oregon trails, historian John D. Unruh Jr. notes: "Encounters with hostile Indians—often much embellished—are far more conspicuous in latter-day reminiscent accounts." In fact, Unruh's analysis of the California/Oregon trails reveals that fewer than 400 migrants were killed by Indians from 1840 to 1860, when approximately 250,000 people took the overland route.[4] The trails to Montana's gold camps in the 1860s saw roughly 10 percent of the California/Oregon trail total (i.e., approximately 25,000 migrants). Yet this smaller migration may have been subject to greater Indian hostilities. This northern trail crossed the bison ranges of the Lakotas and Northern Cheyennes. Also, the record of warfare on the northern Plains between the US Army and Native peoples was far greater during the 1860s than in the 1840s and 1850s. Although more study is needed, the personal accounts from eight emigrant trains that traveled across the northern Plains to the Montana gold camps between 1862 and 1867 reveal that only the 1864 expedition suffered a serious Indian attack.[5] In terms of native hostilities toward emigration parties, even for the trails to Montana, the historical record supports the account in Sanders's diary, whereas the shared or public memory of Montana pioneers (and other overland pioneers) would accept the Indian threat presented in her memoir. By 1897, Harriet Sanders may well have remembered the story of the Indian threat better than she remembered what she had written in her diary, even when she had a chance to reread it. She and her fellow pioneers had told each other the stories of hostile Indians for decades.

Oral historians in the West know that they can hear many stories that sound highly personal and seemingly accurate. Yet all historians have reasons to question the problematic dynamics of memory in whatever sources we examine. I contend that oral historians are especially well situated to question what memory may or may not tell us. Indeed, a healthy skepticism about any source, written or spoken, is a touchstone for historical scholarship. If we have any doubt about our skepticism and want to be skeptical about being skeptical, I strongly recommend deliberating what psychologists and cognitive scientists have been learning about human memory.

Consider the work of Daniel Offer, a psychiatry professor at Northwestern University Medical School. In 1962, Offer interviewed seventy-three boys who were then age fourteen. He was studying the typical American teenager. Thirty-four years later, he was able to track down sixty-seven of these now adult males. He asked the forty-eight-year-old subjects to recall their teen years and answer the same questions from 1962. Offer reported the results in the June 2000 issue of the *Journal of Child and Adolescent Psychiatry*.[6]

In Offer's follow-up, so many answers changed that statistically a person who guessed randomly would score just as well on twenty-five of the twenty-eight questions. Offer did not find that people misremembered basic information. They could get their hometowns right, for example. It was their feelings about childhood events that changed. As fourteen-year-old boys, 82 percent said they were disciplined with physical punishment. As older adults, only 33 percent remembered such discipline. Describing themselves, only 5 percent of the teenagers said they enjoyed mental activity, whereas 23 percent of the men "remembered" it fondly. Asked what they considered worst about their home life, 40 percent of the teens found it physically uncomfortable, whereas 11 percent found home to be emotionally disagreeable. These numbers were more than reversed for the forty-eight-year-olds. Fifty percent remembered emotional discomfort, and only 15 percent felt physically put out at home. Even memories of mothers were different. Only 14 percent of the boys said they were their mother's favorite in 1962, but thirty-four years later, 30 percent remembered being the favorite.

Regardless of whom Mom truly liked more, Offer concluded that as people get older their view of the past, of their own personal histories, changes. This conclusion is not a startling insight. We all change as we grow older, so our memories should change as well. Memory is an active process. It is a construction of the past that is greatly influenced by an individual's ongoing life—the person's family, society, and culture. Maturing beliefs, evolving values, and subsequent experiences all influence what is remembered. In effect, a person's memories can demonstrate his or her present situation. They are a demonstration of the larger context in which they are remembered. Offer considers memories to be "existential reconstructions." As such, it is best for doctors, therapists, and historians to treat all recollections with great care, using discerning judgment to assess what memory tells us about the past.

Oral historians, and all historians, can be skeptical about what we are told in an interview or a written document. That does not mean that when history talks back, those who do the talking will accept any corrections about their memory. The work of Ulric Neisser underscored this point. Neisser, a psychological researcher, carried out an experiment that showed how inaccurate historical memories can become after only two and a half years, not the nearly three and a half decades of Offer's male subjects. The day after the space shuttle *Challenger* exploded in 1986, Neisser asked students at Emory University to write down immediate details about learning of the disaster. Thirty months later, he asked them for the same account. A quarter of the reports were remarkably changed, half had some differences, and less than a tenth had all the details repeated. All were certain their second accounts were accurate.[7]

I believe that Harriet Sanders's response, if confronted with the discrepancies between her 1863 diary and 1897 memoir, might well mirror that of Neisser's students at Emory and Offer's adult men. In the case of Offer's study, when told that the answers they gave as adults did not come close to matching the answers they gave as teenagers, some of the men argued against this information and insisted it could not be true. What they remembered about their teenage life had to be the truth, not what they said at the time. Neisser concluded that people may think they recall an event, but what they remember are memories; indeed, it may be memories of memories. The mind conflates the past through the process of remembering the past.

Oral historians experience these dynamics of memory firsthand, but just because memories may prove inaccurate does not mean they should be discarded. Why people remember what they remember can be more important than the accuracy of the retelling of the past. My most recent book-length adventure in western history, a biography of the Montana pioneer Granville Stuart, underscored this important insight. I wish that oral history could have aided this work more directly. Stuart compiled a two-volume memoir and made letter-press book copies of much of his correspondence. He died in 1918. I did not have the opportunity to carry out interviews as extensively as Sandra Mathews in her chapter here (chapter 10). Even though her aunt, Donna Joy McGladrey, had passed away, people who knew her well could talk to Mathews. None of Stuart's children were alive when I began my research, and only one grandson survived. I spent a day with that grandson in Great Falls, Montana, and had several visits with a great grandson who lived near the same land in central Montana where Stuart had his ranch in the 1880s.[8]

Remarkably, a tape recording from 1958 captured some of the memories of Stuart's daughter, Mary Stuart Abbott. She spoke at a public event in Lewistown, Montana, not far from her home ranch. Eighty-eight years old at the time, Mary responded to questions from the audience in a strong voice. Energetic and direct in her statements, she drew laughs by claiming to have never counted her grandchildren, even though one of her daughters sat near her and spoke from time to time as well. Mary recalled happy days with dances and even roller skating at her father's ranch. Near the end of this event she also provided a story of a killing carried out by vigilantes in summer 1884. Stuart had led this group of ranchers and cowboys who became known as "Stuart's stranglers." During his life, he remained circumspect in publicly discussing the actions of the vigilantes because he claimed family members and friends of those killed might still be alive. The victims were supposedly horse thieves. Mary said her father's men had learned about one thief who had stolen "a little blue mare." After his capture, this man, Sam MacKenzie, was brought to the ranch where that night, Mary learned, he was forced to play the violin and dance a jig. The next day, Mary saw his body hanging from a tree.[9]

Mary had only seen the body and not the other events. She remembered the story, even if she did not observe what happened. As for her father's caution about recounting events, an unidentified speaker in 1958 related in a jocular manner that his mother worked for a Dr. MacKenzie in Lewistown and had told the physician in the presence of his wife that she was sure he was not related to the dead man. "Mrs. MacKenzie spoke up and said, 'Oh yes he was.'"

More than descendants of the stranglers' victim had reasons to recall MacKenzie's death. People of French Canadian and Indian heritage in the area, the Métis, remembered MacKenzie as a popular musician who was one of their own. Years after the hanging, probably in the early 1950s, a local historian interviewed a Métis woman, Isabelle Larocque. She recalled that a friend of her brother-in-law said that Sam MacKenzie had been on his way to a dance and carried his violin because he was expected to provide music at the party. He kept playing all night, unaware that some of the drunken cowboys at the dance were vigilantes. "They took him in the morning and hung him." Did he deserve his fate? Larocque and other mixed-race peoples did not think so.[10] This alternative account indicates a long-standing resentment toward Stuart and his stranglers that stayed alive for some just as long as Mary Stuart Abbott's version of what happened.

The contested narratives of Isabelle Larocque and Mary Stuart Abbott demonstrate the dynamics of memory. They capture racial and generational tensions around and within Lewistown, Montana. No corroborative evidence exists to demonstrate that either story—the hanged horse thief or the unjustly killed Métis musician—is factually accurate. Yet the stories as remembered by those who told them have their own value. They showed the way a daughter recalled this episode connected to her father's life and how Métis peoples felt about the vigilantes' actions. Oral historians often uncover contested and contradictory narratives, sometimes in the same interview. Recognizing the value of these different accounts allows for a comprehensive, yet more complex interpretation of the past. As we move forward into a new era for oral history in the American West, across the diverse peoples and places of the region, the collecting of more memories and narratives will greatly enrich our understanding of the past. Oral historians will help us appreciate that when history talks back we learn more about the lively, complicated human chronicle.

Notes

1. Douglas A. Boyd, *Crawfish Bottom: Recovering a Lost Kentucky Community* (Lexington: University Press of Kentucky, 2011), 88–89, 78, 148.

2. Clyde A. Milner II, "The Shared Memory of Montana's Pioneers," *Montana: The Magazine of Western History* 37 (Winter 1987): 2–13. Sanders's diary of her overland trip in 1863 and "Reminiscences of My Trip across the Plains and of My Early Life in Montana, 1863–1879" are both contained in a bound typescript in the Wilbur Fisk Sanders Papers, Montana Historical Society Archives, Helena. In W. F. Sanders II and Robert T. Taylor, *Biscuits and Badmen: The Sanders' Story in Their Own Words* (Butte, MT: Editorial Review Press, 1983), 4, the authors who used these materials noted, "The text of the diary and reminiscences are typescripts made by Harriet Sanders in the late 1890s. The original of the diary was not preserved."

3. Mary Edgerton wrote letters home to her sisters in Tallmadge, Ohio, and Lucia Darling kept a diary during the overland trip. See Lucia A. Darling Papers, Small Collections 145, and Sidney Edgerton Papers, 1859–1887, at the Montana Historical Society Archives, Helena.

4. John D. Unruh Jr., *The Plains Across: The Overland Emigrants and the Trans-Mississippi West, 1840–60* (Urbana: University of Illinois Press, 1979), 175, 185.

5. Helen McCann White, ed., *Ho! For the Gold Fields: Northern Overland Wagon Trains of the 1860s* (St. Paul: Minnesota Historical Society, 1966), 115–17, 143–53.

6. Daniel Offer et al., "The Altering of Reported Experiences," *Journal of the American Academy of Child and Adolescent Psychiatry* 39 (June 2000): 735–42.

7. Douglas Martin, "Ulric Neisser Is Dead at 83; Reshaped Study of the Mind," *New York Times*, February 25, 2012, http://www.nytimes.com/2012/02/26/us/ulric-neisser-who-reshaped-thinking-on-the-mind-dies-at-83.html (accessed July 3, 2012).

8. Clyde A. Milner II and Carol A. O'Connor, *As Big as the West: The Pioneer Life of Granville Stuart* (New York: Oxford University Press, 2009).

9. Mary Stuart Abbott, Lectures to the Montana Institute of Arts, June 21, 1958, Lewistown, MT, Oral History 66, Montana Historical Society Archives, Helena.

10. Conrad Anderson, "History of Roy, Montana," n.d., 21–23, SC 978.6292, Fergus County Collection 1.12, Lewistown Public Library, Montana; Martha Harroun Foster, *We Know Who We Are: Métis Identity in a Montana Community* (Norman: University of Oklahoma Press, 2006), 159; Conrad V. Anderson Papers, 1954–1974, Collection 362, at the Montana State University Library in Bozeman also contains a copy of Anderson's history of the Roy community. The descriptive note for the collection says this piece was done "around 1954." http://www.lib.montana.edu/collect/spcoll/findaid/0362.php (accessed July 3, 2012).

Contributors

José M. Alamillo was born in Cueva Grande, Zacatecas, Mexico, and raised on a lemon ranch in Ventura County. His family worked in the lemon packinghouses and orchards year-round, which allowed him and his siblings to attend local public schools uninterrupted. At middle school age, he took part in University of California, Santa Barbara's Educational Opportunity Program (EOP) that encouraged minority students to attend a four-year college or university. He is a proud beneficiary of affirmative action programs like EOP. After graduating from the University of California, Santa Barbara, he started graduate school at University of California, Irvine, in the Comparative Cultures Program (ethnic studies).

William Bauer (Wailacki and Concow of the Round Valley Indian tribes) is an associate professor at the University of Nevada, Las Vegas. He has written one book, *"We Were All Like Migrant Workers Here": Work, Community and Memory on Northern California's Round Valley Reservation, 1850–1941* (University of North Carolina Press, 2009) and has published essays in the *Western Historical Quarterly*, *American Indian Quarterly*, and *Southern California Historical Quarterly*.

A native Californian and a folklorist, Barbara Allen Bogart began her oral history career when she was a doctoral candidate at the University of California, Los Angeles. As a faculty member in the American Studies Department at the University of Notre Dame, she created a course on the American West that she continues to teach for the University of Wyoming. She conducted several oral history projects when she worked at the Wyoming State Museum and as director of the Uinta County Museum in Evanston, Wyoming. Almost all of her research and writing has focused on local history and oral narratives in western communities.

Leisl Carr Childers is a visiting professor at Northern Arizona University. She worked on the Nevada Test Site Oral History Project at the University of Nevada, Las Vegas, between 2005 and 2008, interviewing ranchers and radiation monitors, preparing the oral histories for archiving, and digitizing the collection on the university library's website. The interviews she conducted formed the basis of her dissertation, "The Size of the Risk: An Environmental History of the Nuclear Great Basin," completed in 2011. She currently works with history and social studies teachers on a Teaching American History grant in Flagstaff, Arizona.

Jessie L. Embry is the associate director of the Charles Redd Center for Western Studies. She was a member of the first oral history class sponsored by the Redd Center in 1973 and became the director of the oral history program in 1979. She has written ten books and more than one hundred articles, which are nearly all based on oral history. She has taught an oral history class at Brigham Young University and long-distance.

Marci Farr currently works as a manuscript processor at Weber State University, Stewart Library Special Collections. She was a student fellow in 2007 with John Sillito and researched Thomas D. Dee for the Utah Construction Company annual symposium. With the completion of that project, she was hired to interview graduate nurses from the Dee Hospital as well as St. Benedict's Hospital School of Nursing to ensure their stories will be preserved when they are no longer here to share them.

Joanne L. Goodwin is associate professor of history at University of Nevada, Las Vegas, and director of the Women's Research Institute of Nevada. Her publications include *Women in American History, 1585—Present, an Encyclopedia,* edited with Joyce Appelby and Eileen Cheng (M. E. Sharp, 2002); *Gender and the Politics of Welfare Reform* (University of Chicago Press, 1997); and numerous chapters, articles, and reviews in *Gender and History, Journal of Women's History, Signs, Pacific Historical Review,* and the *Journal of Social History.* Her research on the first social welfare policy for single mothers, called mothers' pensions, has been published and reprinted in several collections. Since arriving at UNLV, she has played a major role in the collection, preservation, and dissemination of women's history in the Las Vegas valley. She has published widely in that new area.

Sarah Langsdon is associate curator of special collection at the Stewart Library, Weber State University, where she has worked since 1999. In 2000, she graduated with a master's in history from Utah State University. She coauthored a book with John Sillito in the Arcadia Images of America series on Ogden. She has been involved in collecting oral history interviews from graduates of the Dee School of Nursing and the St. Benedict's School of Nursing in Ogden.

Sandra K. Mathews, professor of history at Nebraska Wesleyan University, specializes in history of the borderlands and the American West. Her books include *Between Breaths: A Teacher in the Alaskan Bush* (University of New Mexico Press, 2006), *American Indians in the Early West* (ABC-CLIO, 2008), *A History of New Mexico since Statehood* with Richard Melzer and Robert Torrez (University of New Mexico Press, 2011), and *Women on the North American Plains* with Renee Laegreid (Texas Tech University Press, 2011). She enjoys camping, bicycling, kayaking, and running with her dog, Dulcinea.

Laurie Mercier is the Claudius O. and Mary W. Johnson Distinguished Professor of History at Washington State University, Vancouver. She is the author of *Anaconda: Labor, Community and Culture in Montana's Smelter City* (2001) and coeditor of *Mining Women: Gender in the Development of a Global Industry* (2006, 2009) and *Speaking History: Oral Histories of the American Past, 1865–Present* (2009). Mercier is a former president of the Oral History Association and coauthor (with Madeline Buckendorf) of *Using Oral History in Community History Projects* (2007).

Linda M. Meyer serves as archivist for the collections of the Agricultural and Natural Resources Archive at Colorado State University Libraries. She earned a master's degree in public history at

Colorado State and has continued to develop her skills in conducting oral history interviews with individuals involved in the history of Colorado agriculture and resource management.

Clyde A. Milner II is director of the PhD program in heritage studies and professor of history at Arkansas State University in Jonesboro. He received his PhD in American studies from Yale University. Before coming to Arkansas State in 2002, Milner served on the faculty at Utah State University in Logan, where he edited the *Western Historical Quarterly* for eighteen years. He has written or edited seven books, most notably *The Oxford History of the American West* (1994). He and his wife, Carol O'Connor, co-authored *As Big as the West: The Pioneer Life of Granville Stuart* (2009), which was published by Oxford University Press. In 2012, Milner received the lifetime Award of Merit from the Western History Association.

Melanie Newport is a doctoral candidate in American history at Temple University. She is a graduate of Pacific Lutheran University and the University of Utah. As a twentieth-century US policy historian, her research and teaching interests include crime and incarceration, state politics, federalism, and modern state-building. Her dissertation is on federal crime control grants and the rise of the carceral state. She resides in Philadelphia.

John Sillito is professor emeritus at Weber State University, Ogden, Utah. A native of Salt Lake City, he has been active in oral history since the 1970s. He specializes in late nineteenth and early twentieth-century US history, with an emphasis on the American left. His most recent book, *A History of Utah Radicalism: Startling, Socialistic and Decidedly Revolutionary,* coauthored with John McCormick, was published by Utah State University Press in 2011. Sillito currently serves as a member of the board of editors of the *Utah Historical Quarterly.*

Skott Brandon Vigil (1977–2010) was a PhD candidate at the University of Wisconsin, Madison. Vigil (Yankton and Southern Ute) earned his BA from Brigham Young University, Hawai'i, and his

MA from the University of Wyoming. He won awards from the Western History Association and the Newberry Library. Skott lived a short but full life, serving on a Mormon mission in Hong Kong, working at a fish cannery in Alaska, and conducting family oral history interviews in Colorado and California.

Claytee White is the director of the Oral History Research Center at UNLV Libraries. She has published a book chapter in *African American Women Confront The West, 1600–2000,* and two articles: "The March That Never Happened: Desegregating the Las Vegas Strip," *Nevada Law Journal* and "Marking the Unique Moulin Rouge Era," *CGI: Casino & Gaming International.* She serves as past president of the Southwest Oral History Association, is a member of the Las Vegas Historic Preservation Commission, and is on the board of Nevada Humanities.

Georgia Wier is a folklorist who has conducted oral history interviews and other forms of documentary fieldwork in the Intermountain states of Colorado and Wyoming as well as in the Northwest, the southern Appalachian region, and her home state of Mississippi. She leads oral history workshops and consults with museums and historical societies on developing community oral history projects. Wier directed the oral history program that resulted in the collection of the interviews examined in her chapter.

Kristi A. Young is the curator of the Wilson Folklore Archive at Brigham Young University. She has a BA and MA from Brigham Young University and a MLS from the University of North Texas. She worked on two folk life projects focusing on agriculture in Utah County. The first deals with orchards, and fruit growers, fruit stand owners, as well as those who used the fruit in cooking were interviewed. The project began as a three-week field school in connection with the American Folklife Center in the Library of Congress. The second project looked at the changing agrarian society in Utah County where Brigham Young University is located. The interviews were primarily conducted by students at the university under her supervision. She is currently working on an oral history project on military wives.

Index